THE
PEOPLE'S
LAWYER

The
PEOPLE'S
LAWYER

*The Life and Times of Frank J. Kelley,
the Nation's Longest-Serving
Attorney General*

Frank J. Kelley with Jack Lessenberry

A Painted Turtle book
Detroit, Michigan

19 18 17 16 15   5 4 3 2 1

Library of Cataloging Control Number: 2015933202

ISBN 978-0-8143-4132-2 (cloth)
ISBN 978-0-8143-4133-9 (ebook)

All photos courtesy of Frank J. Kelley, unless otherwise noted.

Designed and typeset by Bryce Schimanski
Composed in Adobe Caslon Pro

I'd like to dedicate this book
to my wonderful family—my wife, Nancy;
my former wife, Jo; and my three children,
Karen, Frank, and Jane—who helped make
my life and this book possible.

———————

And I also want to dedicate it
to the next generation of young Americans who hear
the call of public service and are determined to do
whatever they can to make this a better nation
and a better world.

CONTENTS

FOREWORD

Jack Lessenberry

Five years ago I went to visit Frank Kelley, who was then beginning to wind down his career as an attorney, government relations consultant, and lobbyist with Kelley Cawthorne, the firm he founded after he left office. I wanted his opinions on some now-forgotten issues of the day. We talked for an hour or so.

I had known him slightly for years. Virtually every serious journalist in Michigan knew the "eternal general," as we all called him, and with good reason. Nobody in the entire nation had ever come close to his amazing longevity on the job.

Thirty-seven years. I knew a few major things about Frank. I knew that, unlike a lot of officeholders, he never retired on the job. I have met congressmen and one statewide official who were literally senile. Frank Kelley walked off the job at age seventy-four as intellectually sharp as the day he was appointed.

What I also knew was that he was candid and honest and that while he was in charge of the legal affairs of the state of Michigan, there was never a whiff of scandal or corruption.

And I knew that he was trusted by the voters in a way that would seem almost unimaginable today. On Election Day in 1982, I asked L. Brooks Patterson, his GOP opponent that year, where he would be when the returns came in.

He looked at me and said, "Down in the bunker with Eva Braun. I'm running against Frank Kelley."

But what I didn't realize is how fascinating a life Frank Kelley's had been, from the rollicking days of Prohibition through his efforts to find himself as a young man trying to make his own way and carve out his own identity.

This was a man who grew up on the mean streets of Detroit and with Great Lakes sailors during the depths of the Great Depression. Later he would be inspired by and spend time with John, Bobby, and Teddy Kennedy, as well as virtually every other major national Democratic Party figure.

As attorney general, Frank J. Kelley went on to essentially invent consumer and environmental protection in the state of Michigan.

He crusaded for civil rights and equal representation before it was popular to do so. He populated his army of the people's lawyers with competent African Americans and women before that was the norm. Throughout his career, he prosecuted wrongdoers whom others wouldn't take on and defended those who most needed defending. Along the way, he helped launch a multitude of political and government service careers. U.S. senator Carl Levin. Governor Jim Blanchard, later an especially distinguished ambassador to Canada. Governor Jennifer Granholm. They all got their start from or were immensely helped by Frank J. Kelley.

Frank J. Kelley made a difference in a way that I think would have made his beloved father proud. It has been an honor—and a lot of fun—to work with him on this book.

PREFACE

Each man's happiness, an ancient philosopher said, is different. Some men's idea of happiness is gold. For others, fame, success, and winning a place in the world for their families after them.

Those are all natural impulses. But then there are those who are motivated to help their fellow man, who are driven to be able to say that they left the world a better place in some way.

That's what I've tried to do with my life. That doesn't mean I am a saint or that I didn't make mistakes. That doesn't mean I did not want to take care of my wonderful family or live as well as I could.

Indeed, my half-joking motto since I left elected office has been, "Vote like you are poor, even if you can live like you are rich." Sometimes, I have to admit, that came out, "Vote like you are a Democrat, live like a Republican."

But I always tried to put public service first, and I think that was instilled in me most of all by my father, Frank E. Kelley, who rose from great poverty to become a prosperous saloon keeper and influential figure in Democratic politics in one of our nation's largest cities.

Dad had few illusions. I'll never forget his telling me: "If you're going to be in public life, and I urge you to, remember this: they stoned Moses, crucified Christ, and shot Lincoln. What do you think your chances are?"

Well, I never would put myself in the same league as Abraham Lincoln, let alone any of the world's great religious figures.

But I will say this: I served as attorney general, the chief legal and law enforcement officer of the state of Michigan, for thirty-seven years. That's longer than anyone in any state in our nation's history.

During that time, I transformed the office from a passive defender of lawsuits against the state to an active and muscular crusader for the rights of citizens. We established one of the first departments of consumer protection in the nation.

We worked hard to break new ground in protecting the environment and to regulate the utilities and other public enterprises for the benefit of the people. As a result, I am convinced we helped millions live happier, better-served, and more affordable lives.

We made a difference, and I am happy about that. Indeed, the world is a far different place than it was when I was appointed attorney general at the end of 1961. There was no Internet then. No twenty-four-hour news cycle. Every reporter at my first press conference was a white, middle-aged man. Nobody would have thought much of the future chances of a squalling four-month-old black infant in Honolulu, Hawaii.

That baby is the president of the United States of America today.

Today, doing what I did would be in one way impossible, since term limits mean every modern Michigan attorney general has to leave office after no more than eight years.

But in some ways, things are the same. The opportunities to serve your fellow man and have a career doing so may be even greater.

If you are a young person interested in politics, or public service, then I want you to know that no matter where your particular interests lie, there is an opportunity to be helpful to your fellow man.

Had I gone in another direction, I likely would have made much more money. Early on in my career, I toyed with the idea of going to the fast-growing state of Florida and setting up a law practice.

But instead of making vast wealth, I think I made a difference. Along the way, I met and got to know an astonishing array of characters, from John F. Kennedy to Steve Allen, from Bobby Kennedy to five governors who were as different as they could be.

I learned from all of them. I won't deny that I have an ego. Nobody can run in eleven statewide elections without one.

Kennedy was my political hero. My father was, and is, my personal hero. Tragically, both men's lives were cut short.

The world knows what happened to President Kennedy. My father died of a massive heart attack in 1954, just as I was beginning my political career. He was only sixty-two. Today, I am almost ninety.

Still, every day, I like to think that he would have been proud of me. He told me something else, not long before he died.

"I know you will do good. But enjoy your life, Frank," he said.

That was more than half a century ago. I like to think that my dad would have thought I did both things—did some good and had a good life. And I want others to know it can still be done.

So this is my story. President Kennedy used to say, "Every person can make a difference, and every person should try." I have lived almost twice as long as JFK did. I've had my sorrows and successes, but I'd do almost all of it again.

And if some young person happens to read this book and is somehow motivated toward a career in public service, well, then, that alone will make having written it worthwhile for me.

ACKNOWLEDGMENTS

Anyone who is even reasonably successful got there in large part by standing on the shoulders of others—and being boosted up by them. That's certainly true for me, in every way.

This book tells how much I owe to my family, as well as some other amazing people, like the priest who talked a somewhat lost young man into going back to school. But in terms of my career, my first real mentors were a group of successful attorneys for whom I worked for two years: trial experts Ernst LaJoie, Frank Neaton, and Philip Neudeck and McKee Robinson, who handled corporate matters.

For the rest of my life, I profited from everything they taught me about being a good lawyer—in and out of court.

I also have to mention the late John Mack, my law school classmate with whom I formed a partnership and practiced law in Alpena for seven years. He was a fine lawyer and a dear friend.

Once I became attorney general, I was helped immeasurably by my various department heads—all fine attorneys and many of them distinguished legal scholars. Among their number were Stanton Faville, legal writer and researcher; Eugene Krasicky, scholar and trial strategist; and Robert Derengoski, who argued so many of the cases we took to both the Michigan Supreme Court and the U.S. Supreme Court. I did indeed argue some of those cases myself but usually with Bob's advice and coaching. Other department heads included George Bourgon, a part-time law professor who also served as a great advisor; Louis Caruso, who was a specialist on highway law; Solomon Bienenfeld, a former law professor and legal scholar; Maxine Boord Virtue, an anti-trust and common law expert, among her many other talents; Gerald White, head of our Detroit office; William Dexter, who was in charge of revenue and tax collection; Leo Maki, who headed up the criminal division; and Joseph Blitzke, who was in charge of regulatory agencies. Thanks also to Hugh B. Anderson, a specialist in public service, and Irving B. Feldman, a renowned expert in public administration and probate law.

I was also fortunate to work with Russell A. Searl, who ran our division on state affairs; Nicholas V. Olds, a conservation law scholar; Charles Hackney, the head of the agricultural law division; Nelson Westrin, who oversaw the lottery; David Brockman, the head of collections; Harry G. Iwasko, a scholar in the fields of commerce, banks, and insurance; Frederick Hoffecker, one of my heads of consumer protection; Keith Roberts, who was in charge of corrections; and Robert Ianni, who was both head of the criminal section and a special advisor to the attorney general.

I'd also like to thank Theodore Klimaszewski, a former FBI agent, who was in charge of organized crime; Wallace Hart, who headed welfare fraud efforts; Terrance Grady, the head of economic development; Gerald Young in education; Stewart Freeman, who was the nationally recognized head of our environmental protection division; my special assistants in the executive division, particularly Kelly Keenan and Heywood Julian; Christine Derdarian, head of the labor division; Gay S. Hardy, Michigan's first female solicitor general; Francis Pipp, a former classmate, who became head of the liquor control division; George Blaty, who was in charge of employment security; Milton Firestone, who headed municipal affairs; Thomas Emery, one of the heads of natural resources; Andrew Quinn, who later oversaw public administration; Robert Taube, who was another division head of public health; and Gary Gordon, an expert on election law.

Finally, I'd like to extend thanks to Don Keskey, who took a turn as head of public service; Michael Lockman, retirement law issues; Richard Roesch, revenue and taxation; Janis Meija, social services; Michael Leffler, tort defense; Patrick Isom, another head of highway and transportation; Eileen Zielesch, workman's compensation; Peter Lark, head of public utilities for a time; and Daniel Loepp, who was my administrative assistant for a time and went on to somewhat greater fame as president and CEO of Blue Cross Blue Shield of Michigan.

I owe special thanks to Sandra Szul, who served for many years as personal secretary for my deputy attorneys general.

But I owe an especially large debt of gratitude to Patricia Anderson, who has been my loyal and most able secretary in public and later private life for more than half a century. Her secretarial skills are superb, and she has the best shorthand in the West. Most of all, however, she was and is a loyal friend.

When it comes to importance, my three deputy attorneys general are at the top of the list. The late Leon S. Cohan (1929–2013), who features prominently in this book, was a brilliant and dedicated public servant. During our dozen years working together, we felt we combined the best aspects of the Irish American and Jewish American cultures and put them to work for the people of Michigan. Sadly, Leon did not live to see this book. But I will remember his devoted friendship always.

My relationship with his successor, Stanley Steinborn, was similar. We met in Alpena in the 1950s, when he arrived as the new attorney in town not long after I was new. He joined the attorney general's office soon after I arrived and became deputy in 1973 after Leon left to work in the private sector.

He stayed in that role for almost a quarter century, retiring in 1997, a little over a year before I did. We remained close friends until his death at the too-early age of seventy-two, in 2004.

The late Joe Sutton, an expert in elder law, served as deputy during my last year in office. Though his time as deputy was brief, his service was excellent; I had witnessed his fine qualities and his warm and outgoing personality over the more than twenty years he spent before that as an assistant attorney general. Tragically, he was felled by a heart attack in 2008.

I also want to say a word about my collaborator on this book, longtime journalist and Wayne State University professor Jack Lessenberry. He helped research a lot of this history, but more important, he helped me find the words I needed to tell my story. I had respected his work for years, but in the process of working on this book we also became close friends.

Lastly, I need to acknowledge that there have been so many other people—fellow lawyers, support staff, friends—who have helped me along the way but whom space would not permit me to name. You know who you are—and so do I. We enjoyed great years of public service. I'll never forget you, and I will be eternally grateful for all of your help.

Frank Kelley,
Haslett, Michigan,
September 2014

1

A SUMMONS
TO WASHINGTON

The phone rang. Washington, D.C., my secretary said. Important. I immediately recognized the voice on the line: Bobby Kennedy. Make that, U.S. attorney general Robert F. Kennedy.

Calling to congratulate me on my appointment as attorney general of the state of Michigan. I'd been on the job exactly ten days. It was January 12, 1962. "I've only been in this job a few months myself," RFK said. "We're both a couple of new Irishmen on the block, and I think we should get to know each other very well."

I thanked him and we chatted briefly. I promised to call his secretary and get to Washington as soon as I could. When I hung up, my head began to spin. "I'm beginning to move in a circle of public servants that would really make my father proud," I thought.

There was still a slight air of unreality about it all.

Less than three weeks earlier, I had been a small-town lawyer in Alpena, Michigan, celebrating Christmas Day with my wife, Jo, and my three children: Karen, not yet sixteen, Frank, thirteen, and Jane, who was ten.

I was in private practice and also handled the city's business. That was my life, and as far as I knew, that's what it would be for the foreseeable future. I was looking forward to my thirty-seventh birthday on New Year's Eve and another year in our mostly peaceful setting.

Eight days later, I was sitting alone in a cavernous office with sixteen-foot ceilings in the state capitol. Governor John Swainson had asked me to stop by his house in Lansing two days after Christmas.

Michigan attorney general Paul Adams was resigning to take a seat on the state supreme court, and he had to appoint a successor.

I knew I was being considered for the job but didn't think I'd get it, mainly because I was too young. I figured the governor would ask me to have a drink in honor of my birthday,

I'd go back home, and that would be that. But when I got there, a maid appeared with three glasses of champagne. "Happy Birthday, Frank," the governor said. "Here's to the next attorney general."

Six days later, I was Michigan's newly appointed chief lawyer.

But my ego wasn't running away with itself.

True, I knew this was a wonderful opportunity. But I honestly wasn't thinking of how I could use it to further my own career. My thoughts were more along the lines of "What am I going to do in this office to further the cause of justice and help my fellow man?"

That's because I had someone's expectations to live up to: those of my father, Frank E. Kelley, whom I always have hero-worshipped. He never had the chance to go to law school or even college. My dad had been orphaned as a young man, in the tough industrial town of Detroit in the days before any safety net existed. Yet he had pulled himself up, literally by the bootstraps he didn't have. He founded successful businesses, raised a family during the Great Depression, and gave us a good life with a cottage up north at a time when other kids my age lacked shoes.

My dad had gone on to become such a respected member of Michigan's Democratic Party he got to cast Michigan's votes for Harry Truman at the 1948 Democratic convention, the first convention ever televised. But I couldn't ask for his advice now.

My dad had died of a sudden, massive heart attack almost eight years earlier. The very last words he ever said to me were: "You'll be successful, Frank, I know it. But remember, it took me a long time to learn this: Worry is a waste of time, because the things you worry about the most in life never happen.

"Enjoy your life, Frank."

Enjoy your life, yes. But I knew he also meant: do something with it worth doing. "I want you to be a lawyer in the service of the public and use it to help your fellow man," Dad told me once.

That's what I felt the Kennedys were doing.

Thinking it over, I realized that Robert Kennedy had called me because, like him, I was an Irish Catholic, in a key state to boot. John F. Kennedy had squeaked into office in one of the closest races in history, and he carried Michigan by an almost equally close margin.

Naturally he wanted me for an ally early on. Regardless of the reasons, I'm glad he called. I would have been on his team anyway.

Within a week I flew to Washington with my very able chief deputy attorney general, Leon Cohan, for a meeting with RFK.

That meeting would help set the course of my professional life. When we arrived, my deputy and I were ushered into Kennedy's reception area and seated on one of two comfortable couches facing the secretarial staff. There were two women manning the desk facing us. They were so flawlessly beautiful they could easily have been movie stars. Later, Kennedy would tell me that he employed these attractive women for a reason.

He knew that half the people who came to see him would never have that opportunity, and the other half would end up waiting a long time before he was able to get to them. That was an era when almost everyone who had official business with the attorney general were men.

As long as the average fellow was allowed to sit there with these beautiful women, he'd be more content to wait. After that meeting, I would make sure that the first person my visitors would meet was a talented, poised, and beautiful receptionist.

You have to remember that this was another era. At the same time, by the way, I was also hiring more women assistant attorneys general, and putting them in more positions of power, than anyone in my office had before or since.

But that wasn't what was on my mind that winter day when I was sitting in the reception area of Bobby Kennedy's office in the Department of Justice. Incidentally, it was about as imposing a room as you can imagine, with a high and cavernous ceiling.

Visitors passed into his office through a wall of solid walnut. His office was enormous—about forty-five feet long and thirty feet deep, with a ceiling that was a good sixteen feet high.

Robert Kennedy sat behind an elevated desk, which made his slight, five-foot, ten-inch frame appear more imposing.

He was eleven months younger than I was, and I was regarded by many Michigan politicians as a kid. But it was an era of young men in power. His brother, President John F. Kennedy, was forty-four.

The governor who appointed me attorney general to fill a vacancy, John Swainson, was seven months younger than I was.

I felt we all had something in common; we felt we could make this world a better place. I was about to find out how true that was.

Our conversation began with Kennedy asking a few superficial questions about my background. Then he launched into a brief lecture.

"Frank," he said, "I intend to use my office as a bully pulpit to initiate legal action against those who violate our citizens' rights. Historically, most attorneys general, federal and state, have waited for something to happen, and then they react. I can't do that. I'm going to be an initiator. I'm going after the injustice I see, and I'm going after the bad people, and I'm prosecuting them.

"I say this to you because, like me, you're new in the job as the chief lawyer of a great state. I want you to be aggressive. I want you to use your bully pulpit. Reach out against injustice wherever you see it and protect the public. If you do that and I do that, the people of our great country will have a new appreciation for the freedoms they enjoy and a greater sense of trust in their government and elected officials. They will see that their government cares about them."

I listened attentively, as if every word he'd spoken was the Sermon on the Mount. He was so energetic, his presentation sounded like a pep talk—the kind of pep talk that my father would have given me, were he still alive to do so.

I told Bobby that I respected him and agreed with everything he said. I wondered aloud whether he, like I, had been conditioned as a youth by his father to believe in the importance of public service. He said he had—something his brother, President John F. Kennedy, would tell me himself later that year.

By the time we met, Attorney General Kennedy had already initiated an investigation against James Riddle Hoffa, the longtime, controversial head of the Teamsters Union, which happened to have its headquarters in my native Detroit. RFK did not bring that subject up, nor did I ask about it. Thirty minutes after it started, the meeting came to an end. Kennedy engaged in some small talk with Cohan, and walked me to the door. He put a hand on my shoulder and informed me that he would keep in touch.

Before we left, he instructed his secretary to give me all his phone numbers in case I should ever need to reach him.

I went back to Michigan deeply inspired by my meeting with Robert Kennedy and determined to make the Michigan Office of the Attorney General a bully pulpit. I vowed to be a strong advocate for the public, and I certainly tried to keep that commitment from that day forward.

What I never imagined, however, is that I would be doing that for the next thirty-seven years, longer than any attorney general in the history of the United States of America.

During my years in office, we established what I believe was the first Office of Consumer Protection in the country—even though I was called a Communist for wanting to do it.

Among other things, we took actions that helped lead to the U.S. Supreme Court's historic one-man, one-vote decision.

We moved to greatly expand the attorney general's office and make it far more of an active crusader on behalf of the people.

Years later, a national class action suit I helped initiate led to the biggest financial settlement in Michigan history: the Tobacco Master Settlement Agreement, concluded in November 1998, just before I left office. This agreement mandated that nearly $6 billion would be paid to the state of Michigan over the following quarter century, money meant to compensate Michigan for the incredible medical and social costs smoking has inflicted on its citizens.

During my time as Michigan's attorney general, we took on and largely tamed Michigan's public utilities, which often acted as though they were something of a law unto themselves.

Early on, we helped legally end the restrictive system—almost unimaginable today—that in the early 1960s was still preventing worthy African American and even Jewish Americans from buying homes, renting apartments, and living where they wanted to.

We did all this through times of enormous national upheaval that no one could then have imagined. I would be in office the day the man who came closer to royalty than anyone I've ever met, John F. Kennedy, was assassinated. I was working to elect Bobby, my mentor as attorney general, president when he was murdered, too.

I was attorney general when Detroit had the nation's worst race riot, an event I saw firsthand in a way that was far more dangerous than I realized. I was there when Jimmy Hoffa disappeared, in what remains one of the nation's most infamous unsolved crimes.

I watched a state and society transform in ways hard to imagine. With a lot of help from superb people, I tried hard to make Michigan a more just society, too.

Along the way I met and worked with more famous and powerful people than I could ever have dreamed, from presidents to show-business types, from Martin Luther King to Danny Thomas.

I worked closely with five governors, helped create law, and helped Michigan orient itself to a brand-new constitution, something that was the equivalent of several seat-of-the pants PhDs.

I made my share of mistakes—personal, to be sure, and a few professional ones as well. I won ten November elections and lost just one, an episode that had a profound impact on my life and career. There were things I wish I had accomplished, and times when I didn't succeed. But looking back, I have to say I have had an interesting life and a career that anyone interested in political science, Michigan, and history might find useful to study.

Maybe, just maybe, young people may look at my life and see something of themselves mirrored here. Perhaps my story will inspire others to chase their dreams.

And sometimes, I allow myself to look back and think, not at all bad for the son of the owner of a speakeasy.

No doubt about it, I've had an interesting life that has taken me through some fascinating times in our state's and our nation's history.

But it all started one New Year's Eve in a booming roaring 1920s industrial town you might have heard of.

They called it Detroit.

2

THE SIDEWALKS
OF DETROIT

I was born on New Year's Eve, 1924, into an era of relentless optimism, perhaps
for Detroit in particular.

"Every indication is that Detroit is entering upon a year whose productiveness
will excel anything in the past," the city's new mayor, John W. Smith, my father's
good friend, had written in that day's *Detroit News*, then the largest of the city's
three flourishing daily newspapers. There was reason for his optimism: the Age of
the Automobile was in full swing, and my town was the center of the automotive
universe. Detroit, which had barely 285,000 people less than a quarter-century earlier, had well over a million residents the day I came into the world.

Detroit and Los Angeles were, in fact, the fastest-growing cities in the
nation throughout the Roaring Twenties. Not that there wasn't a dark side.
Crime was creeping up, and ethnic tensions were on the rise. Mayor Smith, who
was so optimistic about the city's future, had been elected the month before by
barely beating a candidate backed by the Ku Klux Klan.

This was also the era of Prohibition, remember, and dry Detroit was just a
short, clandestine boat ride from wet Windsor.

The very night I was born, Michigan state police were chasing rum-runners
pushing beer-laden rowboats across the ice and busting an enterprising moon-
shiner near Merrick and Twelfth Street.

But I would later learn all about that.

My dad, you see, ran a speakeasy.

The Linden Hunt and Fish Club was, if I may say so, a classy joint. Frank E. Kelley, let me say, never considered what he was doing criminal. Not in the least. During the thirteen years (1920–33) of the nutty experiment called Prohibition, the manufacture, sale, and transport of alcohol may have been forbidden by law, but most people felt this was absolutely ridiculous.

People treated Prohibition much as they treat speed limits now, in areas where they are too slow. They did their best both not to comply and not to get caught. If you had the right connections, getting a drink and getting away with it weren't too hard.

And for the discerning drinker in the dry era, the Linden Hunt and Fish Club was the place to be. In fact, the leading personalities of the day, from mayors to monsignors and an occasional congressman, frequented my father's business.

All knew full well that the only big game there was the occasional olive that could be fished out of a martini.

City councilmen, business leaders, and sports figures were all secret members of "The Club." Well-connected out-of-towners looking for good food and drink would arrange to be admitted. My father, one of the most remarkable men I've ever known, would even issue them an actual membership card.

But I'm getting ahead of my story. That's not surprising, however; I've usually been ahead of schedule, and I was that New Year's Eve. You see, I wasn't even supposed to have come on the scene in 1924. I wasn't expected until the middle of January 1925.

Matter of fact, I completely upset my mother's New Year's Eve plans. Grace Kelley was looking forward to her first baby, all right. But her doctors told her she had at least a couple of weeks. So she had a wonderful last fling planned—entirely appropriate for a beautiful twenty-two-year-old, married just nine months before.

Her younger sister Hazel picked her up in a cab that morning. They lunched downtown, then went to the Adams Theater to see the premiere of the new movie *Janice Meredith*, starring Marion Davies.

It was a silent film about the American Revolution; the "talkies" were still five years or so away. But my mother never got to see the ending because I made my own unexpected early bid for independence. The labor pains started; Hazel and a uniformed usher hustled Mom into a cab, which headed for what was then the brand-new Providence Hospital at 14th and Grand Boulevard.

I hate ruining parties, but some would say I've always had a flair for the dramatic. In any event, at about 7 p.m., one Frank Joseph Kelley made his first appearance on the stage, squalling loudly.

Not for the last time, I might add.

My father was in his early thirties then, a little older and more successful than most first-time fathers. You might say he went a little overboard. They tell me he paid for three large rooms at the hospital—one for my mother, one for a private nurse, and one for himself.

You might say that I came into the world a bit of a little prince, at least as far as my father was concerned. That meant I'd have a somewhat privileged life when I was a boy. But it also meant I was expected to grow up and make a difference, to help my fellow men find better lives in this world.

Eventually I came home from the hospital on a crisp January day, to a Detroit that in some ways still exists—and in other ways is as vanished as ancient Rome. What may be hard to imagine now is that the city I was born in was then one of the most exciting cities in the nation.

California, as far as the rest of the nation was concerned, was a world away, across mountains and deserts in an era before airline travel. Detroit was putting the world on wheels.

The future Motor City was only a large town when my father was born, before a mechanic named Henry Ford got the idea of making a whole lot of cars fast and cheap and hiring armies of men to build them. By 1920, the year the house I grew up in was built, Detroit had exploded to just under a million inhabitants. By the time I went to kindergarten, it had reached a million and a half.

It was a city with a vibrant and brawling working class, with Irish, Polish, German, and Hungarian neighborhoods, and areas of growing middle-class gentility as well. My parents moved into a neighborhood that contained both working- and middle-class families just months before my grand debut—to a brick home just a few houses off of Grand River Avenue, then one of the city's grand thoroughfares. My home, at 8957 North Martindale Avenue, had state-of-the-art modern conveniences, with both oil heat and steam radiators.

There was a living and a dining room, a kitchen, and three good-sized bedrooms. For my father, the son of an immigrant, one of nine children whose parents died when they were young, the ability to buy such a house must have seemed proof of success, that he had, by his own efforts, risen amazingly far in the world.

He would later add a breakfast nook and a half bath, but the home, which is still occupied today, would remain my parents' primary residence for the rest of their lives. Even in its best days the neighborhood was not, however, exclusive or suburban.

While there were other well-kept houses, there were also plenty of multiple-family flats occupied by those who could only afford to rent; before World War II, homeownership was fairly uncommon.

Our family never forgot we were in the center of a vibrant, bustling, growing city. Nor did we want to. After all, my father had strategically selected a home just two blocks from one of what was then one of the city's finest shopping areas.

This was, you have to understand, before anyone thought of malls surrounded by vast parking lots. Believe it or not, almost nobody thought of taking a car to go shopping. Many families still didn't have cars, even in the Motor City, and almost no women drove. What Detroit did have was a bustling system of streetcars.

Shoppers—mainly women—would take the streetcar, shop, meet friends, have lunch, and then carry home what they bought. Thanks to our strategically located house, my mother would walk to the wonderful Joy Road–Grand River shopping center.

Sometimes she'd take me with her, and that seemed like a magical world. There were first-rate jewelers. National and regional retail stores, like Lerner's and Winkelman's.

What interested me most was a Detroit institution, Sanders' Confectionary, where, for fifteen cents, I could sit on a fancy stool at a marble counter and get a huge hot fudge sundae.

There were also two movie theaters. A large Cunningham's Drugstore. Detroit's premier five-and-dime stores, Kresge and Woolworth's. To the west were two blocks of men's shoe stores, barbershops, and other chain stores, all displaying their finest merchandise in huge, shining display windows.

Sometimes I would wander past these stores, alone, losing myself in the magic of this material splendor and the hustle and bustle of well-dressed, well-groomed people.

And to this day, when I think of my youth, I instantly recall the sights, sounds, and pleasant aromas of my neighborhood.

Oddly enough—or not so oddly, given human nature—there were times I felt lonely, frustrated, and sorry for myself.

But my worst days during childhood were nothing compared to the childhood of the man who is still my all-time hero. A man who, in the words of one of the tributes published after his death, "learned his Democratic politics in the days when arguments were settled with baseball bats in labor union halls." But a man who saw that I wanted for nothing, treated me with surpassing kindness, made this city a better place, and inspires me to this day.

I'm talking about Francis Edward Kelley, saloon keeper, product of the mean streets turned respectable party leader, mental health reformer, and part-time country gentleman.

Frank Kelley the first, my dad.

3

THE PATRIARCH
AND THE WORLD HE MADE

I returned, and saw under the sun that the race is not to the swift, nor the battle to the strong, nor bread to the wise, nor riches to the intelligent, nor favor to those with knowledge, but time and chance happeneth to them all.

Ecclesiastes 9:11 (King James Version)

Being poor and Irish was no bed of roses when the twentieth century dawned. My grandfather, Michael Kelley, native of County Mayo, Ireland, came to know that better than most. "Mike" Kelley was one of the best workers Detroit Brass Works ever had. He had a lot of incentive to work hard: a houseful of children.

Before long, he had tragedy and even more incentive. His wife, Maria, prematurely aged from pregnancy after pregnancy, died of childbirth fever shortly after giving birth to their ninth child in 1910. They'd left Ireland thirty years before to escape a second wave of hunger forty years after the first potato famine that devastated the Emerald Isle and sent waves of immigrants to our shores.

For a brief time before leaving for the New World, Mike had worked in England, where he changed the family name from Kelly to Kelley, the more usual English spelling. His reasons were pragmatic: anti-Irish prejudice was huge, and while he wasn't about to change his religion, he thought the Protestant spelling might help him find work.

But before long he went to America, traveling with Maria Maloney, the sister of his best friend. They were only friends when they crossed the Atlantic, but romance bloomed. Four years later they were married, and the children began coming.

And coming. But the hazards of childbirth were great. That was not an era when doctors—if you could afford one—or midwives washed their hands. And the odds caught up with Maria.

Now it was just Michael and nine kids in a small, three-bedroom cottage in Corktown, Detroit's bustling Irish neighborhood. Things went from bad to worse when two years later, on a hot August day on the job, Michael caught a huge piece of iron right in the gut.

It must have hurt terribly, though he tried to conceal the pain. Workers had few or no rights then. Complain, and a man could lose his position. He dragged himself back to work for a few more days until the internal hemorrhaging caused him to collapse and die on the job.

Then his children really were alone. There was no Social Security, no welfare, no workman's compensation. Family was all they had. Fortunately some of Michael's own brothers and sisters had also come to America to escape famine. Michael Kelley's vivid description of seeing one mass grave was enough to keep his son Frank—my father—from ever having any desire to visit the land of his father's birth.

The immediate problem in turn-of-the-twentieth-century Detroit, however, was keeping the Kelley children alive and together. My dad and his older brothers and sisters hit upon a solution. They had an aunt back in Ireland, Margaret, unmarried at the advanced age of thirty-four. Would she agree to cross the Atlantic and care for the Kelley orphans? She would. So her siblings chipped in for the fare.

She crossed the Atlantic and sailed to Detroit. Meantime, her late brother's employer, Detroit Brass Works, had what passed for a twinge of social conscience. Michael Kelley was a good worker, the bosses agreed, and they'd been paying him three dollars a day. So they offered the family a deal. Two of the older boys could drop out of school and go to work full-time in their father's place. The company would pay them each half what their father had been getting. They got two workers for the price of one, and the owners probably felt they deserved credit for their humanity.

The Kelley boys had no choice. Even with their income, however, it was never enough for the entire household. My dad had already gone to work early, dropping out of school after no more than four or five years to help feed his family. Being a paper boy was a potentially good job for a lad in the first years of the century.

But most of the good corners were taken by established newsboys who were bawling out the latest headlines from the *Detroit Free Press*, *Detroit News*, and *Detroit Times*. So Dad became a newsboy for the German-language *Abendpost*, which sold hundreds of copies to immigrant families not far from his neighborhood. The German housewives took an instant liking to him. They knew he was trying to help feed a large family, and on collection day they sent him home with parcels of food tucked into his delivery wagon. That gave him an idea.

Soon he and one of his brothers started the Kelley Sausage Company. Before long, it was supplying sausage to scores of Detroit-area stores. He had a formula for success: when it came to actually making the sausages, no Irish need apply. They could work in the front office or as salesmen—but the boy who grew up on home-cooked German food wanted only German sausage makers in the plant, thank you. But if Frank E. Kelley was successful in the sausage business, he wasn't inspired.

He wanted adventure, and his chance came on April 6, 1917, when the United States declared war on Germany. Dad said farewell to sausages and enlisted. He was only of average height—five feet, nine inches, the same as I am (or was, before the years shrunk me a bit). But by all accounts he was a hero. He never talked much about the war. Most men who have seen real combat don't, though I know he was on the front lines at the epic battles of the Argonne and Château-Thierry. The story was that he once carried a wounded buddy he shared a trench with two miles to the nearest aid station. I have no way of knowing how true that was.

What I know for certain is this: he came home as a man who inspired respect. Frank E. Kelley also arrived home to find the world dramatically changing in one widely unwelcome way. He came home to a country outlawing the consumption of alcoholic beverages. Prohibition, in other words.

A constitutional amendment made the manufacture and sale of alcoholic beverages illegal. The great experiment, it was called. A great failure is what it was.

Not, however, for my dad. Prohibition was the catalyst that made ours a reasonably well-off family—and made him an increasingly prominent and politically important figure in Detroit.

Now, Frank Kelley was an honest, law-abiding man with a great respect for the rule of law. He also was a man who needed to make a living. So he coped with the new order of things in the most intelligent, rational, and moral way he could.

He opened a speakeasy.

Then he made it one of the best ones in Detroit.

Let me be clear about something: Frank Edward Kelley did *not* see himself as a criminal—not in any way, shape, or form. But he wasn't going to put up with any denial of what he saw as the basic, fundamental right to have a glass of beer or shot of whiskey.

After all, his ancestors back in the Emerald Isle had gone through enough unfair government repression for several lifetimes.

So the Linden Hunt and Fish Club was born. Located at the corner of 24th and Linden, it was anything but a cheap "gin joint."

Babe Ruth went there. Ty Cobb and other baseball greats were fixtures at the bar. Jack Dempsey and other boxing legends could be seen there, as were governors, mayors, congressmen, councilmen, and boatloads of candidates for those jobs. Business leaders and priests, too.

It wouldn't be too much to say that Frank E. Kelley was, in a Detroit context, the Toots Shor of his day.

The place was classy, and artfully disguised, thanks to a small grocery store and barbershop in the front. Getting into the "club" was exactly like something in a Hollywood movie. You walked down a hallway, rang a bell, and a small slot slid open.

You then had to produce a membership card, prudently issued by my father. Once Barney, the burly, 230-pound former wrestler of a doorman, was convinced you were all right, the door swung wide.

Then you might find yourself among as many as a hundred men, standing or sitting at a fifty-foot-long bar, trimmed in polished brass. The bartenders were well dressed; there were fine framed pictures of prizefighters, ballplayers, and racehorses on the walls.

There were clouds of cigar smoke in the air and nary a woman in sight. This was a male preserve, and nobody in that era ever thought of challenging that. If you arrived at the club with a female guest or guests, however, things were different. You promptly went past a pool-and-billiard lounge and proceeded right into the dining area, where live music came from a bandstand and a headwaiter would promptly seat you.

Presiding over all this, with cheerfully warm and convivial dignity, was my father, then in his thirties. He was charismatic and had a generosity of spirit I could only envy.

Interestingly, he was never closed down. There may have been a raid or two, but business was never stopped for more than a few hours. Why was that? Well, I don't know for sure, but I was told a great story. Remember the wounded soldier he was said to have saved during World War I by carrying him to an aid station? His name was Bill Burns and supposedly was related to William J. Burns, the famous detective who went on to become the first Prohibition-era head of the FBI.

It was said that word went out from the top: "You can shut down every speakeasy in Detroit—but don't touch Frank Kelley."

True? I have no idea, and even if it was, it doesn't explain how Dad got away with it when Burns was replaced by J. Edgar Hoover, the year I was born. It's probably more likely that my father's growing political ties, especially his close friendship with John W. Smith, councilman and mayor of Detroit, had something to do with it.

But back to Dad. Was what he was doing technically illegal?

Beyond any doubt it was—and there's a dose of irony here. After all, his oldest son—that would be me—would go on to become Michigan's top law enforcement officer. And I grew up surrounded by relative comforts that stemmed from what were technically ill-gotten gains. However, there is a difference, and I don't think I am rationalizing. Dad, who was otherwise as law-abiding a citizen as they came, saw Prohibition as the height of hypocrisy and "an unjust police action."

He resented that it had been enacted by a bunch of moralizing Puritans while he and his buddies were huddled in muddy trenches overseas, getting shot at to make the world safe for democracy.

What makes Dad's attitude far more justifiable to me is that most of the nation soon came to agree with him. They wanted to drink, and Prohibition was repealed as soon as Franklin D. Roosevelt became president in 1933. With the end of the noble experiment came the end of the Hunt and Fish Club.

Dad wanted, all his life, to be respectable and legitimate. So he applied for a liquor license the moment they became available. Within days Michigan's new state attorney general, a genial Democrat named Patrick O'Brien, recommended that the Michigan Liquor Control Commission issue a license to one Frank Kelley.

And so it was done. Not, however, for the old speakeasy but for a new bar, Frank Kelley's Cafe, to be conveniently located on Grand River, right between our home and our church, St. Theresa's.

Things settled down then. I was eight years old.

Father's income declined somewhat when drinking became legit. My parents cut down on frills like custom-made clothes, but we still did far better than the average family. Dad got more and more involved in politics.

We also were able to enjoy life as a family in a way few people were able to do. The Great Depression, remember, was still on. Yet we were able to employ a year-round, live-in maid. We had a cottage at Burt Lake and, during the summer, a cook and a gardener.

Yet odd as it may seem, I didn't realize the extent of my good fortune.

4

COMING OF AGE:
SUCCESS . . . AND FAILURE

Fast-forward to December 7, 1941, the day the Japanese attacked Pearl Harbor, changing our world forever.

Where do you suppose Michigan's future attorney general, the champion of consumer protection, was when the news broke on America's most infamous Sunday afternoon?

Playing football? Returning from church? Studying for finals and thinking about law school?

Well, not exactly.

I was making out with a beautiful blonde named Noreen in my dad's snappy red '41 Buick, a car with highly fashionable whitewall tires. We were cuddling somewhere near (maybe not too near) her home in Detroit. Once a student so promising I was promoted a grade ahead, I was, that afternoon, close to flunking out of my first term in college. I didn't know what I wanted to do or who I wanted to be.

Frankly, I was using my girlfriend (we broke up not long afterward) as a form of escape. Then I heard the announcement over the radio and was stunned.

I was filled with the same shock and patriotic fervor as millions of other men and boys. But I could not go down to the recruiting office and enlist the next morning, much as I wanted to, because I was too young. The minimum age for the military was seventeen.

I wouldn't reach that until New Year's Eve. Now, I looked sophisticated and older than my years and could talk a good game. In my early teens I had gotten away with adding a few years to my age so that I could work as a sailor up north.

Lying to Uncle Sam was a different matter, however, and I feared one that might have some severe repercussions. Nor, frankly, once my flag-waving frenzy cooled a bit, was I all that hot to enlist early. After all, my father had been severely wounded in World War I, and I was in no hurry to outdo him in that department.

Not that I had any thought of avoiding military service; I knew that sooner or later it would be my time. However, I did need to figure out something to do with myself in the interim.

One thing was clear; it wasn't going to be school.

My once-promising academic career had nosedived, badly. My parents had originally sent me to a parochial school—St. Theresa's—run by Dominican nuns. I had a little trouble in first grade, involving temper tantrums that got me exiled under the teacher's desk.

But after that I quickly became a minor star. Thanks to elocution lessons my father insisted I start taking at age five, I was way in front of the other kids in reciting and reading aloud.

I did well in school, even though I didn't study all that hard. Then disaster struck in the seventh grade. The nuns gave us all the standard IQ tests, and the top twenty students skipped eighth grade and went directly into high school.

This may have made academic sense. In fact, every one of those kids earned at least one advanced degree, back in an era when most people didn't go to college. But it was a social and psychological disaster. What's worse is that we were not allowed to assimilate into the regular high school population. Believe it or not, they put us in a special homeroom separated from the other kids by a glass wall. Well, you know what was bound to happen.

We were treated like freaks. We were called "guinea pigs" and "birds in a cage." None of the older high schoolers had time for us, and worse, the three boys who had been my best pals growing up no longer wanted to have anything to do with me. I couldn't take it, and after a year my parents pulled me out of there and enrolled me in University of Detroit High School, a fine institution run by the Jesuits.

Things went much better; for a time, anyway, I tried my best to be one of the boys. I fit in—at least on the surface. I was even popular enough to be accepted into a snobbish fraternity made up mainly of rich and socially prominent kids. These were kids who wore tuxedos to their high school dances and managed to come up with the money to get national names like Gene Krupa to play. But if I was winning acceptance socially, I wasn't performing as well as I should have academically.

The truth was that from earliest childhood I had battled feelings of insecurity and self-doubt. That might be hard to believe for anyone who later saw me running for office. But the Frank J. Kelley who won ten statewide elections, who stood up to governors, mob bosses, and top utility executives, was once a lonely little boy who never really felt good enough. This was in spite of having things much, much better than the vast majority of kids my age, in large part because of my father's success.

My summers growing up were, looking back now, what virtually anyone would have called idyllic. My father was doing well enough by 1927 that he could build a cottage up north, at Burt Lake.

Urged on by a friend named Charles Whitman, who owned a cottage next door, Dad bought an acre of land, hired a work crew of men he trusted, and sent them up north, telling them to build a cottage just like Whitman's—but make every room one square foot bigger and add a real bathroom, not just an outhouse.

You might say Dad could be a bit competitive. He also knew how to pick out workmen he could trust. Anyway, the place was speedily done. Dad took the train up north, looked around, inspected everything, and nodded. Starting that summer, the Kelley clan headed for Burt Lake as soon as school let out every year—something that would remain a family tradition until 1983.

Every summer, we'd head north in a seven-passenger Hupmobile and stay there for more than two months of healthy fun. To say that I was a lucky kid, especially by Depression standards, would be an understatement. When I was five, my dad bought me my own Shetland pony I called Nick, and I soon learned to ride.

We had a full-time cook named "Speedy" Belhardt, and the tables groaned under the weight of the lavish breakfasts and even more sumptuous dinners he laid on. One of the measures of a man in turn-of-the-century Irish-American society was whether he "set a good table," and my father more than overachieved. We'd have pork chops and steak laid on one night, chicken and fish the next.

By this time, our family was growing. The cottage, in fact, was officially named Patricia Lodge after my sister, who was born a year and a half after I was. She would be followed by my brothers Jim, who was four years younger, and Dick, seven years younger.

Additionally, we had an "adopted" sister. Around the time I started kindergarten, a friend of my father's asked him to visit a Polish Catholic orphanage. He noticed one girl sitting alone, looking forlorn, lost, and lonely. He chatted with her for a few moments.

Her name was Mary Olish. She was twelve years old. Although she wasn't an orphan, she was one of seven children whose father had lost his job and whose parents had fallen on hard times.

They felt they had no choice but to put her in the orphanage. My father, just like that, decided to take her home, which says a lot about the kind of man he was—and how different a time it was.

These days, doing something like that would take months, at least, and involve everything from background checks to official legal proceedings. But back then, things were simpler. My father told the attending nun that he wanted to sponsor Mary.

They gathered up her things and told her to be a good girl and help my mother and her maid with the household chores. She was warned that otherwise, she could be returned to the orphanage—though with our family, there was no real fear of that.

And that was that. My father brought her home, and I had a new sister.

Whether my father consulted my mother about this, I'll never know. What I do know is that although they never formally adopted Mary, from day one they treated her like their child. They bought her a new wardrobe and enrolled her immediately in the eighth grade at St. Theresa's. While she did indeed help with the chores, she was one of us. She walked me to kindergarten my first day and comforted me when I was blue. Two and half years later, she made a decision.

Mary, still only fourteen, was determined to become a nun. She joined the Dominicans, in Adrian, the same order to which her teachers at St. Theresa had belonged. Not that she disappeared completely from our lives—she spent vacations with us every year.

It just might be that her constant prayers helped keep me out of more trouble than I've been in. She remained a teacher and a sister all her life, until she passed away quietly in 2008 while watching her beloved Detroit Tigers on TV.

Naturally she also spent summers at Burt Lake with us, where, as a little boy, I was frequently lonely. I loved my sister Patricia, but she was both younger and . . . a girl. Though I am much closer to my brothers now, there was too much age difference then for us to be real pals, though I have fond memories of all of us swimming or playing croquet together. On the other hand, I adored my father and lived for the days when he would take me out on his boat or for a ride in his open touring car—just the two of us.

He was generous with his time, but I couldn't get enough. He taught me how to ride horses and how to judge people. And for that purpose, a summer at Burt Lake was a hell of a laboratory. Everyone who was anyone came to visit.

For example, during one typical summer, my father might host the likes of Jack Dempsey, former world heavyweight boxing champion, and Frank Murphy, the future mayor of Detroit, governor of Michigan, U.S. attorney general, and Supreme Court justice.

Even Kenesaw Mountain Landis, the first commissioner of organized baseball, paid us a visit, as did bishops and priests, journalists and well-known gamblers. Talk about a diverse social circle. What I wouldn't give to be able to go back and sit in on some of those conversations today!

Back then, I was usually happier riding my pony and playing cowboy. Sometimes I'd feel closer to our part-time caretaker, Bill Howell, who stabled Nick, than to my own parents. I thought he understood me better than they did. But what I wanted most of all was my dad's approval. I can tell you I thought I was hot stuff when my father began letting me drive his car on some backcountry roads when I was twelve.

Back then you could get a license at fourteen (not that many young Depression-era kids had access to a car). The fact that I did and that my father let me drive was something truly wonderful.

All too soon, however, every idyllic summer would end—and it was back downstate, back to Detroit, and back to school.

———

But school wasn't going as well as it should have.

Despite my acceptance by the in-crowd at the University of Detroit High School, my grades were mediocre at best. My parents told me they didn't think I was living up to their investment in me.

By the end of my sophomore year, I was miserable but didn't show it. My mother talked to a couple of the nuns from St. Theresa who had been behind my disastrous early promotion to high school. They had both just moved to Visitation High School a couple miles away. They suggested to a worried Grace Kelley that the family enroll me there. So they did.

Finally, things started going better. I was accepted almost immediately, in spite of being the new kid on the block and starting Visitation as a junior. Since I had skipped over eighth grade, I was still younger than the other kids, but few if any knew it.

Those two years at Visitation were the happiest and most normal of my high school career. I acted in plays, something that may have been a good preparation for politics. I even got my picture in the old *Detroit Times* once for being the male lead in a now-forgotten play called *Growing Pains*. I thought I was a big star. What's more, I thought I was a man of the world.

I wasn't, of course—except in one sense.

Unlike any of my classmates, by the time I graduated from high school, I had spent two summers working full-time as a seaman on the Great Lakes. That was really an adult job, but I managed to get away with passing for older thanks to, as usual, my dad.

Even though my father had a better-than-average income, it fell dramatically once Prohibition ended in 1933. As you may remember, thanks to his political connections, he was awarded a liquor license almost immediately. We were never in danger of hunger, but the Depression was still on, and our family started to feel it.

I was more aware than most kids and knew that my father had lost a lot of money in the stock market crash. I felt that I should do what I could to help. As a result, I went into the newspaper business soon afterward. That is to say, I became a paper boy.

I began hawking the old Hearst paper, the *Detroit Times*.

Now to succeed as a paper boy back then wasn't just a matter of yelling loudly, "Read all about it!" The job required business and negotiating skills, considerable diplomacy, people smarts, some self-defense strategy, and intelligence, craftiness, and staying power.

You might even say I learned a whole lot about politics on my corner at Grand River and Beverly. Even breaking into the game took some doing. The really desirable corner was Grand River and Joy, a block away. But that was locked up by a cartel of older Jewish boys. They controlled all the business there. So one day I went to them and asked if they'd let me operate as their "subagent" a block away. I offered to handle the *Times*, which wasn't selling as well as the *Detroit News* or the *Free Press*. I said I'd split the profits with them.

That sounded reasonable to them, so they agreed to my terms. Most people read afternoon, not morning, papers, back then, so I'd hit my corner at 4:30 p.m., sell papers till 6:00, and dash home for dinner.

My profits were a penny a paper, and on an average day I netted fifteen cents. However, the big money came when the papers put out an extra—which was fairly often. There was no TV, radio news was in its infancy, and newspapers were how people found out when something big happened. On extra nights ("Tigers Win Pennant!") I might make a dollar and a half—big money then.

That money didn't come easy, though. Occasionally some new tough kid selling the *Detroit News* would challenge me to a fight for the corner. When that happened, I let my older allies and employers know. My Jewish buddies sent a couple reinforcements. Then the three of us gave the competition a choice between leaving immediately or having some instant dental work done. All this taught me valuable lessons—how to assert myself, how to stand up to bullies, and how to make a sale.

Half a century later, when I was Michigan's attorney general, I was still using those skills. I learned another very important lesson, too, during my paper boy days.

As I said, the circle of older kids who controlled paper sales at Grand River and Joy, who hired me and then became my friends, were Jewish. This was my first real contact with people of a different culture. Now, there was a lot of anti-Semitism at that time. These were the years when Father Charles Coughlin was blaring out his anti-Semitic propaganda to a national audience from his Shrine of the Little Flower Church in Royal Oak.

There was also supposed to be a considerable amount of enmity toward Jews among Irish Americans. But for my dad, the opposite was true. He was sympathetic to all oppressed peoples. "The Irish have been discriminated against for five hundred years," he'd say. "Our Jewish neighbors were discriminated against for five thousand years, and yet they found freedom and opportunity in America and took advantage of it in the best way."

America, he told me, was better-off because both the Irish and the Jews had made it a better country. He was so right. What he couldn't have imagined was that his son would not only be the nation's longest-serving attorney general but also benefit immensely from two superb deputies who were both Jewish.

Leon Cohan and, later, Stanley Steinborn were two of the best assistants any officeholder could ever wish for, and we had extremely close working relationships for many years.

But that was all far in the future then. After only about nine months, I moved on to delivering papers to neighborhood homes. That was tamer, but the profits still weren't that great. By then, I needed to make more money for the same reason that has driven many a teenage boy to work: I wanted to buy a car.

Even though I was only fourteen at that time, it was legal for me to drive. The best job I could imagine was working on the Michigan State Car Ferry line, which took vehicles back and forth between the Upper Peninsula and the Lower Peninsula, across a five-mile stretch of the Great Lakes.

That was important work then. The magnificent Mackinac Bridge wouldn't be built for nearly twenty years. The car ferries were the only way of getting from lower to upper Michigan, unless you wanted to drive hundreds of miles through Indiana and Wisconsin.

Unfortunately, you had to be at least eighteen to get seaman's papers. My father thought that wasn't fair. So he agreed to let me lie about my age. Perhaps Michigan's former chief law enforcement officer shouldn't admit this . . . but I became a forger.

I doctored up my birth certificate, and my dad got me an appointment to apply for a job. He paid my train fare to Mackinaw City, and, thanks to his influence, I got a job working on the docks for a not-so-princely $97 a month. I found a room in a boardinghouse, with a bath and shower down the hall, and Dad got me a 1935 Ford with wire wheels and a tendency to burn almost as much oil as gas.

After making a car payment and paying my room and board (I got two meals a day as part of the deal), I didn't have a lot of spending money left. But nevertheless, this was a golden opportunity for me to get practical experience and street smarts beyond my years.

This was in the summer of 1939. World War II was fast approaching, and before the summer ended, the world would be plunged into the biggest and bloodiest war in human history.

How much I was aware of any of this, I can't say. What I was aware of was that I was endlessly frustrated because I didn't actually get to work on the boats themselves. Instead, I was made a dock worker. The ferries would arrive every twenty minutes, and I soon learned how to expertly and quickly catch a heaving line, pull a heavy cable, and tie a couple knots to secure it.

These car ferries had multiple levels and were fairly huge, so it took maybe ten to fifteen minutes to load and unload the cars, and then we'd load them up again, unloose the cables, and the ship would cast off. Then we'd get ready for the next one.

That was really an incredible summer, healthy and stimulating. I was popular, in part, I'm sure, because I was one of the few guys who had a car. We'd spend some time with the sailors from the boats, most of them regular seamen from the Upper Peninsula.

Some of them remained friends for life. They taught me a lot, and once in a while, much later, I was able to return the favor. Tommy Jewel, for example, was an older wheelman who went out of his way to be good to a punk teenage dockhand named Frank Kelley. Many years later, when he was captain of a boat with the enchanting name of *Chief Wawatam*, and I was attorney general of the state of Michigan, I had an opportunity to repay the favor. The railroad that owned the vessel was threatening to take it out of service. That was not at all justified, and I went to federal court and got an injunction that kept the ship running and Tommy on the job. Five years later, he was able to retire with a decent pension, something for which he was forever appreciative. And I was just extremely grateful that I had the chance to do it.

The experience was wonderful. Not every moment, of course. During your first year, you weren't allowed to go out on the water. As the newest and youngest dockhand, I was saddled with the unlovely chore of cleaning the restrooms of every boat.

In the evenings, I got an education of a different kind. I'd pick up some of the other guys in my car, and we'd head off to town. Mostly we'd go to the Gold Front in Cheboygan, which was a dance hall attached to a bar. Or else we'd head for the Dixie Tavern in Mackinaw City, which was a bar attached to a dance hall.

I grew up fast. You learned very quickly that the crew of a ship was your second family. It was one for all and all for one, on deck, in town, and especially when your shipmates got into a brawl.

Yes, sailors did indeed like a fight now and again. Nobody had any idea how young I was, but they knew I was small. Once, when a melee started at the Dixie, a big guy on our ship picked me up and put me on the piano: "Stay there, and don't hit anyone until I bring them over for you to hit." Which he proceeded to do. I was getting quite a deck-smart education. While other kids my age were learning how to tie knots in the Boy Scouts, I was tying them for real on Great Lakes freighters, being accepted as a man among men.

Thanks to my seaman's papers and my car, everyone thought I was eighteen or nineteen—even though I was four years younger. Fortunately, I didn't start drinking. Not that I didn't occasionally sample a beer, but everyone realized that somebody had to be sober enough to drive.

But I did use my "older man" status to flirt with some very attractive girls who had no idea I wouldn't even turn fifteen until that coming New Year's Eve. These were harmless flirtations—though I won't deny sneaking in the occasional cuddle or quick kiss. Beyond that, I'm of the generation where a gentleman just doesn't tell.

Small wonder, then, that when fall rolled around, plane geometry didn't seem that much of a thrill. My second summer on the waterfront was even better. My father had helped arrange for me to be a real seaman this time, and I worked mainly on a ship called the *City of Cheboygan*, though I was occasionally loaned out to another ship, the *St. Ignace*. So I was a seasoned mariner at fifteen.

Not that this was all that glamorous of a job. Yes, I finally did have a place to sleep—the absolute worst berth on the boat. It was below decks, next to the fire hole, and no matter the weather, the temperature down there was never less than 110 degrees.

That didn't matter. This future attorney general didn't dream about suing for unfair working conditions. By the time my shift ended, I was normally so exhausted I could sleep anywhere.

Essentially I was the deckhand to the boatswain's mate, which is a romantic, nautical way of saying I was his maintenance stooge. I polished more brass than you can imagine, day after day. I also painted lifeboats and did other odd jobs. I had one near-death experience: that first year, I was pulling a cable up to secure an arriving boat when the machine evidently broke and the cable jerked me right into the water—less than ten feet from the churning propeller of the giant boat. Suddenly a hand reached down, grabbed the neck of my overalls, and pulled me out as if I were an oversize kitten. The hand belonged to the University of Detroit's great Italian American football star of that era, Al Oliveto, who saved my life. We both later became lawyers, and I remained his close and forever grateful friend down through the years.

The summer of 1941 was my last on the straits, mostly on a ship called the *St. Marie*. I had graduated from Visitation High School that June and was getting ready to go to college. The most dramatic thing happened toward the end of the summer.

I sold my car the day before I was to leave and, with my paycheck, had $200 in cash—an enormous sum in those days. I stashed it in my cabin—and when I came back from breakfast it was gone. My mood turned to panic, and I told the captain.

He stopped the ship in the middle of the straits and called everyone together. Doing so was relatively easy because there weren't any passengers then; we were on our way over to pick up a load of cars. The captain told them that somebody had taken Frank Kelley's money, and they had better 'fess up—or by God, he'd have the state police board the *City of Cheboygan* and search everyone.

Within a few minutes the ship's fireman went to the captain. He had six or seven kids, a tough job, and a prior jail record. He handed him the money. The skipper told him he wouldn't turn him in—this time. But the captain, a wiry little man of French descent, told the fireman he would keep an eye on him. I did not feel any bitterness—getting my money back was one of the happiest moments of my life. Instead, as time went on, I was more and more impressed with the way the captain had handled things. Had he turned the thief in, he would have gone back to prison—and who knows what would have become of his family and all those children?

Maybe that example helped shape the way I looked at human frailty years later, when I would spend most of my adult life as the top law enforcement officer for the state of Michigan.

In any event, with that dramatic episode, my career as a sailor ended. When the ship pulled in for my final time, my mother was on the dock with my dad's Buick. Within a day or so, I would go back to start life as a college man, at the University of Detroit, then a very strict Jesuit institution.

What I can say is those summers on the Straits of Mackinac were about the most ideal coming-of-age experience a young man of my generation could have had. We worked hard, but it was satisfying work; as I said, we were completely wiped out by the end of the day. It built my muscles, I can tell you that. The pay wasn't spectacular, but they fed us mountains of great food, something I especially appreciated as I was, in my early and middle teens, in my rapid growth phase. I've been to many of the world's finest restaurants since then, but I can honestly say that I cannot recall any time in my life when I enjoyed food as much as I did back then.

Frankly, those summers were some of the most wonderful of my life. How many kids could have had a similar adventure? This was mostly because of my wonderful dad. We never talked about it, but I have a sneaking suspicion that my father knew I was going to grow up fast working on those docks and aboard those ships—and that was just fine with him. He had had to become streetwise himself at a very young age and thought giving me that experience was the best protection he could give me. Nor did he ever utter a word of reproach. "You know right from wrong, and don't do anything that would make your mother ashamed," he told me when I was a boy, and that was about it.

My dad allowed me to make my own way. He believed if you were sharp and had a good mind, you could do anything. And he always backed me up. Sometime that first summer, I wandered into the Gold Front Tavern and decided it was time to try a beer.

Back during Prohibition, the Gold Front had been a barbershop, and in fact, I got my first haircut there in the summer of 1926, when I was just a year and a half old.

They brought me one. Later I found out that the bartender told my father about it. "How old did he say he was?" Dad asked. Twenty-one, the bartender replied. Well, I was two-thirds that age. Dad just nodded. "Then that's what he is."

I do have to mention a sadly amusing postscript to my summers on the straits. You remember I had sold my trusty 1935 Ford just before I came home for good? Well, a few days after I returned home, I happened to pick up the

Detroit News, only to see a big picture of my old car riddled with bullet holes, as though it had belonged to Bonnie and Clyde! Seems the man I sold it to was having a secret rendezvous with an old girlfriend who happened to be a newly married woman. That didn't set well with her new husband, who ventilated the dockworker and my old car. The man was killed more or less instantly.

The husband was eventually found not guilty by a jury. They seemed to take a very dim view of cheating up north.

Sadly, however, my career as a college student didn't turn out to be what I had expected—at least not, that is, my first time.

Remember that I was only sixteen when classes started. Nevertheless, I thought of myself as an extremely mature young man, especially after three summers palling around with a bunch of much older college students and professional sailors.

But once I started college classes, reality hit me like the proverbial ton of bricks. Make that, two tons with the mortar attached. First of all, I'd never really known how to study. That would have made things hard enough, but then add that the University of Detroit was a very rigorous academic institution in 1941. The professors were stern, no-nonsense men, half of them Jesuits. Many of my fellow students were academic stars, and I soon began to fall behind. A combination of false bravado, ignorance, and insecurity prevented me from getting the help I needed.

When the first semester ended, my grades were mostly Cs and Ds—plus one big fat F. That was enough to get me put on academic probation. Did I do the right thing? Adjust my attitude and start learning how to study?

Hell no! I was a kid, just about to turn seventeen, and I decided to quit. Though I didn't formally withdraw till January, I had effectively given up by the time America was suddenly and violently attacked and dragged into the bloodiest war in human history.

You might expect that my sense of patriotism would have driven me to again lie about my age to enlist. However, although I felt intensely patriotic, I wasn't one of those kids who imagined that nothing could happen to them. As I mentioned, my father had been wounded in World War I. I figured this war, like that one, would last years, and I knew I would be the right age to join the armed forces soon enough.

Meanwhile, I felt I could at least do my part for the war effort. So after dropping out of college, I got a job making aircraft parts.

The lingering effects of the Depression vanished the moment the United States entered World War II. Suddenly there were more jobs—good-paying jobs—than there were workers. I soon found myself toiling away for an outfit called Continental Motors, working ten hours a day, six days a week. I cleaned scrapings off freshly made pistons and polished them. I made spectacular money for a seventeen-year-old kid—$125 a week. That was more than twice the earnings of the average worker.

And I hated every minute of it.

Soon I got the idea of getting into the Merchant Marine, which seemed logical after my car ferry experience. That way, as I saw it, I could do even more to help with the war effort by transporting troops, at least until it was time for me to fight.

What I didn't know then was that the Merchant Marine had an extremely high casualty rate—higher than most branches of the fighting service. The problem, however, was my ears. I had had recurring middle-ear infections since I was a child, and there were no antibiotics back then like there are today that can solve the problem in a matter of days. I knew I would have to pass a physical to get onboard ship, and the doctors told me my ears would never heal without an operation on my nose. Such a procedure would open up my breathing passages and help my ears heal. They also told me that after the operation, I should go to a dry climate for a while. That was a time-honored cure back then.

I told all this to a fellow I worked next to at the piston plant, Harvey Hunyady, a former star tennis player who, like me, had dropped out of college. "Listen," he said. "Let's both go. We'll get out of this factory and enroll in college in Arizona this fall."

Sounded good to me. This way I would at least know somebody out in the Wild West. Besides, Harvey had a car, a four-year-old Ford convertible. I was sold. Besides, I figured I needed a little adventure.

5

FROM ARIZONA TO ALPENA

The operation on my nose went well. The next step was to persuade my parents that going to Arizona made sense. When I explained, they agreed.

So Harvey and I set off on a beautiful fall day in September 1942. We were bound for Tempe, the home of what is now Arizona State University but was then just a small "normal," or teacher's, college. A trip like that was far more of an adventure than it would be today. There were no freeways—we're talking two-lane highways.

Nobody was making new cars during World War II, and if Harvey's Ford broke down, it was anyone's guess whether we would be able to find a mechanic with the parts to fix it. But we did make it, somehow.

We endured scorching heat and humidity that knocked the car out for a while in St. Louis. We watched jackrabbits big as terriers jumping over our open convertible as we drove through the Texas Panhandle, on a beautiful starry night I will never forget.

Stopping at a motel in New Mexico, we saw real cowboys riding horses on unpaved streets and a sheriff's deputy wearing boots and a white ten-gallon hat, complete with a white-handled pistol in a large leather holster. The next night we drove across the state line in the dead of night and slept in the car, on purpose.

We had been told we should cross the border into southeast Arizona at sunrise. What we saw when we woke up at 4:30 a.m. was beyond all description, the most breathtaking sunrise I have ever seen. There was a gorgeous mountain range with a timberline. Strange, saguaro cactuses dotted the entire landscape.

Vivid, multicolored wildflowers were interspersed everywhere. Arizona then had fewer than half a million people—less than a tenth the number it would have by the end of the century. That summer taught me to appreciate forever the wonder of the Earth's unspoiled natural surroundings.

The next seven months passed quickly. Ironically, although Harvey and I rented a room from an elderly lady, we didn't spend much time together. But I soon met three guys, fellow students from Clawson, Michigan, not far from Detroit. We spent Thanksgiving eating sandwiches at Roosevelt Dam, fifty miles from any other living person. There was also one interesting twist in which I helped launch a major broadcasting career.

Actually, it happened because I turned *my* back on a radio career. One day, for the fun of it, I auditioned at what is now radio station KOY in nearby Phoenix. In those days, stations generally preferred clear, deep, "unaccented" midwestern voices. They liked mine and offered me a job. But the pay was peanuts, and after I paid the bus fare to and from the station, it was even less. That didn't do it for me, but I had a bright idea.

I recommended another guy from the Midwest, a kid from Chicago I'd become friendly with. He was there, like me, for his health, trying to get over his asthma so he could get into the war. They offered him the job, at $1.25 per hour, and he enthusiastically took it. That was the beginning of what would become one of the most successful careers in show business.

His name was Steve Allen, and he would go on to have his own long-running network TV show, become the first host of the *Tonight Show*, and have a spectacular career in show business. Years later when he came to Detroit and I was attorney general, we'd get together and talk about how lucky we both were . . . and how far we'd come from our adolescence in the Arizona desert.

Naturally I made friends with local kids, too, some of whom invited me to their family ranches. There, they took me riding across that amazing landscape. But these were not just any horses! They were magnificently trained, utterly gorgeous Western saddle horses, huge animals, fifteen hands (five feet) or more. Seventy years later, I still remember riding through the purple-tinted desert, framed by the tall, tree-like saguaro cactuses. What I'll never forget was that it was far more beautiful in reality than any cowboy movie I've ever seen, before or since.

Yes, I took some classes, but that wasn't the main thing I got out of my Arizona odyssey. The new sights, adventures, and people I met helped me mature—really grow up—fast. Within a few months, I could tell my ears had healed considerably, and my breathing was much better.

So six weeks after my eighteenth birthday I decided it was time to try to get into military service. My goal was to enter the U.S. Navy's famous V-5 aviation program for college students, designed to lead to a commission as an ensign. Everything was going well until the incompetent local physician examining my ear flushed it out with a syringe too large for the job and broke the nicely healed scar tissue.

The pain was excruciating, and what happened as a result hurt even more. Not only was I not admitted to the naval officer program, I couldn't even pass the physical to be drafted into the army. Specialists later told me I would have had no trouble getting in if that clumsy doctor hadn't damaged my ear. I was devastated.

Later, back in Detroit, I did get called up by the draft board. Again I failed the physical because of my ears. While I was disappointed once again, today, with the wisdom of hindsight, I realize that this may have been a blessing. The men who took the physical right before me and right after me were both boys I knew, and both ended up being killed—one in Europe, one in the Pacific.

After my ears were damaged by that reckless desert doctor, I knew the military wasn't in the cards for me and that it was time to get serious about the rest of my life. I called my father. I now knew what I wanted to do; it was time to come home. I told him I had a new sense of purpose. I would work, go to night school, and after that go to law school and on to a profession.

I think my parents were delighted. My dad promptly wired me a hundred dollars for train fare and expenses, and a few days later I was on the Southern Pacific, bound for Detroit.

———

I went back to school, but it took me a while, partly because I felt I first needed a job. But I was also embarrassed about how poorly I had done my first time in college. I didn't really know how to start.

It took me more than a year to get back in school, and it happened then only because of one of those chance encounters that can change your life. One day in the summer of 1944, I happened to be standing in front of a building at what was then the University of Detroit's old main campus on Jefferson, looking over a bulletin board. Suddenly, a kindly priest appeared in his shirtsleeves.

"Can I help you, young man?" he said.

"I don't think so, Father," I said, a bit dejectedly. "I've already had my chance at U of D." To my surprise, he said, "I'm here to give you a second chance. Come into my office."

He turned out to be Fr. Henry J. Wirtenberger, a highly respected Jesuit who was the regent of the University of Detroit's College of Commerce and Finance.

He took me inside, and I told him my story. "We'll enroll you for ten credits of night classes," he said. So with the Allied armies pushing across Europe, I went back to college in September 1944. This time, I was an immediate success from the start. I went to school for almost three years at night.

That completed my pre-law requirements. The U of D had a combined program leading to a law degree, and I immediately went to law classes. In June 1951, I emerged a newly minted lawyer. In the process, I had met and sat in classrooms with some of Michigan's most important future leaders. I went to school with future congressmen, judges, mayors—influential people of my own generation who helped shape my city, my state, and, to an extent, the nation for years to come.

But that was all in the future. What I did know, however, is that I was graduating with more than a law degree. Frank J. Kelley, brand-new attorney, emerged from a very difficult education with a wife and two kids.

———

Naturally, I'm getting ahead of my story. Well, as both my supporters and opponents can tell you, I don't do things halfway.

I did not intend to get married so young, much less start a family. But suddenly, the woman I thought was the most beautiful girl in the world appeared before my eyes, and what else could I do? We met not long after I came home from Arizona. Ironically, she had been dating one of my old friends from childhood who had left to join the Marine Corps. Eventually, I asked her to go with me to a dance.

There was a hot new singer performing there named Doris Day, who of course would later become internationally famous. But that night I only had eyes for my date, Josephine Palmisan. That, I soon learned, wasn't her real name—it was Palmisano, a lovely Italian name. She had dropped the vowel so she wouldn't seem quite as "ethnic" to her classmates at Central High School. What was ironic is that most of them happened to be Jewish. Central High School was where much of Detroit's Jewish community went back then. But regardless of what name she went by, Josephine was lovely, inside and out. In fact, she had been voted the most beautiful girl in her school in both her junior and senior years.

But when I met her, my life was anything but beautiful. I had found a job in a tool shop, where I was fairly miserable—that is, till I met Josephine. Almost from the start I knew she wasn't like any other girl I'd ever met. Within a few weeks, I'd met her parents, who had a cottage up in Ontario, and she was able to travel to Burt Lake to meet mine. To my relief, my parents fell in love with her, too.

Everyone did. She was able to pull me out of my shell and make me want to be a better person. At the same time, she was able to show this brooding, prematurely morose Irishman the fun side of life and teach him how to play. Josephine, who had just graduated from Detroit's Central High School, also gave me the courage to quit my awful job and look for another. For a while I worked selling shirts on Michigan Avenue.

That was supposed to be just a temporary job over the Christmas holiday rush—but the spirit of tolerance my dad taught me helped me succeed in life, not for the last time. The United Shirt store was managed by a fine Jewish guy of Dutch descent named Sam Van Horn. Anybody who lived in the Detroit area in the 1950s and 1960s likely remembers the clothing store his brother Neil later started in the yet-to-be built Northland Mall: Van Horn's Men's Wear.

They were gentlemen. But that was a different era, and many customers would make anti-Semitic remarks, especially when they came to return items. That didn't sit well with me. "We're just normal people like you," I would say. I later learned that this made me a hero in the eyes of the Jewish clerks and customers, and my comments were reported back to the owner.

"Keep him on for as long as he wants," Sam said.

Consequently, I was the only Gentile retained after the Christmas rush. I didn't stay long, however. Within a short time, I got a much-better-paying job in what was called the safety department at Ford Motor Company, thanks to my Uncle Charles, who for some baffling reason we called "Uncle Chink."

Now here's a revelation. My many longtime union supporters may be horrified to hear this, but I got that job because of my uncle's friendship with one of the biggest enemies the United Auto Workers (UAW) union ever had: the infamous Harry Bennett, an ex-boxer and street tough whose goons had beaten up Walter Reuther and other UAW leaders years before during the legendary Battle of the Overpass.

By the time I came along, however, the UAW had managed to unionize the company. Legend has it that Henry Ford gave in and recognized the union in 1941 because his wife, Clara, was sick of the violence and threatened to leave her husband otherwise.

I knew something about Bennett's anti-union tendencies back then, but I didn't have to work with him; the union—whose goals I would have fully supported from day one—had won long ago. In any event, I needed a good-paying job so I could go to school.

Ironically, Josephine and I split up briefly over some silly argument in September 1944. That may have been a blessing in disguise for a couple of reasons. Without a steady girlfriend, I could really apply myself to my studies. Plus, our separation may have helped me realize how much I really needed and wanted her. We finally got back together right after Christmas. Had I been healthy enough to have been drafted, I might then have found myself fighting for my life in the Battle of the Bulge. If I had succeeded in enlisting in the navy, I might easily have been risking my life either in an airplane or fighting in some tropical jungle in the Pacific—and probably never would have met Josephine. Though I had been terribly upset that I couldn't get into the military, my bad ears may have been a lifesaving and life-altering condition. Josephine and I knew we wanted to get married.

Within a couple months, I screwed up my courage and told my father. To my surprise, the patriarch heartily approved. He thought a lot of Josephine. He was a shrewd judge of character and correctly calculated she would be a good person for me. Dad also knew I was more mature than most boys my age and figured I would be able to handle marriage. Fortunately Josephine's parents also approved. We had a big summer wedding at Visitation Catholic Church, followed by a reception at the Fort Shelby Hotel.

The date was June 30, 1945, and our wedding was a fairly extravagant affair, given that the war was still on. The Nazis had surrendered, but our war with Japan was still raging in the Pacific and was expected to last for at least another year. Nobody knew then that the atom bomb, the war's biggest military secret, was close to completion in the New Mexico desert and that within six weeks World War II would end. My thoughts, however, were primarily about getting to Mackinac Island for our honeymoon.

I had wheels again—a black 1934 Ford with a sound body and a V-8 engine, quite a prize in an age when no new cars had been made for four years. I managed to acquire it for a hundred dollars. We drove to Bay City, where we unfortunately spent our wedding night in a hotel that was hosting a convention of World War I Marine Corps veterans, who paraded up and down the halls all night singing songs like "The Halls of Montezuma." I knew better than to try to argue with a company of Marines, regardless of how old they might be. So we had a pretty sleepless night but afterward an idyllic honeymoon on Mackinac Island.

Politics was never too far from the surface in our family, though I didn't give the idea of running for anything myself a single thought. Flashback to the late 1930s: my father got more and more involved in politics after Prohibition ended. He ran for the state senate in 1936 and 1940, narrowly losing in the Democratic primary each time. He probably would have won easily if the Irish vote hadn't been split, thanks to crafty opponents who made sure the ballot was packed with a lot of Irish names. I really wanted him to win the first time he ran and was very disappointed when he lost.

How could people not vote for my dad, the best man in the world? The second time, however, I felt differently. I had met some political figures and was street-smart. I knew that when the legislature was in session, there was a lot of drinking and dissipation. Not that I worried about my dad's morals, but I did worry about his health. So when he lost I was quietly relieved and elated. Dad never ran for anything again, but his political career did take off.

He was named to the Wayne County Board of Institutions about the time I came back from Arizona. That was an important job back then. His fellow members promptly elected him chairman of the board, a job he would hold for the rest of his life.

Even those who may have been politically opposed to Frank E. Kelley agreed that he was a rare, excellent, and honest public servant. The last time he was up for reappointment, he faced a vigorous challenge. But in the end, Dad won by getting dozens of Republican supervisors to vote for him, a staunch Democrat. That was a victory for the people. Dad's services to the mentally ill were perhaps his greatest contribution.

After he died in 1954, the *Detroit News*—normally no friend to Democrats—ran an editorial praising him to the skies for the way he ran what was officially known as the Wayne County General Hospital but which everyone knew by its nickname, "Eloise." At that time state government still believed that it had a responsibility toward the mentally ill. Eloise was built before his time, but he spent every moment he could fighting with the legislature and the county to get them to appropriate more money for the hospital, which had been founded in 1839 and was in dire need of upgrades and improvements. As the newspaper reported, "It was Mr. Kelley who fought consistently for more and better physicians and surgeons for the hospital, and a larger staff of psychiatrists. For the meager salary of $3,500, the county had in him a servant worth 10 times that amount," adding, "it is probable that he spent it all and more in private charity."

That was my dad.

But there were other perks that went along with being a prominent Democrat. Probably his crowning glory came during the campaign of 1948. He was the chair of Michigan's delegation to the Democratic National Convention in Philadelphia that summer. That was the first convention shown live on the new medium of television. I would have loved to have gone with him, but there wasn't any way I could have done so; I was just starting law school, married with a full-time job and a baby.

So on a hot night in July 1948, I sat in Detroit, twisting the dials to bring in a grainy picture on a small, black-and-white TV set in Dad's bar. Finally the presidential balloting began. I waited forever till the clerk intoned "Michigan!" and watched the camera zoom in on my father. "Michigan casts forty-two votes for that Great Commoner from Missouri, the next president of the United States, Harry Truman," Dad said, as the convention cheered wildly and I was filled with pride.

Suddenly I saw what my life held in store. I was flooded with overwhelming certainty that my destiny was set, that I would be my father's son and fulfill the dreams he had for me. And maybe also fulfill his frustrated ambitions. I couldn't have told you then what that meant beyond this: I was determined to become an able, honest lawyer whose career would be dedicated to public service, to serving the people. But that was still a long way off.

By the time Dad came home from Philly, everyone knew the election was hopeless. Most of the Southern Democrats, or Dixiecrats, walked out of Convention Hall in disgust over Truman's support for civil rights. They nominated Strom Thurmond as their candidate. Meanwhile, those on the left also broke away and formed the Progressive Party, mainly because they thought Truman was being too tough on the Soviet Union and "Uncle Joe" Stalin.

The Progressives nominated Henry Wallace, who had been FDR's vice president before Truman. With three Democrats on the ballot, Republican nominee Thomas E. Dewey looked like a sure thing. The one man who disagreed was Harry Truman. He insisted he was going to win. None of us believed that, but we were loyal.

My father had one greater thrill ahead: he was invited to ride on the president's famous "whistle-stop" campaign train when Truman arrived to campaign across Michigan that September. Not only did he get to meet the president in person, but according to Dad, they shared some good bourbon and a few hands of poker. For the rest of his life, Dad maintained that Truman was not only his favorite president but one of the best men he'd ever met.

On election night, I was out with some friends in a sound truck, driving around, trying to scare up a few Democratic votes. We didn't think Truman had a prayer, but we had some hope that our young candidate for governor, G. Mennen "Soapy" Williams, might score an upset.

We stopped for dinner after the polls closed and heard some incredible news. President Truman was *ahead*. By the next morning, it was clear that he had won the greatest upset in American political history. Truman narrowly lost Michigan, which was Dewey's birthplace. But Soapy Williams had won by a landslide, beating Kim Sigler, the ineffectual Republican incumbent.

It was a tremendous night for Democrats. When it was over, I knew politics would be in my blood, though it would turn out to be fourteen years before I would run for office myself.

Ironically, the first time I ran, it was as an incumbent for a statewide office I already held. But once again, I'm ahead of my story.

———

Between working and going to school and learning how to be a proper husband, I had precious little time. You may know that apartments were hard to come by right after the war.

For a brief time, we lived with Jo's generous parents at Outer Drive and Seven Mile. Within a few months, however, a family friend helped us find an apartment. Life was good. My father helped Josephine get a good-paying job working for Wayne County.

But after about six months she started becoming violently ill every morning. Soon we found out why. To put it in my father's words: "Well, she might as well quit her job. She's going to be a mother." Which meant yours truly, Frank J. Kelley, was about to become a father at the ripe old age of twenty-one.

That didn't worry me, however; my life on the docks and assorted other experiences had helped me grow up. Actually, I was thrilled. Our apartment was barely six blocks from my parents' home. The shopping center at Grand River and Joy Road was still excellent, even if an almost imperceptible decline had begun.

Josephine brought out the best in me. So much so that after we were married, my pre-law grades steadily improved—in spite of the increased responsibility of marriage, fatherhood, and working at Ford full-time during the day.

Remember, too, that we were living in what was then still the vibrant arsenal of democracy in the first years after America had won World War II, the greatest war in history. We felt that we could do anything.

Our daughter Karen, who today is a vivacious and highly successful travel agent, was born in October 1946. Naturally she was the most beautiful baby who had ever been born.

We hit a bump, however, when there was a cutback at Ford, and I lost my job a year later. So what did I do? I answered an ad in the paper and soon had a new career as a baby photographer! Talk about needing the gift of gab. In fact, back in those days they called it a "kidnaping" business. All you really wanted to get away with, however, was a bit of the proud parents' money.

Henry Harbican Studios was the name of the business, and it was perfectly legitimate. The idea was to wander around various neighborhoods, take pictures of babies—and then present the proud parents with the proofs and try to get them to buy the photographs.

If you have a hard time imagining how I could possibly make a living that way, consider this: these were the years of the famous baby boom. Millions of people had had to put off having children during the Great Depression and then World War II. Now they were making up for lost time. Most families didn't have sophisticated camera equipment then, and many parents wanted a proper studio-quality photo of the next generation. As a result of this trend and my sales techniques, I was soon making twenty dollars a day, enough to support my family in 1947.

Granted, none of my baby pictures was ever nominated for a Pulitzer Prize. But I kept that job and my own baby in diapers for nearly two years, until I had completed my pre-law studies.

Incidentally, soon after I became attorney general, I learned to my delight that Mr. Harbican was still alive—and proud as he could be that one of his photographers had become such a success.

I fell into a better job just as I was starting law school. More on that shortly. But what was interesting is even before that, my embryo political career had started to bloom. During fall term, 1948, there was a university-wide election for the board of the University of Detroit student union. This wasn't a post of great power.

But it was something. I decided to run for vice president, which was nervy in itself. For one thing, I was a night student on a downtown satellite campus, six miles from where most of the students took classes full-time. Almost no one knew me. Matter of fact, no night student had ever run for a campus-wide student government office. The U of D rented the old Mercury Theater for a big political rally. My main opponent was a decorated World War II veteran who appeared wearing his Purple Heart.

My spirits sank. What could I say? How could I possibly compete with a deserving war hero? Then I remembered my motto: Never Give Up. I was no longer the first-term freshman who had flunked out seven years earlier. I was about to graduate.

I was a successful husband and father. I was done running away. Fortunately my opponent spoke before I did—and laid an egg big enough for an ostrich. The veteran was arrogant and patronizing. He felt his fellow students owed him the job and said as much.

Within five minutes, his formerly admiring classmates were booing him! Then it was my turn. I went up onstage. By this time the angry audience was howling. They didn't want to hear any more politicians. I stood there coolly, smiling.

Finally, in a loud but warm voice, I began, "Gentlemen! Gentlemen of this university!" (There were then very few women among the student body of this Jesuit school.) The audience quickly got it. They realized they'd been behaving boorishly and rudely, and began laughing and applauding. I continued by simply saying, "If you men will vote for me tomorrow, I will humbly represent you with all my heart."

The next day I learned to my astonishment that I had been elected student body vice president by the largest margin in the history of the University of Detroit. That was my first election. There would be a few more along the way.

Suddenly things were starting to fall into place. Within a few weeks after my election—and the (slightly) more historic national Democratic sweep—I managed to get what was really my first truly professional, career-related job.

The newly elected Wayne County sheriff (a friend of my father's, naturally) agreed to hire me as a deputy in the civil division at the beginning of 1949. I wouldn't be wearing a badge and uniform, however, but a suit and tie. My job was to receive and serve various civil papers, summons, subpoenas, and other legal documents. Half the lawyers in the county preferred to have papers served by the sheriff, and so I had more than enough work to keep me busy. I was paid well enough to meet the needs of our now-growing family—our son, Frank E. Kelley, would arrive that April, entering the world on the same day his dad was taking an exam.

Just as important, however, the work was flexible enough that I could manage to go to law school. Frankly, from the standpoint of training for my future careers in politics and law, I doubt that I could have had a better job. I saw the gritty end of the legal process up close. And between the sheriff's office and law school, I met a generation of rising young stars who would dominate legal and political life in Michigan for decades.

Remember: Wayne County in those days wasn't just the biggest county in the state. It dominated public affairs. Believe it or not, Wayne County had the largest tax base of any county in the United States, thanks to the auto companies. A third of the state's population lived in the county, most in Detroit, and the county housed most of the lawyers, the most important professional classes, and virtually all the significant media in Michigan.

I met men (and a few women) who would shape my life. First, however, I had to get through the tough law school curriculum itself—which turned out to be far harder than I expected.

My first year was the worst. Miraculously, once again, the good Father Wirtenberger was my salvation. I was in danger of earning a D in one of my classes, but my mentor told me, "Don't worry about it." I ended up with a C, and that was the closest brush I had with academic disaster. I put together a study group with two other men like me who already had full-time jobs. Don Harrington was an engineer at Ford. Frank Pipp worked for the Detroit Water Board.

We got together three or four times a week in our each other's homes, had dinner, and studied hard for two hours. We learned how to study, create outlines, and write legal language. By the time we were seniors, we were sailing through our exams. What's even better is that we became lifelong friends.

Finally, in June 1951, graduation came. But that isn't the end for any newly minted lawyer; our minds were focused on passing the bar exam. Otherwise, the degree itself was pretty meaningless.

I took the exam in September—froze on two or three questions and fell just short of passing. That was depressing, but I have since learned that some of the nation's best lawyers have failed on their first try—including one of the best men Michigan ever sent to the U.S. Senate, the late Phil Hart.

Resigned, I kept studying and took the exam again in April 1952. Back then, it took months to get the results. In July, Jo and I went up to my parents' cottage for a little vacation. She would soon give birth to our third and final child, Jane.

We wanted to get away from it all before the baby came, and Burt Lake was the place to do that—especially since Dad had never installed a phone in the cottage. We were completely out of touch.

Then one night, Dad and I were sitting out in the backyard as the sun was going down. We were smoking cigars and talking politics. Suddenly we heard a truck headed for our cottage.

Our caretaker, Bill Howell, burst out of the truck. He was out of breath. "Frank! Frank Senior," he told the patriarch.

"Tell Frank Junior that he got his bar license. They gave him a license for his bar."

I jumped out of my chair, happy and stunned.

I was a lawyer.

6

YOUNG MR. KELLEY
GOES NORTH

I don't remember when our caretaker figured out I wasn't going into the saloon business, but I do remember what happened next. I jumped out of my chair, hugged my dad, and ran to the house.

"Did you hear? Did you hear?"

I hugged my mom, kissed my wife, and Dad announced: "Frank and I are going down to the tavern to have ourselves a little visit."

That was one of the happiest moments of my life. I can still remember every word my father said. "Always be honest," he told me, his voice suddenly taking on a serious tone. "Remember that the reason I wanted you to become a lawyer was so that you could carry knowledge around in your head. As long as you are honest and have that knowledge, people will come to you. You can always be independent, always be happy, and always be honest. And remember, Son, don't ever lose your integrity. Otherwise, there's no point in being a lawyer."

Some young men might have resented being lectured to. But all I remember is his beaming pride and confidence in me. Besides, both he and I knew that I wouldn't have done it any other way.

The rest of that vacation was a blur. A few days later, I was in the old Veterans' Memorial Center in Detroit, where a group of us, including my "study buddy" Frank Pipp, were sworn in to both the state and federal bar at the same time.

I was introduced to another young attorney that day in what would turn out to be one of the most fateful meetings of my life. He was seven months younger than I was and tall, clean-cut, and good-looking. I took an immediate liking to him. Afterward, a few of us went out for a drink. I noticed he was walking a little stiffly—and then someone told me something I found hard to believe. My new friend was walking on artificial legs. He was a war hero; his legs had had been blown off below the knee in France when he was barely nineteen.

His name was John Swainson, and he would go on to become one of Michigan's youngest governors before his career was destroyed by events that could have been the stuff of Greek tragedy.

But that was all years in the future. What I was thinking about that summer of 1952 was getting a job practicing law. As usual, my father had a hand in things. He contacted Phil Neudeck, a man he considered a model lawyer, and asked him to consider hiring me. Trouble was, another politically connected Irishman named William Cahalan also needed a job.

Neudeck, a wise man, solved this dilemma by hiring us both for slightly less than half what he would pay one baby lawyer. That meant I began receiving the princely sum of thirty-five dollars a week, in addition to which my secretarial expenses were covered. We also got to keep half the profits from any business we brought the firm.

Bill Cahalan, who later became Wayne County prosecutor and then a fine judge, and I each jumped at the opportunity. My daughter Jane had been born that April, and naturally, with a wife and three kids, I also needed to hang onto my job at the sheriff's office.

Soon, however, we moved to a newer neighborhood. And though money was still a bit tight, within a few weeks after landing my first job as a lawyer, I decided to buy a new car. That may not have seemed fiscally prudent, but thanks to my father, I knew that appearances matter, especially in any job where you need to win the confidence of the public. If you wanted to get clients, you had to have good clothes, freshly shined shoes, and nice wheels.

The salesman easily talked me into ordering a new Buick Special—a small, striking, black two-door sedan. I thought the salesman took an authentic liking to me, and two weeks later a phone call from him proved I was right.

"Well, you're going to be able to pay for that new car of yours," he said. Seems he had another client, a drummer in a band, who had also bought a new Buick from him. The poor fellow was on his way to play in Toledo when a drunken superintendent from one of the glass companies smashed into him and totaled his car.

I went to see the poor drummer, who happened to be African American, and signed him to a contingency fee contract. That meant he'd have to pay me only if I won—and then I'd get a third of whatever we were awarded. This was my first big case.

And it went well. With the help of Frank Neaton, a senior lawyer in my firm, I filed a suit in U.S. Federal Court in Toledo—after a former classmate from the glass city helped me find the building. After a few pre-trial hearings, the company threw in the towel and agreed to an $18,000 settlement. That was reasonably big money in 1953. My firm got a third of that, half of which, $3,000, went to me. That was nearly twice my meager base salary. I was extremely satisfied.

I felt I was on my way.

But I was restless. One hot summer day I drove home in bumper-to-bumper traffic. Neither my car nor my house was air-conditioned. I started daydreaming about country breezes and open spaces. After dinner, my wife and kids and I walked to our nearest branch library. "Do you have any books about rural lawyers?" I asked the librarian. She nodded yes. "I've got a book you'll just love," she said. It was Bellamy Partridge's *Country Lawyer*, the story of his father, a small-town attorney in upstate New York. I stayed up half the night reading.

The next night, I finished it. I was, as they'd say today, blown away by the story of this small-town lawyer, a man of great respect and a pillar of his community, the portrait of a sort of northern Atticus Finch, years before *To Kill a Mockingbird* would be written.

"What a wonderful life! What a great way to raise children," I thought. My own world was very different. I was scratching for a living in the hustle and bustle of Detroit. I've always had the ability to see around corners a little bit, to have a sense of what was coming. Even though Detroit was strong and muscular and had nearly two million people, I wondered about the Motor City's future. Evidence was already beginning to surface of the complex problems that were soon to plague the city—racial tensions, for example. Historian Thomas Sugrue, himself a Detroit native, paints a compelling portrait of the injustices stemming from segregation and the festering resentments felt by both black and white in his masterful book, *The Origins of the Urban Crisis*.

The U.S. Supreme Court's *Brown v. Board of Education* decision ending school segregation was still a year away, and the civil rights and voting rights acts of the 1960s were still a decade off. But something else was also beginning that very year.

The freeways were beginning to cut through the city, opening up an easily commutable path to suburbia. The very next year, Northland Center in Southfield would open at the end of what would become the Lodge Freeway, and the city would begin emptying out. People would leave in ever greater numbers, depriving the city of the tax revenue needed to provide services to those who remained. I can't pretend to have seen all that coming.

But I knew that things would be difficult—and besides, I wanted a change of pace. So I decided to seek the advice of the man whose judgment I respected most: my father.

You might have thought I had hit him with the proverbial ton of bricks. My father's dreams had always centered on my being a lawyer—a steadily bigger and more important lawyer—in Detroit. Like many fathers, he wanted me to be the personification of his dreams so that he could mentor me and, yes, brag about me. He was a saloon keeper with little formal education. Having a son in town who was a lawyer was the culmination, in a way, of his whole life. (Imagine what they would say back in County Mayo!) The last thing he wanted was me hundreds of miles away in some small town nobody had ever heard of. Seeing how hurt he was, I dropped the subject . . . for a while.

But a couple of months later, I came back to it. I told him something he could understand, that I thought this was the only way I could become a trial lawyer in a hurry. Otherwise I would have to work in the dismal Wayne County criminal courts for years, prosecuting petty hoodlums as a poorly paid assistant prosecutor, maybe until I was middle-aged. But in a small town, there was a chance I could quickly become a known trial lawyer.

Naturally, I added, I could always move back. I told him I had done some research and was thinking about moving to Alpena, a town of about 13,000 on Lake Huron, almost exactly 250 miles northeast of our home in Detroit.

Dad didn't say much. But not long afterward, unbeknownst to me, he and a few friends drove over to Alpena and talked to the editor of the local newspaper, an Irishman himself. They talked to various businessmen, asking politely whether there was room in town for a good, young, Irish Catholic lawyer. He was so warmly received that he began to change his mind. Then one Sunday afternoon, he asked me to come over. "Frank, I didn't tell you this, but I went up to Alpena, and maybe that idea isn't so bad after all." You could have knocked me over with a feather.

Well and good. But what I hadn't done is take any concrete steps to make any of this happen. Then, suddenly, an amazing lucky break. One of my law school classmates, John Mack, had already moved to Alpena, though he hadn't found a practice yet.

Then lo and behold, our governor, G. Mennen "Soapy" Williams, appointed the only Democratic lawyer in Alpena, a fellow named Philip J. Glennie, to a vacant judgeship. The new judge suggested that Mack and I take over his law practice. That was what I needed. When I told the lawyers I was working for about my plans, they were surprisingly supportive. They explained that they liked me but that there were too many lawyers in Detroit—and too few beyond the city. There were only nine lawyers in Alpena when I arrived; I would be the tenth. My bosses even offered to advance me money for up to a year and allow me to repay them later, when I landed on my feet.

Still, I hesitated. My father's approval was important to me. Now it was early June 1954. If I was going to make the move, it would make sense to do so before school started. Karen would be entering second grade that fall; Frankie would be starting kindergarten.

"Look," Jo said. "On your way down to the law office, why don't you stop in the old neighborhood and see your dad before you go to work. Talk to him about the move."

Dad was, as always, glad to see me. He was sitting in the living room in his bathrobe, sipping a ginger ale. I think he was tired of my indecisiveness. "It wouldn't be too bad a move, but I worry about you, Frank. You have a lot of ambition and drive, but you worry too much." We glanced at the clock, and he began walking me back to my car. "You'll be successful, Frank, I know it. But remember, worry is a waste of time. It took a long time for me to learn this, but the things you worry about the most in life never happen."

"Enjoy your life, Frank," he told me.

He and my mother were leaving to go up to Burt Lake that day. I backed out of the driveway, waved to him, and drove off.

The next morning I left for the office. As I was pulling up to the old county building, I heard a bulletin on the car radio: "This just in: Frank E. Kelley, prominent Democratic leader of the City of Detroit and chairman of the Wayne Board of Institutions, suffered a fatal heart attack at his summer home in northern Michigan."

I pulled over, ran into a nearby bar, and called my cousin Tommy Kelley, whose dad had built a cottage nearby. They had a phone; my parents still did not. "Is it true?" I asked.

"It's true, Frank," he said. The date was Friday, June 18, 1954. Later I learned the full story. Father, who was considerably overweight, had gotten up early that morning as he always did and had gone downstairs to read and listen to the radio and wait for my mother to come downstairs and fix breakfast. Suddenly he began having sharp chest pains. He struggled up to my mother's room and collapsed.

She screamed loud enough for the next-door neighbor, an elderly man named Charles Whitman, to dash over to help.

Dad was sprawled partially across the bed, his head and shoulders in my sobbing mother's arms. To the last, he thought of his family, not himself. "Stay calm, Grace," he said.

"My lungs are filling up, and I may not make it," he told her, and then added: "Tell Frank he should go to Alpena." He told my mother that he loved her and that they'd had a great life. Mr. Whitman pressed a glass of brandy to my father's lips, but it was too late. He died in my mother's arms.

————

Frank E. Kelley's funeral was an event. Hundreds poured into the now vanished McInnis-Desmond funeral home on Woodward in Highland Park to pay their respects to the patriarch. The mourners included everyone from the governor and the mayor to business leaders and more than a few poor wretches, some in questionable occupations, whom he had gone out of his way to help over the years. The priests who had enjoyed Dad's Prohibition whiskey three decades before mysteriously reappeared.

Moments before he died, Father told Mother I'd take care of everything. When the body was ready, I gazed down into the casket. "That's not my father," I thought to myself. "He's not here. This is just an image created by a few dollars' worth of chemicals."

This helped me stay emotionally strong. The procession to the cemetery was two miles long. But something did touch me deeply. Governor G. Mennen Williams went to my mother's side and spoke with her for five minutes. As I watched, Grace Kelley's spirits were lifted. For a few minutes, she was relieved of her sorrow. I've always remembered that. Years later, when I became attorney general, time and again I visited funerals and sent letters of condolence to surviving and grieving spouses and children.

Belated thanks, Soapy, for that lifelong lesson.

————

With that, my immediate future was clear.

I went to Alpena, all right—even before I went to Alpena.

The very day after my father's funeral, I was in a car with a psychiatrist, heading north to try my first case there—and it would be one of the most risky and controversial ones I ever argued in court. Lest you think I was leaving town with indecent haste, this was a case I had been brought into before Dad died. The psychiatrist had worked at Wayne County General Hospital and had known and liked my father. This helped me to talk with him on the long drive north.

What was even more helpful, in terms of escaping the pain, was immersing myself in my first big legal challenge. Turns out my first case in Alpena was one that could have gotten me ridden out of town on a rail. I was going to be defending an escaped prisoner who was—get this—a convicted criminal sexual psychopath. Well, never let it be said that Frank J. Kelley was afraid of a challenge. The man, one Harold Arden, had escaped from the state prison in Ionia and managed to flee all the way to Alaska.

But after a few years on the lam, he called what would soon be my law office, the one John Mack and I were taking over from the attorney who had been appointed to the bench. Arden claimed to have been wrongly accused and charged, and wanted to clear his name. He told John that he'd been framed by his former wife, who had accused him of molesting his stepdaughter, divorced him, and then taken virtually all his assets.

What he wanted was a chance to face the music—and, he hoped, clear his name. That was impressive; in those pre-Internet days, he might have been able to live out his life without being caught in a place thousands of miles away; Alaska then wasn't even a state. I soon talked with him on the phone. Attorneys develop an instinct for whether a client is telling the truth, and after I spoke to him I believed that he had been railroaded. I told him to go to Detroit because I could easily arrange to have him examined there by two prominent psychiatrists before he went back to surrender himself to the authorities in Alpena.

That was fine with Arden, which to me was another good sign. However, if I'd been thinking only of myself, I might have wondered if I was the one who should have had his head examined. After all, Alpena was a somewhat sleepy, conservative, small town. You could argue that taking on a controversial case like this was neither wise nor prudent. But the challenge motivated me. More important, I believed the man was innocent. "If I'm any good as a lawyer, I should be able to prove it," I told myself.

My suspicion that Arden had been framed grew even stronger after he walked into my Detroit law office. He was a handsome, athletic man in his mid-forties. Two psychiatrists then examined him and came to the same conclusion; there was no sign that he was a "criminal sexual psychopath." What's more, they would testify to that under oath. So we filed a petition with Alpena Circuit Court and waited for the fireworks to start. Word travels fast in small towns, and on the morning of the hearing, curious citizen spectators crowded into the courtroom.

There was no jury—only the judge, the same Philip J. Glennie whose practice John Mack and I had assumed. He expressed concern over the gathering crowd, which added tension. No matter; a little pressure helps shape a good trial lawyer. I thoroughly examined the psychiatrist. Then the judge did the same.

Finally, after a grueling two and a half hours, the judge was finished. He said his decision would come quickly; in the meantime, the defendant would remain free on his personal recognizance.

But what was the judge thinking? We didn't have a clue, and we were nervous wrecks. We knew that losing this case would be a major blow to our ability to practice law in Alpena.

That night, I stayed in a motel. The next day, we received a call from the court. The judge would render his verdict at 1:30 that afternoon. We may have been nervous, but that was nothing compared to the state Harold Arden was in. His entire life was at stake. We sat in the courtroom and waited for the judge, who wasted no time whatsoever: "In the case filed against the defendant by the people of the state of Michigan, there is sufficient evidence to show that Harold Alden was improperly charged."

We were stunned. The judge threw out the case against Arden as "illegal, void, and of no force and effect." We had cleared our client and given him his life back. There are few better moments a lawyer can experience than that. He hugged us, and we could feel his body shake with his sobs.

The next day, Harold Arden returned to Anchorage to live out his days as a successful businessman. I returned to Detroit to settle my father's estate and get ready to move my family north.

Frank J. Kelley was cleared for landing in Alpena.

———

Life in Alpena turned out to be good—surprisingly so.

Soon we were renting an old lumber baron's spacious home on Dunbar Street. Business started to come in—the fact that we'd gotten our names known during the Arden trial didn't hurt.

My family happily adjusted to Alpena, and my law partner and I had both a good working relationship and a friendship.

Josephine made a new set of friends. We joined a local Catholic Church, St. Bernard's, and were warmly accepted by the congregation. The kids adjusted quickly to small-town life, and I was soon sure I had made the right move.

Within a few months, I landed another big case. A group of citizens marched into my office. They were upset that the county board of supervisors had decided to build a new jail next to the town's beautiful courthouse, and they wanted it stopped. "We know you are from out of town and aren't afraid to take on controversial cases," their spokesman said.

Well, here I go again, I thought. Wild Irish Frank Kelley, taking on the town establishment. Could I do it a second time?

The committee took up a small collection to pay me, and I figured out a strategy: I would request a special meeting of the Alpena County Board of Commissioners to reconsider the vote.

Not only did I file my petition with the county, I gave a copy to the local newspaper—which promptly did a big, headline-grabbing story. I made sure that the petition was signed by a number of Alpena's leading businessmen, doctors, and religious leaders. The commissioners might be able to ignore some young punk lawyer from Detroit, but I knew they couldn't ignore them.

Sure enough, the chairman of the board reluctantly announced they would convene a special meeting in ten days. I then rounded up twenty of the county's top citizens to speak against the jail location.

When the meeting began, I briefly explained why we thought the building plans were imprudent and asked them to allow each petitioner to speak for three minutes. They could scarcely say no. They were steamrollered. When my clients were done, the Alpena commissioners quickly voted to reverse themselves and find a new location for the jail. That night, I thought that this was one hell of a lot better than running around serving papers in Detroit.

Where else other than in a small town like Alpena could a young, ambitious, but mostly inexperienced young lawyer take on such rewarding and controversial cases? How else could I have gotten such phenomenal on-the-job experience so rapidly?

Not that all of my cases were earth-shattering—far from it.

This was, after all, a semirural practice in northern Michigan in the 1950s. I had to argue cases in what amounted to the backwoods, before justices of the peace who were barely literate. Needless to say, they weren't even lawyers. Some cases resembled bad comedy, including one farmer who sued another, claiming he shorted him two bales of hay. The bales were worth about a dollar each, but the farmer spent about eight hundred dollars on the case. On top of that, he lost! Before you laugh too much, think of the vast sums the rich waste in nasty celebrity divorce trials. Silliness and spite are no strangers to any class.

What made me proud is that I seem to have earned the entire town's respect in a very short time. I made friends with brewers and bank presidents and was on good terms with Republican leaders. Actually, you pretty much had to be; Democrats were fairly rare birds in Alpena County, then a great GOP stronghold. In 1956, for example, the Republican presidential candidate got 71 percent of the county vote.

However, something truly astonishing happened two summers after I arrived, a few months before that GOP landslide. One day there was a knock on my office door. I opened it to find the mayor, Harlo Herron, a hardware store owner and farm implement salesman in his mid-fifties, and the entire city council on the other side. I was startled. I brought them into our conference room and said something like, "Mayor Herron, what brings such a distinguished group of dignitaries my way?"

The mayor cleared his throat. "Frank, the council and I have talked it over, and we've decided that we want you to be our city attorney." I was flattered, honored—and astounded. "Why, thank you. But you know I'm a Democrat." Every man there was a rock-ribbed Republican. "Don't you think this might make it difficult for me to be your city attorney and advisor on governmental affairs?" The mayor grinned. "We've talked that one over, Frank. You take care of guiding us on the law; we'll take care of the politics."

What could I say?

I agreed to take the appointment for a year, though as it turned out, I kept being reappointed as long as I lived in Alpena. They must have thought I was doing something right—and so, evidently, did the citizens. Republican though they may have been, Alpena voters supported me for attorney general every time I ran.

I didn't make a lot of extra money as city attorney—maybe $1,500 a year. But with three kids, every little bit helped.

As I entered my mid-thirties, my life was pretty wonderful. My career move had been a success, and the town was good for us as a family. We had plenty of time together. Jo and I developed a nice social life, and I was active in everything from our church to the usual service clubs. Additionally, every few weeks I took one of the kids for a "night out with daddy," to a restaurant and usually a movie.

Looking back, I don't think I really appreciated how good it was.

But then, seven years into my Alpena odyssey, I started to get a little restless. It was the spring of 1961, and John F. Kennedy had just become the first Roman Catholic ever elected president. He was Irish, to boot. I had heard him challenge the country, saying, "I think we can do better." JFK told the nation it needed to get moving again. "Well," I thought, looking in the mirror, "what about me? Do I really want to spend the rest of my life in this small community?" I had just turned thirty-six and was, as I used to joke, still a brunette. I had a law school classmate who was doing well in Florida.

Should I uproot my family again?

I started taking some steps to study for the Florida bar. Then, in November, I got a call out of the blue from Governor John Swainson's executive secretary, which is what they called the chief of staff back then. What was this all about? I wondered.

"The governor just appointed Paul Adams, the state attorney general, to the Michigan Supreme Court," he told me.

That wasn't surprising. Most attorneys general in that era stayed a few years and then tried to get appointed to a judgeship. Few made any lasting impact.

The governor, he explained, had to appoint someone to fill the vacancy, and they were putting together the best list possible for him. They had settled on twenty Michigan lawyers. "What I am about to tell you must be kept in strictest confidence," he said. "You're on that list."

I was completely and utterly stunned.

7

A STUNNING
APPOINTMENT

I was flabbergasted. From that point on in the conversation, I had to concentrate hard to make sure I understood what he was saying.

The governor's secretary was Zolton Ferency, who later became a hero to left-wing students, breaking with the Democrats and starting the short-lived independent Human Rights Party. But in 1961 he was just another young political apparatchik, a couple of years older than I was. He explained that Governor Swainson, who had been in office less than a year, was taking a lot of criticism over his appointments. "By God, we're not going to give them any more ammunition with this one," he said.

They had to make the right choice.

Now this was very much a young man's era. Swainson was seven months younger than I was; he'd been elected governor at thirty-five. Jerry Cavanagh, thirty-three, had just been elected mayor of Detroit. John F. Kennedy, the young-est man ever elected president, was just forty-four. Compared to Cavanagh, I was an elder statesman of thirty-six. But I knew there was no way I was going to be appointed attorney general.

No way. Oh, I knew more than my share of big-name Democratic politicians in the state. But that was partly due to geography. There weren't a lot of Democrats that far north. We used to joke that our office was the only place north of Lansing where a traveling Democrat could use the bathroom, freshen up, and receive a sympathetic ear.

So maybe including my name was a bow to geography.

Ferency continued: he, the governor, and four prominent Democratic community leaders would meet weekly to narrow down the list. If I survived the next cut, he would let me know. And that was that.

I sat there for a few minutes assessing my chances. Nah. No way. They were surely going to appoint someone older and more experienced to the post. Well, it was flattering to have been called. I made a quick call to my wife, of the "You're not going to believe this" variety, and put it out of my mind.

Then, on December 10, I got another call.

"Frank," the always serious-sounding Ferency said, "you're still on the list." Now it was down to ten candidates. "Keep this confidential," he said. They would further narrow the field to five, and then the finalists would be interviewed by the governor and the full selection committee.

Well, what do you know? I thought when we hung up.

Suddenly it seemed really possible that I might become Michigan's next attorney general. That appealed to me—a lot.

Why?

Even then, I knew that being attorney general was the most important job any lawyer in Michigan could have. Here's why: the attorney general is the chief lawyer for the state. The top attorney, that is, for the government, for its officers, and for all civil and criminal matters involving the state. Being attorney general would give me an enormous chance to make a huge difference in the lives of my fellow citizens. And that was what really mattered.

First of all, that's what my father always taught me, and corny as it may sound, I wanted to live up to his hopes for me. As a matter of fact, I am still very much my father's son, though I'm now far older than he was when he died. These were also the Kennedy years, and we had a handsome young Irish president whom I very much idealized.

People of my generation believed government could make a positive difference in the lives of our fellow citizens. It is sad that young people today have such a hard time imagining this. One of JFK's slogans was "One person can make a difference, and everyone should try."

I believed that wholeheartedly.

Still do.

Michigan has had an attorney general since 1836, a year before it officially became a state. The office, like that of governor and secretary of state, was created by our first state constitution.

A lot of people think of the attorney general as the "lawyer for the governor." Well, that's true—but that's only one part of the job. Michigan's attorney general does act as an attorney for the executive branch, down to every last state department and employee. But he or she also represents the interests of the legislature. When I was attorney general, my assistants and I had to be available as counsel to any member of the state house or senate. We were also their official legal advisors. That meant we had to offer opinions and interpretations regarding any laws or proposed laws whenever they asked.

But the job didn't stop there. We were also the attorneys for the judicial branch of government. Whenever the state was in court for any reason, we were there representing it—sometimes as plaintiff and sometimes as the defendant. Additionally, the Michigan Supreme Court would often ask the attorney general's office to present arguments to the court on both sides of some important issues.

But I'm getting ahead of my story.

You may have realized by now that I am anything but passive by nature. Once the list of contenders was narrowed down to ten, I wondered what I could do to improve my odds.

I called my good friend Stanley Steinborn, a Chicago native and Northwestern law grad who had ended up practicing law in Alpena. Years later, he would become my chief deputy. He came to my house for dinner and we came up with a strategy:

I would call the top Democrats around the state I knew well—and could trust to keep my confidences. I would swear them to secrecy—and then let them know what was going on. The theory was that they then would boost my candidacy without letting on that I had told them; after all, they'd love to be able to say that the attorney general was their friend.

Stanley Steinborn, on the other hand, would call people I didn't know. He would tell them that he'd heard I was being considered, provide a brief sketch of my background, and tell them why I was qualified.

We went at it for a week, calling perhaps thirty prominent Democrats. From their comments I got a sense that my being from outstate Michigan was a real plus. Most Democratic officeholders back then were from industrial cities, especially Detroit.

I had grown up in the Motor City, but officially I was now the candidate from Alpena. Whomever the governor chose would have to run for reelection the following year, and every ticket strives for geographic balance. I also had to be careful not to push too hard. Appearing overambitious or aggressively campaigning for the job might well ruin my chances.

Steinborn then had a brilliant idea: "Frank, for the last seven years you've helped all the labor unions in town, usually free of charge. I think they should call their main offices in Detroit and sing your praises." Immediately he went to work, and it paid off. The chief AFL-CIO representative in northern Michigan suggested driving me to Oakland County to meet with the powerful August "Gus" Scholle, who was the labor federation's head man in Michigan. Getting to his Birmingham home took five hours. Scholle questioned me thoroughly about my beliefs regarding organized labor. The fact is that while I was sympathetic, I wasn't a zealot.

While in Alpena, I represented many small businessmen who had problems of their own, and I knew union men weren't always saints. I would defend the right to organize to the death. But I also knew there had to be a balance between management and labor. My feeling was that if a company treated its workers well, government shouldn't interfere with the conduct of their business.

Fortunately, nothing controversial came up during our meeting. Gus seemed more interested in my general philosophy and in what I knew about organized labor. Fortunately I had read a lot on the subject in my youth and knew the background of many labor leaders.

I was supposed to be there for half an hour, but the meeting lasted three times as long. At the end, he got up and walked me to the door.

"Frank, I'm endorsing you," he said.

That made for a happy trip back home. But that meant, at most, one vote out of five, that of Mildred "Millie" Jeffrey, one of the highest-ranking women in the UAW.

The others on the selection committee included the chairs of the Michigan and Wayne County Democratic parties, Neil Staebler, the Democratic National Committeeman and a power in state politics for years, and a fifth member, first among equals: Governor John Swainson.

Two days after my audience with Scholle, Ferency called to tell me that I was on the list of the final five. He told me to come to Lansing—alone—the day after Christmas to be interviewed by the committee.

Suddenly it occurred to me that while it was amazing that I'd made it this far, thinking that I would actually be appointed attorney general was absurd. Here I was, this young guy from Alpena who had never been elected to anything. I was probably window-dressing.

Well, I thought, maybe this would lead to the governor appointing me to a vacant judgeship down the line. The next day the phone rang, and it was Millie Jeffrey. She was a tiny powerhouse who had far greater influence than most knew. "You are supposed to show up for your interview alone," she said, "but bring your charming wife, and you'll throw them off." This was the woman who had helped deliver Michigan's votes to John F. Kennedy at the Democratic convention the year before. I wasn't about to second-guess her. "If you say so, Mildred," I said.

That's exactly what I did. The day after Christmas, Jo and I got in the car to begin the long drive to Lansing. It was a Tuesday morning, and fortunately there wasn't a snowstorm.

All the way down, we tried hard to anticipate what I might be asked and rehearse answers to questions they might ask.

Late that afternoon, we checked into the famous old Jack Tar Hotel, which today has been renovated into the George W. Romney office building, where the governor has his main office.

We made our way—nervously—to the interview location, which was in a large house that was then the main headquarters for the Michigan Democratic Party.

The interviews began at seven that night. They put us all in separate little rooms. I was scheduled to go third. I had no idea who the other finalists were. Much later, I learned that they included Avern Cohn, a prominent lawyer from Detroit who later became a distinguished federal judge and a good friend. The others were Tom Foley, a Detroit circuit judge, Joseph Kadans, an attorney, and one exceptionally qualified candidate—Robert Derengoski, then the state solicitor general, the man in the attorney general's office who handled all the major cases that had to be argued in the Michigan Supreme Court.

When my turn finally came, I startled most of the committee by walking in hand in hand with Jo. They were all polite, however. Nobody asked her to leave, and then they began: Why did I feel qualified to be attorney general? What was my view of the office? What would my priorities be if I were chosen?

Well, I figured all I could do was answer the questions as well and as honestly as I could. I remember telling them I had been an attorney for ten years and had practiced many different kinds of law. I noted that in addition to my private practice, I was the city attorney for Alpena, and the laws pertaining to that small city happened to be the same as those for Detroit—and any other city in the state. Other questions flew across the table.

I explained my views on integrity. Public service. The role of the attorney general as an advocate for the people. On and on. I just tried to be myself, and if I told you I remember exactly what I said, I'd be lying. Finally, after a little over an hour, it was over.

My wife and I left for a late dinner. We discussed what had gone on during the interview. We both came to the same conclusion: the committee liked me all right but felt I was too young for the job.

So we went back to our hotel and went to sleep. I was philosophical; even being considered for the job would be good for my career. The next morning, we had breakfast in the hotel coffee shop before heading back to Alpena. We were surprised to see James Burns, an old college classmate who had become a prominent Lansing lawyer, walk in.

I told him what was going on. Burns agreed with me that in all probability it wasn't in the cards. I told him I expected to get a call from the governor anyway. "He knows my birthday is New Year's Eve," then four days away. "My guess is he will call me before I leave town and ask me to stop by so he can wish me a happy birthday."

Believe it or not, at that precise moment the bellboy dashed up. "Mr. Kelley, sir, you have a call from Governor Swainson."

I was literally speechless. "Hello, Frank," the governor said when I finally reached the phone. "Come by the house before you head back to Alpena. Let's have a birthday drink."

I thanked him, returned to our table, and announced that my prediction had become a reality. After we all had a good laugh, my college chum said, "Well, go get your drink and go back to Alpena."

Today the governor lives in an official, 8,700-square-foot Wallace Frost mansion in an exclusive Lansing neighborhood. Back in 1961, however, the governor's residence was just a rented house.

That afternoon, we parked at the governor's house and walked up to the front door. John Swainson himself answered, shook our hands, and gave Jo a warm peck on the cheek.

The governor moved his hand slightly, and a maid appeared with three glasses of champagne. Swainson lifted his. "Happy Birthday, Frank. Here's to the next attorney general of Michigan." I was dumbstruck. I couldn't believe it.

He did almost all the talking. "I will be issuing an official statement about your appointment later today." he told me. For now, he told me to get back to Alpena, get my affairs in order, and then come back for a press conference. "Plan to stay over so you can attend my New Year's Eve party. You will be sworn in at noon on January 2, the same day Paul Adams will take the oath as a justice of the Michigan Supreme Court." That way, he said, there would be no vacancy in the office of attorney general. That much I understood.

What I never dreamed was that I would stay in that post longer than any man has held it, in this state or anywhere, and that I would gradually reshape what it meant to be attorney general.

When I finally left thirty-seven years later, the Michigan attorney general's office was a skilled and muscular watchdog for the citizens, a nationwide leader in the new field of consumer protection. We more than doubled the number of attorneys we had when I started and became national pioneers in environmental and other areas of law.

But all that lay off in the future. For now, I had a whole lot to learn and not much time. The next day I was startled to see a huge headline in the *Detroit Free Press*: "Alpena Dem Named Attorney General." In today's world, I would have been lucky to have my appointment make the front page at all on a slow news day. But back then, the media paid more attention to politics and government.

The governor took pains to make sure I would get a warm welcome. "I have known Frank Kelley for some time and believe his background in law and the high respect he has won from other attorneys make him eminently qualified," he told the press, adding that I was a "distinguished son of a distinguished father." I was glad that the coverage was overwhelmingly favorable.

After I drove my wife back to Alpena, I turned around and jumped on a chartered plane to return to Lansing and be sworn in. When I got there, Paul Adams gave me a warm welcome. He showed me around his (soon to be my) spacious office, which was every bit as big as the governor's. He gave me a tour, handed me the key, and said, "Frank, my dear friend, I wish you well. I'll never interfere with you and never second-guess you." He paused and chuckled, adding, "I couldn't if I wanted to."

Adams was not, however, the first person I met that day—or, as it would turn out, the most important as far as I was concerned. That would be the young man who met me at the airport, someone who would prove to be the biggest asset I could possibly have during my first decade on the job: Leon Cohan, the deputy attorney general. Leon was then barely thirty-two and had risen rapidly in the ranks since Adams had hired him in 1958. He might have been young, but as I soon found out, he had what it takes.

His own story was fascinating. Later I learned that he had served in Army Intelligence in Germany right after the war, where he had fallen in love with a beautiful blond German woman named Heidi. He had brought her back to the States, managed to win over his parents, and married her. That wasn't easy, given that he was Jewish and she wasn't; she also had a child by a Nazi soldier, and this wasn't long after the Holocaust.

Leon helped me set up my first press conference (first of about a million) and filled me in on the logistics of the way the attorney general's office worked. We clicked instantly. I could see that despite the differences in our personalities, he thought the way I did.

I think I had a pretty decent legal mind. Very few of my opinions were ever overturned while I was attorney general. But my instincts have always been especially strong when it comes to judging people.

I could see that Leon was worried that his position as first deputy was about to end. We sat together in my office that first afternoon, poring over a chart of the sections in the attorney general's office and the various departments of state and going through who was who.

Finally I broke the ice. "By the way, Leon, you are going to continue on as deputy attorney general. I hope you will quickly brief me on all the workings of this office." I saw a broad, relieved smile that told me I had made the right choice. I needed him, too. There were more than eighty assistant attorneys general then, plus support staff.

I needed to know—quickly—how everything came together, who they were, and what they did. Only then could I start to make the necessary changes to improve things and put my stamp on the office.

I needn't have worried. Leon remained at my side for eleven years, and we solved many a problem and weathered many a crisis together. He finally left when his children were getting close to college age and Detroit Edison made him a financial offer he couldn't refuse.

All that, however, was history yet to be written. All I could see on that day in January was that I had to do a lot.

Fast.

8

ATTORNEY GENERAL:
BAPTISM UNDER FIRE

There was one big reason I had no time to lose.

I became attorney general ten months prior to a statewide election in which millions of voters, most of whom had never heard of me, would decide whether to keep me in my job.

What this meant was that I had to do good work and attract public attention—and do that quickly. First on the agenda, however, was making sure that the machine was well-oiled and in good order.

Leon Cohan and I spent a day or two analyzing the organizational charts. I saw that he had good instincts, but to be on the safe side, I also consulted a couple of the top lawyers on the staff, men who were senior in ability, if not always years of service. As I noted, there were more than eighty lawyers working in the department, all with the title "assistant attorney general" but differing a great deal in interests, experience, and expertise.

Soon I came up with a plan. I announced about ten changes in division heads and a number of other new working assignments. Word from the water cooler was that the changes were well received, but more important, they showed I was in charge, and my move communicated to both the staff and those who followed the workings of the office that I knew what I was doing.

I realized that I would have to win the public over through the press—what today political consultants call "free media." That meant mostly newspapers.

Though local television and radio news did exist, they were relatively primitive by today's standards. Newspapers were where people went for serious news.

Here I had an advantage, in that both Leon and I were serious students of public policy in addition to being lawyers. Both of us had read widely throughout our lives and had studied politics and the media.

He swiftly agreed that if we wanted to be taken seriously, we couldn't flood newsrooms with press releases announcing "puff stuff"—routine lunch speeches, crowning beauty queens, and so forth. We knew we had to make significant "hard news" that would interest the public.

But we were not tempted to stage trumped-up crusades or witch hunts. My philosophy was that if we did meaningful good work and found a way to let the public know about it, the politics would take care of itself.

Indeed, that is what ended up happening. But I knew enough to know the press liked scandals—and sometimes would settle for just the appearance of one. Perhaps more than any other public office, that of the attorney general depends on public trust. Though the word "transparency" was not yet being used, I knew I needed to make sure everything was clean beyond the shadow of a doubt.

Accordingly, I quickly hired an independent auditing firm to track anything of value I earned or received. The firm's accountants were instructed to inform me immediately if anything looked even remotely suspicious. I knew that if I were going to survive, my finances, both public and private, had to be above suspicion. Frankly, I couldn't have lived with myself otherwise; I was, remember, Frank E. Kelley's son.

That decision paid off.

When I retired nearly four decades later, an editorial in the *Detroit Free Press* observed that "as the curtain rings down on the longest-running show in Michigan politics, what you see are 37 years with no scandal [and] an enduring popularity with the voters."

Not a bad career epitaph.

Except what it didn't say was that what I was running was a lot more serious than a show. The attorney general's office is a vastly powerful one—in Michigan more so than in many other states.

The moment I took the oath, I became the chief law enforcement officer for the entire state. Not just the governor—though at least one of "my" governors made the mistake of thinking that I was "his lawyer." My staff attorneys and I represented every official and every branch of state government.

That was the case for all matters, civil and criminal, executive, legislative, and judicial. We were the only ones who could sue on behalf of the state—and we were there to defend the state if any person, corporation, or other state sued the state of Michigan.

But that wasn't all. We were available as counsel to all members of the legislature and were their official legal advisors, whom they could ask for advice on the constitutionality of proposed legislation or for opinions on the meaning of existing law. This was a highly important service. Most legislators were not attorneys, and most who were knew enough to know they weren't constitutional experts. Many lawmakers from both parties later told me that we helped save them from proposing and passing laws that would have been struck down by the courts as unconstitutional.

Additionally, I was sometimes asked to issue a formal opinion on the meaning and constitutionality of existing law. Such an opinion then had the effect of law unless it was overturned by the courts.

I often issued as many as a hundred opinions in a year—and very few were ever overturned, in large part because I had an excellent staff of brilliant legal experts. As the years went by, I continued to build this staff until I had what might easily have been the best law firm in the state—virtually all of whom were working for a mere fraction of the salaries they could have commanded in the private sector. Some are there even as I am writing this, more than fifteen years after I left government.

But our duties did not stop there. We were also attorneys for the third branch of government—the judicial branch—especially the Michigan Supreme Court. The Office of Attorney General stands in the unique legal position of being above conflict of interest. That meant, as I have said, that in many complicated and important cases, the justices would often ask our office to present arguments to the court on both sides of an issue. This was so that they could make sure they understood every legal aspect before they made a ruling. Whenever this happened, I would assign one team of attorneys to research and argue one side of the case and an equally skilled set to present the opposing view.

All this meant that the attorney general's office was always busy, highly challenged, and overworked. And yet the vast majority of my staff was eager, stimulated, and professionally fulfilled. They weren't necessarily getting rich—but they were doing important work they believed in. Additionally, as many of them told me, working for the Michigan attorney general's office was about the best training any lawyer, especially a young lawyer, could have. That's because they were able to gain more experience in more areas of the law than they could have gotten in years of private practice. I also took pains to make sure that our office was a supportive and collegial place to work. That, I believe, is why so many turned down better-paying jobs and stayed so long. When many did eventually leave for other opportunities, I had the satisfaction of knowing I had helped produce some of the state's best-trained attorneys.

But there was still another vastly important aspect of the job: Michigan's attorney general has the constitutional right and duty to independently sue on behalf of the public. As attorney general, I could also intervene in any case, anywhere in the state, in which I determined that the greater public interest was involved.

This has been true ever since Michigan was first admitted to the union in 1837. That's not the case in every state; in some, attorneys general have far more limited powers. But I had the ability to use my office not only as a bully pulpit but to battle on behalf of the people.

I won't deny that I wanted to be elected in my own right or that I wasn't thinking about that, to some extent, from the very first day.

But not simply because of my ego.

My reasoning was this: if I could become known well enough in the early months as attorney general, I could win election to a full two-year term. Then if I managed to do enough good for the public in that time, maybe I'd be able to have a rather long-term career in this job.

That wasn't how most of my predecessors had thought about being attorney general. None had stayed in the job longer than five years. Most stayed barely two or three years, often in the hope of being appointed to a judgeship, maybe the state supreme court. Still others ran for office elsewhere.

Most of Michigan's attorneys general had primarily been "reactors." They were mainly involved in weathering or trying to ward off crises and defending lawsuits filed against the state. They didn't have, or didn't take, the time to initiate legal action on behalf of the public interest.

Which got me wondering: What could I do to make the public see me as an attorney general who fought for them? What legal areas were open to me?

I quickly studied what was happening elsewhere in the nation. Some attorneys general in other states had filed isolated lawsuits in the area of civil rights. For example, employers had been charged with failure to consider qualified African Americans for certain jobs. Today federal law outlaws such discrimination, but that was not the case in 1962. You could only try to bring such civil rights cases to court if a particular individual state outlawed discrimination.

There was another kind of case that intrigued me as well. I saw instances where a state attorney general had brought actions to set aside shady contracts in which new homeowners had been pressured to have garages constructed at what were wildly exorbitant prices. What these attorneys general were doing was referred to in the press by a term that was unknown at the time: *consumer protection*. Eventually my office would help make those two words part of every citizen's vocabulary. But first I had to establish myself.

Before long, I had a routine. I would meet with the governor for at least half an hour in his office, twice a week or more, primarily to discuss any state legal problems that had arisen or that were outstanding. I had liked John Swainson from the start, but I gradually developed a real appreciation for his courage and abilities.

Think of it: when he was nineteen years old, both his legs had been blown off by a land mine that left him close to death. He battled back, went to law school, bucked the party establishment, and got himself elected governor at age thirty-five. That was amazing.

We were less than a year apart in age, and ten days after I was sworn in as attorney general, I got a call from another man who outranked me considerably—but was also a little less than a year younger than I was: Attorney General Robert Kennedy.

This book begins with the story of that meeting, which, as you can imagine, had a powerful effect on me. The Kennedys were magic, it's true. But you also need to remember that this was an era when people had much more respect for government than they do now. Presidents were seen as huge, larger-than-life figures. High-ranking figures in their administration were revered as statesmen.

This was before the Vietnam War and the Watergate scandals tore the country apart. Nobody reported on politicians' sex lives.

More important, perhaps, we thought government—and those of us who worked in government—could make a difference.

The Kennedys deeply inspired lots of people, including me. Like me, the Kennedys were Irish Catholics. Unlike me, they were royalty, princes of the realm. "I'm going after the injustice that I see, and I'm going after the bad people," RFK told me. "Reach out against injustice wherever you see it, and protect the public. If you do that and I do that, the people of our great country will have a greater appreciation for the freedoms they enjoy and a greater sense of trust in their government."

That was all the encouragement I needed.

Soon after I got home from my meeting with Robert Kennedy, I threw myself into a case that screamed of injustice—and learned a painful and very valuable lesson from it.

The case involved a young black man named Grady Little. If his name sounds familiar, it's probably because another man of the same name later was a successful major league baseball manager. "My" Grady Little was dead before I had ever heard of him. He had been strolling through Palmer Park in a nice part of Detroit on an early fall evening in October 1961 when I was still in Alpena. He was confronted by a group of white young men, and a fight broke out. Grady Little and a nineteen-year-old white man named Fred O'Dell fell into a clump of bushes. After a struggle, O'Dell came out.

Grady Little lay dead, stabbed with a knife.

The Detroit police investigated the case and recommended that Wayne County prosecutor Samuel H. Olsen issue a warrant for O'Dell's arrest. In most cases, a warrant would automatically follow.

But not this time. Olsen refused to issue a warrant, saying O'Dell was entitled to a presumption of innocence. I was startled.

The black community was outraged. "Was Olsen up to racist politics?" I wondered. This was back when African Americans made up less than a third of Detroit's population and a smaller share of the rest of Wayne County. The prosecutor was fond of talking about cracking down on inner-city crime, and he ferociously prosecuted blacks, something that seemed calculated to win over white voters.

My attention had been first drawn to the case by one of the top lawyers in my criminal division, Irving Beattie. Beattie was a well-respected attorney and former small-town prosecutor who had enjoyed a brief moment of fame a few years earlier when George C. Scott portrayed a character based on Beattie in the movie version of Robert Traver's* brilliant novel, *Anatomy of a Murder*. However, the real-life attorney was nothing like the overbearing character the future star of *Patton* invented.

The real man was soft-spoken and scholarly—but just as concerned about injustice. After Beattie told me about the incident, I sent him to Detroit to investigate. When he came back to Lansing he told me, "This case stinks to high heaven," adding that all the authorities wanted to sweep it under the rug, presumably because they were afraid of stirring up racial tensions. Few remember it now, but there had been a vicious race riot in Detroit in 1943.

Nobody wanted a repeat of that, nor did anyone dream that a far more destructive riot was only a few years away. But I felt that I had gotten into this job to see that justice was done.

Leon Cohan agreed. "There is sufficient evidence here not just to justify but to require us to ask for a warrant," he said. "This is not a question of guilt or

---

* Robert Traver was actually a justice on the Michigan Supreme Court named John Voelker. He used the pen name Traver because he thought that being a novelist might be seen as a questionable hobby for a judge on the state's highest court.

innocence but of probable cause, of whether a crime was committed and who did it." That was more than enough for me. I called a press conference in early March and announced that I was taking over the case and filing a first-degree murder charge against Fred O'Dell.

And all hell broke loose. The Wayne County prosecutor said I was incompetent. "I've been a prosecutor for years, and Frank Kelley doesn't know what he's doing," Olsen said. He then proceeded to stack the deck against me. He swiftly got the case before Recorder's Court judge W. McKay Skillman, who did not have an enlightened reputation on racial matters. When we showed up for jury selection, we discovered there were no blacks in the pool of available people.

Once the trial got under way, the judge did all he could to beat me. He swiftly knocked the charges down to manslaughter. Then, in a most unusual move, O'Dell's defense called the Wayne County prosecutor as a witness—and the judge allowed Olsen to give his opinion regarding the defendant's guilt or innocence.

I was flabbergasted. That violated all the rules of evidence and fairness, and should have been inadmissible in any court of law.

We were not surprised that we lost the case. On July 9, the jury took only ten minutes to find Fred O'Dell not guilty. Afterward, the judge told the jury he agreed with the verdict and denounced me: "The attorney general should not use the power of his high office to supplant the local prosecuting attorney unless there has been a clear and wrongful abuse of discretion." He added that in his opinion, "this warrant for murder should never have been issued."

You might have thought that left me with egg on my face. Well, yes—and no. I responded to the judge's tongue-lashing by saying, "It is not the function of the prosecuting attorney, or the attorney general, to determine guilt or innocence." A young man had died violently, and I felt this was a case that a jury needed to decide.

Fifty years later, I still firmly believe that—and I will be convinced until the day I die that the jury was wrong. I am also still convinced that the Wayne County prosecutor's decision not to bring charges was politically motivated, opportunistic, and racist.

But I made my share of mistakes, too—and learned some valuable lessons. Frankly, the brashness of youth and a sense of righteousness had made me behave like the proverbial raging bull. By charging in and intervening, getting my own warrant and prosecuting O'Dell for murder, I did more than just overrule and embarrass the prosecutor. I turned a significant part of the community against me. By bringing the power of the state sweeping in, I had actually inflamed their prejudices by making them mad. Instead, I should have quietly started my own investigation.

However, the press largely supported me and gave me credit for trying. The civil rights movement was getting fully under way. People had seen the Freedom Riders beaten up and buses burned on the nightly news, and there was a growing sense that it was time for more justice in America.

Needless to say, I was suddenly a hero in the black community, praised as a courageous, new "man of justice."

But I learned something about justice in the process: try as we might, justice cannot be imposed. Our Founding Fathers gave us guarantees of freedom of speech and of the press. But not even Thomas Jefferson or James Madison could guarantee justice. All they could do was allow us to pursue it. Human nature being what it is, the best we can hope for is to manage to get something approaching justice . . . most of the time.

Injustices are bound to occur. For Grady Little, like countless other murdered black Americans in our history, there was no justice. But at least I had tried. I had learned some important lessons, too. Never again would I use my power to suddenly overrule the final decision of a county prosecutor. Instead, I learned that by building bridges and using friendly persuasion, you can get a lot more accomplished.

That turned out to be true in my dealings with everyone from local prosecutors to U.S. attorneys to federal agencies.

I also learned that justice has a better chance of prevailing when everybody has the opportunity to look good and save face.

When the verdict came back in the Grady Little case, I had just completed my first six months in the attorney general's office. It had been, I realized, a baptism under fire.

And the day the voters would decide whether I could keep my job was fewer than four months away.

9

WINNING ELECTION
ON MY OWN

There was something else I realized after the bitter outcome of the Grady Little case: the importance of the media—both print and broadcast. That was a relatively primitive era by modern standards.

Television news was very local, mostly evenings only and broadcast in often grainy black and white. National news was only on for fifteen minutes in the evenings. Nobody ever imagined all-news stations and channels, and newspapers were still king.

But one thing was as true then as now: all politicians, all public figures, have to find a way to shape their image and prevent the media from defining them in a way that could fatally damage their careers.

First impressions are very hard to change. That's even more true today, thanks to the ever-present, twenty-four-hour news cycle. Remember what Texas senator Lloyd Bentsen did to Dan Quayle during that otherwise forgotten vice-presidential debate back in 1988? When he looked at him and said, "I knew Jack Kennedy. Jack Kennedy was a friend of mine. Senator, you are no Jack Kennedy," Quayle looked like a young deer caught in the headlights of a hunter's pickup truck. His career never recovered.

Ironically, Democrats lost that presidential election largely because nominee Michael Dukakis allowed the Republicans to use the media to define him as a bumbling liberal who was eager to let dangerous felons out of prison.

But from the moment Bentsen pointed his finger at Quayle, the future vice president was doomed to be mostly the punch line of late-night comedy routines. The media eagerly looked for everything that would reinforce the image they were determined to create, pouncing triumphantly when Quayle misspelled "potato" at a spelling bee. When he did try to run for president a few years later, his candidacy was laughed to death before the first primary.

All that lay far in the future when I was a young attorney general. But I was determined not to let the press define me in a way that prevented the public from knowing who I really was.

Incidentally, you might be wondering why I never appealed the Grady Little decision, since to me it was clearly a miscarriage of justice. For one thing, getting a reversal would have been virtually impossible. Our legal system is set up to protect the innocent. Thanks to the doctrine of double jeopardy, once anyone has been acquitted of a crime, it is beyond difficult to reopen the case. The only possibility would have been to convince the higher courts that the trial judge had made grave errors in conducting the proceedings. Frankly I thought that had been the case.

However, I have always believed in paying attention to the experts—and the seasoned appellate lawyers in the attorney general's office told me the odds of being granted leave to appeal were slim indeed. The odds were I would just look like a sore loser.

Now, I would have been perfectly willing to challenge the system and the odds if it were a case where the public interest was truly at stake—to save an innocent man from conviction, say. But Grady Little was dead, and there was nothing I could do to bring him back to life. If I were really going to make a difference in the coming years, I was going to have to get elected in November.

Reluctantly, I let matters rest. But that doesn't mean I was determined to avoid controversy until the election. In fact, I was about to take up a case that angered some very rich and powerful people: reapportionment.

Today we operate under the principle of "one man, one vote," meaning legislative and congressional districts have to be essentially the same size. Congressional districts, in fact, have to contain exactly the same number of people. They can vary by only a single person—based, that is, on the most recent U.S. Census, the population count held on April 1 every ten years.

State legislative districts are legally allowed to vary a little more, to keep areas with common interest together, if possible. Every ten years, once the census results are known, lawmakers have to go to work, drawing new boundaries to fit new population patterns.

But that was not the case when I became attorney general. Although the state house of representatives was reapportioned every decade, and the legislature created districts that were roughly equal, the Michigan Senate was another story. Those making the rules divided the seats up by area, not population, a system deliberately rigged to give rural areas far more influence. For example, after the census of 1950, one Upper Peninsula district had 61,008 people. Meanwhile, one Wayne County district had 544,364! That meant a resident of the Keweenaw Peninsula had nine times as much representation as someone in Detroit.

That was outrageous. Plus, since rural voters tended to vote Republican, that meant the GOP virtually always kept control. For example, Democrats won all the top state offices in 1960, and John F. Kennedy narrowly carried Michigan in the presidential contest. Democrats and Republicans ended up exactly tied in the state house. But thanks to this unfair system of apportionment, Republicans kept an overwhelming, 22–12 edge in the state senate. Naturally the GOP had absolutely no incentive to change.

But it was monumentally unfair. Three years before I became attorney general, Gus Scholle, the leader of the state AFL-CIO, had sued over this clearly unfair "malapportionment." The suit reached the Michigan Supreme Court, which ruled in favor of the Republicans.

Four justices held that this grossly unequal system of allocating seats didn't violate the U.S. Constitution. A fifth justice said he thought that while a violation did exist, Michigan's highest court was powerless to grant relief.

So what could I do? I suddenly remembered what Bobby Kennedy had told me only a few weeks before. He told me to use the court as a "bully pulpit," to crusade for what was clearly right.

Morally, and I believed legally, there was no question. Or rather there was a question—one of fundamental justice. The fact that rural voters were wildly overrepresented violated, I felt, the equal protection clauses of both the state and federal constitutions.

I decided, come hell or high water, I was going to go ahead. But would I be just beating my head against the wall? Eugene Krasicky, one of my assistant attorneys general who really was a legal scholar, reassured me. "Don't worry," he said. "Either you'll win or, at the very least, you will obtain a good solid dissent from the appellate courts, one that will really help make your reputation as a fighter for justice." So I filed a petition to intervene in a new case Scholle had launched over the same issue.

Fortunately, someone else intervened in a way that really helped me: the U.S. Supreme Court. A similar case from Tennessee had reached the high court, a case every law school student knows as *Baker v. Carr*.

Sometimes people call this the case that established equal representation, or "one man, one vote." That's wrong. But it was the case that opened the door to that principle eventually becoming the law of the land. Here's what happened. Charles Baker was, ironically enough, a Republican who complained that there hadn't been any redistricting in his state since 1901—and his Memphis-area district now had ten times the population of some rural districts. The case was so divisive that the justices insisted on hearing it argued twice.

One justice, Charles Whittaker, was so conflicted he refused to take sides and afterward, his health broken, resigned from the court. The issue dividing them was not whether the system was fair. What they were trying to decide was whether this was properly a question for the judicial branch of government to decide. The great Felix Frankfurter argued that it wasn't, saying: "courts ought not to enter this political thicket." But in the end, Justice William Brennan convinced a majority that it was a matter of constitutional protection.

The U.S. Supreme Court did not, however, order the Tennessee districts redrawn. They sent the case back to the federal district court in that part of the country. Logically, it followed that the same thing would happen in Michigan, especially because our case had been combined with the Baker case on appeal. Sure enough, the high court shortly did exactly that. (Look up *Scholle v. Hare* if you are interested.)

Clearly the side I was on was winning, and the implications were obvious. And that provoked a fiery and explosive reaction from my opposition—especially the Republicans in the state senate. They knew they would be the big losers if the courts were to order all legislative districts to have about equal populations.

Some senators pugnaciously threatened to try to impeach me, though I don't think anybody ever actually moved to do so. No newspapers went that far, but a number of those with conservative editorial pages held that I had gone too far and had no business intervening. All I did was say, "Well, let the courts decide."

Now if you were around at the time and had any instinct for politics, you might well have said, "Frank, what the hell were you thinking?" Here I was, new to the job, relatively unknown—and in a few months I had taken on two high-profile, controversial cases. Not only that, in both cases the positions I took deeply upset the establishment, and I was about to face my first statewide election in what many thought would be a Republican year.

But my intuition told me something else. I believed that there was really no problem wading into controversy, as long I appeared to be fighting fairly, honestly, and on behalf of the people.

However, I have to confess I was a little worried about the reapportionment case and how that would play with the voters. So I confided this in an old friend, a retired newspaperman who had trouble with the bottle—but superb instincts about mankind. "Don't worry, Frank. This whole apportionment business is too complicated for the average person to get involved with. When it comes to complex matters, the public ignores what it doesn't understand," my now long-departed friend told me.

Throughout my career I learned over and over again that he was right. Whenever my office did have to weigh in on a complicated matter, I tried to explain it as well as I could. But for the most part, the public didn't concern themselves with the merits of a case, though I would like to think that most people believed I was trying to do the right thing. The election returns showed, over and over, that they gave me the benefit of the doubt.

There was one notorious exception to this: school busing. But that was ten years in the future, and my civil rights and reapportionment stands appeared not to have hurt me a bit in that first campaign.

My side completely won the reapportionment argument, of course, though it took a while before the nation's highest court finally ruled in our favor. That summer of 1962, the "Con-Con," or Constitutional Convention, was wrapping up its work. Most of the delegates were Republicans, thanks to both malapportionment and the fact that we Democrats aren't always so good about showing up to vote.

The new constitution they produced came up with a complicated formula for reapportionment that was based in part on past practices and still didn't provide for equal representation. But higher authorities took it out of their hands. Two years later, on June 15, 1964, in *Reynolds v. Sims*, the U.S. Supreme Court ruled 8–1 that state legislative districts had to be roughly equal in terms of population. "Legislators represent people, not trees or acres," wrote Chief Justice Earl Warren, one of the court's all-time giants. Four months earlier, in *Wesberry v. Sanders*, the nation's highest court had issued a nearly identical ruling that said all congressional districts in a state had to be as equal in population as possible.

Democracy, and one-man, one-vote, had won.

But that was still in the future in the summer and fall of 1962, and I had to get myself reelected. George Romney, the handsome American Motors chairman, had become a national figure through his sponsorship of the popular Rambler, America's first really successful compact car. Romney then got his feet wet in politics by pushing for the Constitutional Convention and artfully used that as a vehicle it to win the Republican nomination for governor that year.

Governor John Swainson knew he faced a tough opponent—and he had been through a bruising first year and a half in office. What's worse is that all statewide officials had to run for reelection every two years at that time, something that was finally and sensibly changed to four years in 1966. Swainson, an amazingly accomplished man, was still popular. But he had great difficulty getting any of his programs through the legislature, in part because of the GOP lock on the Senate.

Romney, a man with a take-charge attitude and movie-star hair and chin, presented a confident, can-do attitude. Plus, Democrats had controlled Michigan's statehouse since 1948. There was a strong feeling in some quarters that it was time for a change. So much so that President Kennedy later told me that his key political aides didn't want him to waste time going to Michigan to campaign for Swainson, whom they felt was a goner. When they told him that, JFK blew up. "That boy got two legs blown off fighting for this country in the war!" That had happened in France, the same theater, in fact, where JFK's brother Joe had been killed when his bomber exploded just months before. "He's a Democrat and one of ours and I am going there and campaigning for him."

That led to one of the most memorable days and conversations of my life. It was October 5, 1962. Air Force One swooped into Detroit Metropolitan Airport, and within a few minutes, John Swainson was introducing me to the president of the United States: John Fitzgerald Kennedy. That was an era before the Vietnam War and the Watergate scandals started to make us cynical about our leaders. It was a time when presidents, all presidents, were seen as superhuman figures. Kennedy was especially magnetic, and what made this all far more special was that he was of my blood, in a manner of speaking. He was, indeed, an Irish prince, the first and so far only Roman Catholic ever elected to the world's top job.

Thanks to my father, I had managed to make it into the middle class. But the Kennedys were royalty, and I immediately saw that everything I had ever heard about JFK was true. He had all the graceful bearing you'd expect of a prince, from his casual yet perfectly tailored Savile Row suit to his clearly custom-made shoes. Not only that, he had the tanned face of a hero and a unique voice that was equal parts upper-class Harvard and New England. He was, simply, the most charismatic person I'd ever met.

"When were you elected attorney general?" he asked me when we got into the presidential limousine, en route to the first of many stops that day. I explained how I came to be appointed. "I'm not going to worry about you," Kennedy said, with that famous grin. "With that Irish name, Kelley, and your good looks, you are as good as elected. We have to focus on Governor Swainson here. They are outspending him terribly, and I think they are buying the election," he said. "We've got to stop them," he said, meaning, of course, the Republicans. "Hear, hear!" the governor said.

The rest of that morning was a blur of motorcades and parades, of speeches and large, enthusiastic crowds. Michigan voters, like those in so many places across the country, seemed genuinely thrilled by the presence of their beaming young president. Early that afternoon, we all went to the Sheraton-Cadillac Hotel on Washington Boulevard in downtown Detroit. For fifteen minutes or so, various important people and politicians were allowed to walk through JFK's suite and shake hands with him.

Then the room was cleared. The president went into a private bedroom to make phone calls and lie down for a few minutes. Half an hour later, he emerged and ate a quick buffet lunch with Swainson and me. "Governor, how many newspapers are endorsing your reelection?" Kennedy asked. Swainson smiled bravely. Republicans then owned almost all the newspapers in the state, and poor John had to confess he might not get any of them.

"It takes extra courage to run without any newspaper endorsements," President Kennedy said gallantly. This was, remember, an age when computers didn't exist, and voters turned to TV for entertainment and still depended on papers for news.

"I remember my dad wouldn't let me announce my first run for Congress for three months while he worked on the editor of one of the Boston papers to secure my endorsement in advance," he said, as Swainson and I sat there, fascinated. "It was tough going, but the old boy came through," he said. I don't think it had occurred to either the governor or me that politics might be a little easier with an influential millionaire dad.

After a while, the governor excused himself. Few people knew it, but walking all day on artificial legs exhausted him. He needed to lie down for half an hour or so. He left.

President Kennedy and I were alone.

Less than a year earlier, I had been a country lawyer in Alpena. Now here I was, the attorney general of a major industrial state, sitting with the most powerful man in the world.

I wonder if my father would have believed it. After all, Joseph P. Kennedy and Frank E. Kelley had more than a little in common. They may not have been on the same scale, but both were a couple of struggling, hardworking Irishmen, eager to come up in the world and take care of their families. (And not inclined to let a silly and outrageous law, such as Prohibition, stand in their way.)

I knew that the elder Kennedy had been stricken by a stroke the year before, just before Christmas. I wondered how he was doing. "My father is working feverishly on the campaign," the president said, "offstage and behind the scenes." This was probably untrue; though Joe Kennedy's mind wasn't impaired by the stroke, he lost all power of speech and was partly paralyzed.

When you are royalty, however, appearances matter. I asked JFK if his father had lectured about public service at the dinner table, as mine had. A big smile came over the president's tanned face. "Quite often, and let me tell you, in a most persuasive way." I listened, spellbound, as he described what it was like. "My father was at the head of the table. To his immediate right was my brother Joe, who was killed in World War II. I sat opposite Joe, on my father's left. Bobby sat next to Joe, then came the girls. Little Teddy, the youngest, was way down the line." JFK said the patriarch used to tell his four sons, "You boys are privileged, and I want you to take that opportunity to serve the public. Now, I was in business and succeeded at it. But most of the people I met in business were bad, and I don't want you boys mixed up in it."

The president then added a surprising aside: "My dad said the only businessmen who had a social conscience were the Jewish men in Hollywood that he met when he was in the motion-picture business." The elder Kennedy was often said to be anti-Semitic, but JFK's reminiscences were clearly sincere. At that point the refreshed governor emerged from the bedroom, and all three of us got up from the table and went down to Washington Boulevard, where a thousand people were waiting to get a glimpse of their president. Kennedy then flew off for a campaign stop in Flint.

He never came to Michigan again. Two weeks later, campaigning elsewhere in the Midwest, his press secretary suddenly announced Kennedy had a cold and was returning to Washington. In fact, it was the beginning of the Cuban Missile Crisis, the closest the superpowers ever came to nuclear war. My family, like families all over the nation, watched, worried and nervous, as we waited to see whether the Soviet Union would back down.

As you probably know, the Soviets did. They announced they would pull the missiles out of Cuba. That result led to a surge of support for President Kennedy's Democrats. Normally the party that doesn't hold the presidency makes big gains in the off-year elections. That didn't happen that year. But I had no idea what would happen, and I had the toughest race I would ever face to keep my job.

My GOP opponent, Robert Danhof, was the same age I was and from Grand Rapids. But while I'd been struggling to support a family and go to law school at the University of Detroit, he was sailing through the University of Michigan. President Eisenhower had appointed him U.S. District Attorney for the western half of Michigan. He had been a delegate to the Constitutional Convention and was a tough opponent.

Somehow I managed to come up with a campaign budget of $60,000 or so. That was a lot of money back then but not a huge amount, even by the standards of that era. I ran a few commercials, mainly on the radio, but without major funds for broadcast, I instead turned to an innovative sign campaign.

Today this might sound corny, but this was at the dawn of the space age. I blanketed much of the state with an innovative campaign of signs, about four feet by six feet, with my name on a red, white, and blue rocket. When election night came, I felt pretty good—nervous but good. Slowly, the returns came in. Slowly, I inched ahead. But what was troubling was that the man who had given me my big chance was not faring as well. I was ahead in Wayne County by 294,000 votes; Swainson led by only 217,000.

Meanwhile, while we were both losing traditionally Republican counties, the governor was running behind me there, too. Both races were close, but by midnight I knew.

Romney's magic and money had done it.

I had been elected attorney general in my own right, with a hair over 52 percent of the vote. But my friend and patron, John Swainson, had lost by an even narrower margin.

President Kennedy's campaigning had certainly helped us. Democrats won the state's other top jobs—lieutenant governor and secretary of state. But it hadn't been quite enough to save Swainson. Now I was the state's top lawyer—but the state's top official would be a man who had openly hoped for my defeat.

I knew life was clearly going to be different.

What I never suspected is that it would be another twenty years before Michigan would have another Democratic governor. (The night John Swainson lost, the next Democrat who would be elected governor was a sophomore at Michigan State University.) Nor could I have imagined that two decades later, I would still be attorney general. But that's the way it worked out.

But not without a bit of drama along the way.

10

RESHAPING THE ATTORNEY
GENERAL'S OFFICE

I felt compassion in my heart on New Year's Day when I took the oath of office, as I watched Swainson, the man who had given me the chance to become attorney general, gallantly turn over his job to George Romney.

Compassion—and a bit of apprehension. Now I really was on my own. As I mentioned, I had known the outgoing governor since the early 1950s, when as young lawyers we used to talk politics while grabbing a quick bite to eat in Detroit. Swainson and I were, in many ways, two of a kind. Romney, however, was an entirely different creature, a corporate executive who was used to behaving like a captain of industry. When he was running American Motors, he barked orders and his underlings scurried around in an effort to do his bidding. He would soon find out that state government didn't work like that—and early on, he and I would have one major brawl.

More on that a little later; back to the attorney general's office. I had made up my mind even before I was appointed that I was going to be an activist attorney general, and now, in the winter of 1963, I felt I had even a freer hand.

The voters had elected me in my own right. I already had shown where I stood on civil rights and equal voting rights, with my battles over the Grady Little case and unfair apportionment. But now I turned my attention to the consumer. Michigan in the early 1960s was a place where it was far easier for consumers to be ripped off than it is now. The prevailing philosophy in many areas was caveat emptor—let the buyer beware.

That's not how I saw it. I wanted the attorney general's office to be a watchdog and a bulldog for the people. So we started looking into all sorts of consumer complaints, for example, those having to do with trading stamp companies. Back before coupons were the rage, grocery stores commonly gave shoppers stamps (the most famous were S&H Green Stamps), which could be pasted in a book and redeemed for prizes. I don't believe we ever prosecuted a trading stamp company, though we made them aware we were looking at their activities very carefully to make sure they kept their promises.

We did find plenty of authentically bad actors. We went after the well-known Holland Furnace Company, which specialized in phony furnace inspections. Their scam was fairly simple. They would offer free inspections to homeowners and then tell them their furnace needed cleaning, which was often true. However, the company would then recommend the furnace be resealed. If the homeowner agreed, he would soon find the parts strewn all over the basement floor, and the Holland man would say, "I'm, sorry, you need a new furnace," which much of the time wasn't true. We went after them in Michigan. Eventually the Federal Trade Commission ordered them to cease and desist, and a federal appeals court upheld that verdict.

But it seemed like there was no end to various crooked schemes and frauds. Past attorneys general tended to wait until cases were brought by local prosecutors in local courts. But my philosophy was that we were going to be a fighting attorney general's office—fighting for the little guy. I would use my office as both a bully pulpit to alert the people and as a command center from which we would dispatch legal teams to fight corruption.

Harry Truman, my dad's old hero, once said that there were a few million people who were rich enough to have their own lobbyists in Washington. He felt his job was to represent all the rest.

That's exactly how I saw my role, too.

One very common rip-off back then was interstate land scams. When World War II ended, plenty of veterans had saved a little money and wanted to invest in land. I had known since my days working the car ferries on the Great Lakes that money draws crooks as surely as fresh meat draws flies. Land scams were no exception.

The way it worked was simple. These companies would buy cheap land in various states for a few dollars an acre. Then they would peddle it in other states as "choice, beautiful building sites." Naturally the reality was that most of it was poor land hundreds of miles from anywhere, with no access to utilities and good roads, and with almost no chance of being improved enough for development.

You have to remember that back in the early 1960s, you couldn't get on the Internet to find things out. Long-distance phone calls were far more expensive than now, and it was much harder to check anything. So some trusting consumers really got ripped off.

Fortunately, I had begun to make a study of such things, and I am proud to say that my office managed to stop many of these shady land companies from doing business in Michigan.

Nor am I too proud to mention that we took pains to let the press—primarily newspapers and the wire services—know what we were up to. That doesn't mean we took causes for their publicity value alone. What it does mean, candidly, is that we weren't averse to blowing our own horn. For one thing, I knew I would have to run again in two years. I needed to let the public know what I was doing.

But I did not do this by myself. Leon Cohan, my deputy, and I saw eye to eye. He agreed with my approach. We very occasionally differed on tactics but never on basic philosophy or overall direction. Not only that, he shared my sense of drama and appreciation of suspense. And he was a wonderful writer.

Years later, he confided that he sometimes would actually even write stories for certain members of the press, some of whom were perhaps better at gin rummy than at understanding and explaining the fine points of legal actions. We never, ever, lied to reporters, and we tried whenever we could to make their jobs easier.

Somehow, I don't think it was an accident that the attorney general's office—and yours truly—got generally fair, even favorable treatment at the hands of the working press.

And while I was refocusing the attorney general's office in the direction of consumer protection—though nobody called it that yet—we were moving in other directions as well.

When I took the reins, there were fewer than a hundred lawyers in my office looking after the interests of the entire state of Michigan and what was then a population of eight million people. No more than a handful of those were women. But the ones who were there were some of the most dedicated public service lawyers I have ever seen, anywhere, and the most outstanding one was a woman with an incredible background, Maxine Boord Virtue.

Fifteen years older than I, she was one of the first women ever to graduate with high honor from Yale Law School. She was subsequently appointed clerk to U.S. District Judge Harold Medina. She helped him do research for a series of famous Cold War trials of American Communists and became involved in helping his colleague, Judge Irving Kaufman, with one of the most dramatic cases of the twentieth century: the trial of the alleged "atom spies" Julius and Ethel Rosenberg. She did a lot of background research for the judge, who later sentenced both Rosenbergs to die in the electric chair for their role in helping the Soviet Union get the A-bomb.

They were both put to death in 1953. Ironically, Maxine once confided to me that like me, she didn't believe in capital punishment. But she had a ringside seat at what was the biggest trial of the Cold War.

"Max," as her friends called her, had gone on to become quite a legal scholar and had written and edited a number of books. Normally someone with such credentials could command her own price in the private sector. But she had a burning desire for public service, and the Michigan attorney general's office was lucky enough to have her because her husband took a job as a professor at Eastern Michigan University in Ypsilanti. Talk about dedication: she drove something like 150 miles every day, sometimes through rain, snow, and sleet, to get to the office.

From the start, it was clear to me how valuable she was. Michigan's first consumer protection act was still four years away when I first took office, but as Max told me, things were stirring. Rumblings were being heard in Washington and in a number of other progressive states that government should do more to protect people. Virtue strongly urged me to act. "The average citizen is highly vulnerable to any number of cheats and chiselers, con men and crooks," she told me.

I saw that she was right. So one of my first innovative acts—and one I remain proudest of today—was starting an actual Consumer Protection Division in the attorney general's office, which was either the first such division or one of the first of its kind in the nation.

Virtue was named to run it, naturally, and two other lawyers were assigned to work with her. The number would gradually grow to more than ten attorneys and a support staff to assist them, but it was a start. Later, once Michigan passed its first Consumer Protection Act, the division really started making its mark.* I'll talk about some of those major landmark cases a little later. But I want to note that consumer protection wasn't the only new division, or special section, I would create.

We were living in an era of increasing specialization, and within a short time after taking office, I had conceived a plan to gradually create, staff, and move lawyers to a number of these sections. We eventually had teams of attorneys

---

* For the Michigan Consumer Protection Act, see http://www.michigan.gov/documents/consumer_protection_act_54984_7.htm (accessed November 19, 2014).

specializing in various areas, including civil rights, environmental law enforcement, and utility rates and insurance abuses.

I put the civil rights division in our Detroit office, which was where I knew it would be most needed. I also put a young assistant in charge of it named Carl Levin, who later was elected to the Detroit City Council and then became the longest-serving U.S. senator in Michigan history. Throughout his career he remained a loyal friend of mine, and is one to this very day.

I was deliberately reshaping the attorney general's office into an active, muscular, watchdog agency. Prior to World War II, most Michigan attorneys general hadn't seen their role that way at all. They mostly just functioned as lawyers for the governor, the legislature, and various governmental agencies. They were mainly reactive and seldom initiated legal action.

That started to change somewhat after the war, especially under my immediate predecessors, Thomas Kavanagh and Paul Adams. But I wanted to build a completely new image for the office, though I knew I needed to do it carefully and gradually, not getting too far ahead of what my office could do or the people were ready for.

Fortunately the public and press reaction was, by and large, overwhelmingly favorable. The early 1960s were at the dawn of the era of consumer consciousness, and in any event, rip-off artists and con men have never been popular with the public. We continued to take on consumer protection cases whenever we could. And in that scantily regulated era, there was no shortage of them.

One of the biggest scams was run by Koscot Enterprises, which was a classic pyramid scheme offering people franchises to sell cosmetics. People were pushed to buy franchises to mainly sell more franchises. What this meant was that a few people at the beginning might do well, most would lose their money, and the promoter of the whole scheme, namely Koscot and its owner, Glenn Turner, stood to make millions by selling a deception. The battle took years, but eventually the Michigan Court of Appeals (37 Mich. App. 447, 1972) ruled that Koscot was an illegal lottery and a deceptive trade practice.

The ruling was a victory for those conducting business honestly, as well as for the people. There were many other similarly shady operations, including a nationwide scheme called Holiday Magic, a cosmetic sales company that was eventually dealt with by the Federal Trade Commission (FTC). An administrative law judge held in 1974 that their practices were "false, misleading and an unreasonable restraint on trade." That was an especially interesting one because the company's founder, William Penn Patrick, was an extreme right-wing character, you might say, kook, from California who wanted to use the proceeds from a number of his dubious businesses to finance his political ambitions. Suffice it to say he thought Ronald Reagan was way too liberal, was a proud member of the John Birch Society, and once ran for vice president on something called the Theocratic Party ticket.

However, by the time the FTC issued its final verdict against Holiday Magic, he wasn't around to see it. He had flown a World War II fighter plane he owned into a mountain the year before, killing his managing director along with himself.

You do come up against some interesting characters when you are engaged in defending the people's interests via the practice of law. And politics is never far from the surface, in any elected position.

From the start, I had decided that I would do my best to shield the attorneys who worked for me from partisan politics. The rules were simple: follow the law, let the chips fall where they may, and keep me informed. Otherwise, we would have quickly lost all credibility. Plus, I wanted to build a new kind of attorney general's office that would continue to be a watchdog after I left.

Building the office was my first priority. During my first decade, we managed to double the number of attorneys from around 75 to about 150, with the additional clerical and secretarial support needed.

How did I do this on a limited state budget? In my opinion, in the best possible way. I hired young and aggressive attorneys fresh out of law school in part because, as in the old saying, they didn't have to unlearn a lot of bad habits. I thought I could train them from the start to be watchdogs for the public. Most hadn't yet been exposed to the fee-is-everything mentality of many private firms, where justice often takes a back seat to billable hours. I had another huge advantage, too: women. The number of female law school graduates was increasing dramatically in the mid-1960s. But the big private firms were still very reluctant to hire them, at least as full-fledged attorneys.

By that time, I knew that women could be every bit as effective at practicing the law as men—and possibly even better, since many were still striving to prove themselves. Thanks to this, my staff soon had a higher percentage of female attorneys than any other "firm" in the state. Eventually almost half the lawyers in the attorney general's office would be women.

That provided me with a great sense of quiet satisfaction.

I believed then, and believe now, in hiring the best lawyers and turning them loose to do their jobs creatively, giving them guidance where needed, yes, but in putting together a team of self-starters.

However, I did establish some basic policy rules: we were, indeed, going to reinvent the attorney general's office as an activist team of attorneys working for the people. But we developed these basic guidelines: we would initiate any action—an investigation, a lawsuit, or even a simple move to enforce an existing rule or law—*only* if we were convinced that what we were doing would have an important and lasting influence in one or more of a number of areas. We wanted make sure that our actions would (1) establish sound legal precedent; (2) have a telling impact on law enforcement itself; (3) protect the public in some new way; (4) enforce a state law; or (5) uphold the constitution of the state of Michigan.

We would leave local crimes to the county prosecutors unless one of them specifically requested our help or if the crime involved a state officer or multiple counties.

I also wanted to be extremely careful about issuing official opinions that would set legal precedent—opinions that had the force of law unless overturned by the courts. My policy was to do this only when the subject was of more than local interest.

When it came to our taking on cases that involved public protection matters or consumer fraud, we looked mostly for activities likely to affect a lot of people. Additionally, whenever we took someone to court we wanted to make sure we were legally authorized to get involved, either by statute or through the authority of the state constitution.

Even the strictest possible interpretation of those rules would have left us extremely busy. But that wasn't all we had to cope with. What we couldn't control was the exploding number of cases that were being filed against the state or one of its agencies.

When I first arrived in Lansing, the attorney general's office defended five or six cases a year. But suddenly that turned into dozens and then into hundreds. The activist, litigation-minded 1960s were beginning to fully flower. As lawsuits against the state continued to increase, it meant that my staff of lawyers had to be dramatically increased, if only because we had to spend half or more of our time defending lawsuits.

Now I have to admit that in some cases, those suing the state had legitimate grievances. But most of the lawsuits filed had no merit. Prisoners with too much time on their hands would file suit for being served cold food or stale, broken cookies. These were mostly thrown out of court immediately, but it still took staff time to prepare a case asking judges to do just that. Many of the inmates who filed such suits were lifers who didn't have to worry about court costs or about wasting their own time. Prisoners weren't responsible for all frivolous suits, however; some people involved in automobile accidents sued the state highway department in an attempt to blame them for their own bad driving.

More dangerous, however, were the cases brought by shrewd lawyers who were attempting to get into the "deep pockets" of the multibillion dollar state treasury. We were a tempting target. Personal injury and a lot of other attorneys who sue for damages tend to take cases on a one-third contingency basis. That means that if they win, for example, a $300,000 lawsuit for their client, they get a cool hundred grand. But that doesn't do them much good if the case is against a client who lacks the ability to pay. Corporations also tend to drag such cases out for years, and most lawyers need cash flow. But states have money—are always "collectible," in other words—and are historically less likely to drag matters out. Lawyers knew that, and the temptation to make a quick killing was too much for some of them. Fortunately they didn't get away with it, most of the time.

Now I don't mean to suggest that trial lawyers aren't necessary. In fact, they are essential to democracy; they are often the only recourse a citizen has to get justice from powerful institutions. However, not all are perfect, and being a watchdog for the people, in my view, also meant preventing the people's money from being looted by the unscrupulous. During the years I was in office, we won more than 90 percent of all our cases.

———

While I was setting policy and attending to administrative details, I was also acutely conscious that I would be facing another election in 1964. Polls, my gut instinct, and what I saw in the newspapers told me my popularity was continuing to rise. But I also knew perfectly well that the politician who takes the voters for granted pretty quickly becomes a politician out of a job.

Only a few months after my first victory, we found ourselves facing another vote that had enormous implications for Michigan. George Romney had risen to political prominence and power by spearheading a drive for the state's first Constitutional Convention in decades, which was held in 1961–62. He had ridden the Con-Con, as everyone called it, right into the governor's office. Now, in the winter of 1963, the proposed new constitution had been finished and was about to be submitted to a vote of the people.

Frankly, I didn't like it. The convention that wrote it had been heavily Republican, and it showed. The constitution did not provide for equal representation and legislative districts with the same population—what back then we called "one-man, one vote." It outlawed a graduated income tax, meaning that poor people working part-time and billionaires would be taxed at the same rate.

Two-thirds of the delegates to the Con-Con had been Republicans. The Democratic delegates had voted 40–5 against sending the final document to the people for a vote.

Democratic officeholders felt the same way. But could we do anything to stop the voters from approving the proposed new constitution? A group of us met confidentially with Lou Harris; he and George Gallup were the nation's two top pollsters. Harris told us that the proposed document was hugely popular with the people. If we campaigned against it, not only would we fail to defeat it, but we would hurt ourselves politically.

So we mostly did nothing.

The constitution was taken to the people in a special election on Monday, April 1, 1963. Turnout was, as you might expect, low. That night, to my astonishment, I heard the vote was too close to call. As a matter of fact, throughout much of the night, the vote to reject the document was ahead. Finally, late-reporting Republican areas pulled it through—barely. The vote in favor of the new constitution was 810,860. The vote to reject it, 803,436.

Afterward I reflected that the election had been held on April Fools' Day—and we Democrats ended up being the fools. If a few of us had made just a few speeches against it, the flawed document undoubtedly would have been turned down.

In the long run, things weren't as bad as they might have been. As I have already mentioned, the U.S. Supreme Court soon ruled that flamboyant malapportionment was unconstitutional and made one-man, one-vote the effective law of the land. Because the U.S. Constitution outweighs any state or federal law, any time the nation's highest court rules that something either violates that document or is required by it, their ruling invalidates any laws to the contrary.

There was one other good thing about the new Michigan constitution. Terms of statewide officeholders were lengthened from two to four years, which was a very welcome and sensible change. This meant that beginning in 1966, I would only have to run for office half as often, which would make my life much easier. All things considered, my first full year as an elected official had been a very good one.

I have always been a strong believer in exercise—and swimming has been one of my favorite activities. Late that year, most of the major legal battles behind me, I went over to the Lansing YMCA to swim on a Friday afternoon just after lunch. The next week was Thanksgiving, and Christmas was coming. Everything in my life was pleasant. Suddenly, while I was swimming I looked up and saw Leon Cohan, my deputy, walking toward me. But he wasn't dressed for swimming. He had his winter coat and hat on.

I took one look at his face and was struck with horror. The thought hit me: something has happened to one of my kids.

"Frank," Leon said. "The president has been shot."

I dressed in a blur. We got back to the office as quickly as possible. My secretary was there, tears streaming down her face. "President Kennedy is dead," she said. The Department of Justice had just called. I was numb. For the next few days, I was in a fog.

A few days after the assassination, I went to make a previously scheduled speech in Pontiac. To my unpleasant surprise, I began crying while I was addressing the audience. I have never been one of those politicians who turns on the tears. The audience was unnerved, and so was I. Three months went by before I made another speech in public.

John F. Kennedy was dead. It may be impossible today for young people to understand how much we looked up to him—especially a guy from a middle-class, Irish Catholic family like me.

Remember this: When I was growing up, it was taken as a given that no Catholic could be elected president. Kennedy changed all that. He made us feel that we could do anything. When he said "one man can make a difference, and every man should try," he made us believe it.

After JFK was slain, the writer Mary McGrory told Daniel Patrick Moynihan, the future U.S. senator, "We'll never laugh again." Moynihan, who then worked in the Kennedy White House, told her that of course they'd laugh, "but we'll never be young again."

Ironically, less than five years later, I would sit next to Moynihan on the *Caroline*, the Kennedy family airplane, as we returned to Boston after Robert Kennedy's funeral.

Sometimes life really can break your heart.

I've met nearly all the presidents since JFK and admired some of them greatly. But Kennedy remains my prince.

And that day I spent with him in Detroit remains as vivid in my mind as ever, more than half a century after he left the scene forever.

11

ASSERTING MYSELF—AND THE
OFFICE OF ATTORNEY GENERAL

During my first year in office, as an appointed attorney general, I never had the slightest difficulty working with the man who put me there, Governor John Swainson. And that wasn't because I owed him for the job. The secret to our success was that we both understood the nature of the office. While I had the responsibility of legally representing all of Michigan government, the attorney general's office is an entirely separate and independent branch. He would no more have tried to tell me what cases to prosecute than I would have suggested what his agriculture policy should be.

The fact that we were both Democrats with similar goals and values didn't hurt. It also helped, I'm sure, that we were the same age and from roughly similar backgrounds and had had known each other since law school. The bottom line, however, was that we were professionals in the art of politics.

George Romney came from an entirely different background. He wasn't a lawyer and had never been in public office. He had been an auto executive, used to giving orders to subordinates that were immediately followed. And that led to the biggest knock-down, separation-of-powers clash of my career.

Late in December 1962, a few days before the inaugural ceremonies (newly elected or reelected state officials in Michigan take the oath of office on New Year's Day), governor-elect Romney came to visit my office in the capitol. He was warm and charming—maybe a little too much so. I remember thinking that he came across as if he were an honor graduate of one of those Dale Carnegie "How to Win Friends and Influence People" courses that were all the rage in the 1950s.

That approach seemed to me based on the idea that in order to win people over, you have to flatter the hell out of them, something that struck me as intellectually dishonest. Now, don't get me wrong. I am a politician and have flashed more smiles and kissed more babies than I can count. During one of my later elections, I told an opponent that I was a million handshakes ahead of him—and I don't think that was all that much of an exaggeration. But Romney wasn't there to court my vote; we weren't ever going to vote for each other, anyway.

We were going to be two colleagues who, whatever our political differences, would be working together for the good of the state.

By the way, you may well think that I was predisposed not to like George Romney. Believe it or not, that really wasn't the case.

Do I wish that he had failed to beat my friend John Swainson? Absolutely. Even before that, I have to admit I was a little cynical about his featuring himself in American Motors ads pushing his Rambler, America's first really successful mass-market compact car, as an alternative to other automakers' "gas-guzzling dinosaurs."

Nor was I impressed by his posturing as an "independent" when he was running Citizens for Michigan, the group formed to lead the drive to get the voters to approve a constitutional convention. From the start, I guessed that this was a vehicle to launch his campaign for governor, and it indeed succeeded brilliantly.

But I had learned some very valuable lessons as a young country lawyer in Alpena, a Democrat in a largely Republican universe. Mostly I learned that in order to function in a bipartisan world you cannot remain partisan after the campaign is over. Most of the time, you are going to have to govern with people from the other party. What I knew was that in November Michigan voters had chosen Republican George Romney as their governor—and Democrat Frank Kelley as their attorney general.

What they wanted, I was certain, was for both of us to work together for the good of the state with its best interests in mind. I still believe that—in fact, the voters eventually reelected me seven more times on days when they also chose various Republican governors.

So right from the start, I made up my mind that I would do my best to get along with the new governor and his GOP appointees. Unfortunately, the feeling wasn't mutual. Only a few weeks after he took office, Romney began making statements on legal matters, saying he didn't feel certain welfare practices were lawful.

My top lawyers were taken aback. They felt his office should have contacted us first for an opinion on the legality of this issue before he began making pronouncements. Romney, by the way, was not a lawyer; he hadn't even graduated from college.

Finally I was forced to issue a press release expressing my disagreement with the governor. "The legal opinions of state government are to be rendered by the Attorney General elected by the people for that purpose, and not by the governor," I wrote.

George Romney's reaction wasn't long in coming. Half a century later, his youngest son, Mitt, would be criticized for showing a lack of spontaneity and genuine emotion when he ran for president. His father was entirely the opposite. Within a couple days—at most—after my statement, I got a direct call from the governor—and he was steaming mad. "Kelley!" George Romney shouted. "How dare you criticize me in public as doing something wrong! I have every right to speak out as governor." I replied just as calmly as I possibly could. "You can say anything you want, Governor Romney. But you're not going to infringe on my power and duties as attorney general." Romney's voice got even louder. "I want you in my office as soon as possible so we can thrash this matter out," he barked. "I'll be there in thirty minutes," I said.

Leon Cohan walked in from his adjoining office. My secretary had told him the governor was on the phone, and he figured I might want to see him. I shook my head. "Leon, I knew Romney was supposed to be intense. But in that call just now he was out of control, shouting over the phone." I filled him in. "I'm going over to see him now. You had better come with me, and bring a copy of the statute on the attorney general's powers." Leon's face fell. "Christ, my dad's in my office. I promised I'd take him on a tour of the capitol and arrange to have him meet the governor." I knew he was thinking, so much for that idea. "No, we'll take your dad over and park him in the governor's reception room until we are done arguing. If the mood isn't too bad, we'll have him meet Romney afterward."

Back then both the governor's and attorney general's offices were in the capitol building, just one floor apart. We put Leon's father in an area safely out of earshot of the governor's office and went into the lion's den. Romney was standing, wearing a blue sweater. His legal advisor, the young, affable, and aristocratic Richard Van Dusen, was there as well.

Romney pointed an angry forefinger at me. "Look here, Frank Kelley, who do you think you are, trying to embarrass me with some cheap shot? I've been in chief executive positions and a leader in industry for many years. I've dealt with the best and brightest corporate lawyers and they would never do what you did the other day and criticize me in public!" As he spoke his face got redder and redder.

Finally, he poked his finger in my chest, shouting, "When I want your legal help I'll ask for it, like I would as president of American Motors! The governor is the chief executive officer of this state, and I am not going to take any crap from you or your lawyers."

Dick and Leon looked straight ahead, their faces expressionless but barely hiding their disbelief at the scene. I suspect nothing in his Harvard Law School education had prepared Dick for this.

I had had all of the governor's bluster I could take. No longer calm, I nevertheless remained as collected as I could and spoke in my best courtroom baritone: "Governor, your outburst is absurd and out of line. I've planned since the election to make an effort not only to make sure I was nonpartisan in my legal obligation to you but also to be patient and understanding of the fact that you are not a lawyer. You don't understand the relationship between state constitutional offices like governor and attorney general. Your analogy of comparing a private corporate chief executive and his lawyer to the public positions we now hold is untenable. Both our offices are created by the state constitution. We are mandated by law to share power. I'm not your employed lawyer."

While I was speaking I saw that Romney was trying to calm down and regain his composure. It wasn't easy for him. Possibly because I had been provoked myself, I couldn't resist adding: "As a matter of fact, I got more votes than you did." I later found out that that wasn't true. I had, however, been elected by a bigger margin, which was what I meant.

I knew it was time for me to throw down the olive branch. "I'm sorry if I provoked you. Let's try to calm down." The governor didn't directly apologize, but he clearly knew he had gone too far. "Let's have Dick here and your Leon work out some guidelines for us to look at," he said. That was fine with me.

I held out my hand. Romney responded with a very weak handshake, but at least he shook on our deal. A bit dazed, we walked out of his inner office only to find Leon's smiling elderly father, whom we had both momentarily forgotten.

I took him by the arm and rushed him into the governor's office. "Governor, this is Leon Cohan's father, Maurice, who is visiting the capitol today." George Romney had completely recovered. He gave him a winning, million-dollar smile. "How very nice to meet you," the governor said. "I want you to know you have a wonderful son in Leon. You must be very proud."

Mr. Cohen beamed. In a voice rich with the accents of his native Poland, he said, "Thank you, thank you, thank you so much. It is a rare pleasure to meet you."

The patriarch, Frank E. Kelley (1892–1954).

Frank with his mother, Grace, Detroit, 1927.

Frank and Frank, 1927.

Patricia Lodge, 1930s.

Burt Lake, ca. 1930. Frank and a young friend.

Sister Patricia, in front of the Patricia Lodge, ca. 1940.

Adopted sister Mary Olish.

Frank at sixteen.

Frank in Arizona, autumn 1943.

Studying for law school, ca. 1951. *Left to right*: Don Herrington, Frank, and Frank Pipp.

Burt Lake, ca. late 1950s. *Left to right*: Jane, Karen, Frankie, and Jo.

Grace and Frank Kelley's twenty-fifth wedding anniversary, 1948.
Left to right: sister Patricia, Frank Sr., brother Dick, mother Grace, and Frank.

Frank with Governor John Swainson and outgoing Attorney General Paul Adams.

Frank with President Kennedy and Governor Swainson, Detroit, 1962.

Democratic dinner, 1964. *Left to right*: Margaret Price, Hon. Theodore Souris, Frank, and Jo Kelley.

Dedicating Democratic headquarters in Lansing, ca. 1964. *Left to right*: Ted Kennedy, Phil Hart, Millie Jeffrey, U.S. Senator Patrick McNamara, Frank Kelley, Adelaide Hart, Zolton Ferency, Martha Griffiths, Neil Staebler, U.S. Representative Charles Diggs.

Inauguration day, January 1965. George Romney is in the first row, far right.
Frank is third from the left in the same row.

Swearing in Carl Levin as assistant attorney general, mid-1960s.

Campaigning in Michigan for Robert F. Kennedy with Ted Kennedy, 1968.

Frank with Hubert Humphrey and brother Jim Kelley, 1968.

To Frank J. Kelley
With best wishes,
Lyndon B. Johnson

Frank with President Lyndon Johnson and U.S. Attorney General
Ramsey Clark, 1968.

Union supporters in Frank Kelley's U.S. senate campaign, 1972.

Frank and others are burned in effigy in protest during the PBB scandal, mid-1970s.

With Malcolm Dade.

With Henry "Scoop" Jackson, 1976.

With President Carter, 1976.

With Tip O'Neill, early 1980s.

Frank and Teamsters president James P. Hoffa.

Visiting Michigan prison inmates as attorney general, ca. 1980s.

Frank and Deputy Attorney General Stanley Steinborn, 1990.

Frank and Nancy Kelley, 1986.

Frank and President Bush, 1992.

Frank with the Clintons at the White House, December 17, 1993.

To Frank Kelly
With best wishes,

Al Gore

With Vice President Al Gore and Detroit auto dealer "Hoot" McInerney.

Frank with Rosa Parks.

Frank and three of his five governors. *Left to right*: William Milliken, John Engler, Frank Kelley, and James Blanchard.

Frank with Lieutenant Governor John Cherry and Governor Jennifer Granholm.

With Governor John Engler, 2011.

Kelley with his children, Frank, Jane, and Karen, on Mackinac, 2013.

At the Capitol Walkway, October 23, 2013. *Left to right*: Bill Schuette, Frank, Governor Rick Snyder, Gretchen Whitmer, State Senator Steve Bieda, Dan Loepp.

Dick, Frank, and Jim Kelley at the Capitol Walkway named after Frank, October 23, 2013.

The governor replied, "The pleasure is all mine." I've always wondered if Maurice Cohan went to his grave thinking George Romney was the most easygoing man on the planet.

His son and I knew differently. Later, back in the office, we talked about what had happened. What worried us most were two things: one, George Romney had a dangerously low boiling point; and two, it was already very clear that he saw the governorship as a stepping-stone to the presidency of the United States. Was this a man whose finger should be anywhere near the nuclear button? You could always hope he would mature, but at the time of our confrontation, he was about fifty-five years old.

As it happened, of course, he never got to the White House; his campaign for the 1968 Republican nomination collapsed early, thanks to some off-the-cuff comments he made on a local Detroit TV show about having been "brainwashed" by the generals in Vietnam.

I have always wondered whether George Romney's impetuous ego and tongue were the main reasons his son seemed so carefully packaged and scripted during his two runs for the White House.

Eventually I developed a more favorable opinion of the elder Romney, as I will discuss later in this book. Meanwhile, however, our "scream summit" ended up having a positive effect.

Leon Cohan and Dick Van Dusen talked, and we eventually came up with an agreement for them to consult on a regular basis and thereby minimize unnecessary friction. My position was that the Michigan constitution provided for only one legal authority in state government: the Office of the Attorney General. Naturally, several hundred full-time attorneys are needed to meet the needs of a modern state.

But the two offices wouldn't work together smoothly until we went through one more explosion, caused largely by the famous Romney temper. This time, what happened was much more public.

Fast-forward to October 1964, when both the governor and I were in the middle of reelection campaigns. Nationally, it was clear that it was going to be a tremendous Democratic year. President Lyndon Johnson was on his way to a landslide victory over Barry Goldwater, the Republican nominee. Goldwater was widely perceived as a radical right-winger who might start a nuclear war and privatize Social Security. What's more, he had opposed the breakthrough bill passed that year, the Civil Rights Act of 1964. That caused George Romney to refuse to support his own party's presidential nominee.

All these factors would lead to Goldwater becoming the first and only major party presidential candidate ever to lose Michigan by a million votes.* With the national tide running so overwhelmingly Democratic, I wasn't too worried about my own chances.

Romney, on the other hand, had to be running scared. He was going to need a near-record number of voters to split their tickets and vote Democratic for president—and Republican for governor.

Soapy Williams had gotten Michigan voters to split their tickets the other way, twice, but that was after he had been around for a while. Romney had been governor for less than two years, and Barry Goldwater was going to lose far worse than Adlai Stevenson had.

So the governor needed to look strong and in control. About a month before the election, rumors reached both the governor's and attorney general's offices that there were serious problems developing in the Michigan National Guard, specifically, charges that top officers had been abusing their privileges.

What the governor's office should have done was simply check with my folks. I would have assured them that we weren't about to use whatever was going on for political purposes in any way. We didn't know what was going on or who might be at fault, and in any event, any investigation would take time. Nothing would surface till after the election was over.

But that's not what happened. Evidently the governor and his top advisors saw a chance for Romney to look like a tough, strong, and morally alert leader, out to end corruption wherever he found it. Within days, without a word to me, he summarily relieved the top three officers of the Michigan National Guard from duty.

Huge, front-page stories followed. The dismissed men were Major General Ronald McDonald, the guard's highest-ranking, or adjutant general; Brigadier General Carson Neifert, the quartermaster; and an aide to Neifert, Lieutenant Colonel Versel Case Jr.

The press's and the public's first instincts were to indignantly condemn the men and support the governor. The charges, incidentally, weren't all that earth-shattering and involved neither death nor sex. According to Billie Farnum, the state auditor general, they involved "administrative irregularities," such as improper sales of state-owned land and mishandling of money and liquor sales.

---

* Lyndon Johnson swamped Barry Goldwater in Michigan, 2,136,635 to 1,060,152. I handily beat my Republican opponent, Meyer Warshawsky, a future judge, by more than half a million votes. Romney, however, survived, thanks to an avalanche of ticket-splitting, beating Neil Staebler, 1,764,355 to 1,381,442.

But after a day or two, some editorial writers had second thoughts. Was it really fair to end three military careers without even a hearing, or at least a court-martial? McDonald in particular had a distinguished military record and had served on General Douglas MacArthur's staff in the Pacific during World War II.

Fearing a backlash, after a few days the governor's office finally asked for my legal advice. Knowing that would take a day or so and with the election fast approaching, I sent Mr. Romney a telegram. "I advise you that your action . . . was illegal," I told him, adding that the men should be reinstated immediately. "There is no legal justification for dismissal," I wrote. If, after a proper investigation, the governor decided that disciplinary action was warranted, he should "proceed by court-martial in accords with the statutes of the state of Michigan." I then sent him my formal written legal opinion.

George Romney then went ballistic, this time in public.

Going before the cameras, he raged that he had sought my advice but that I was grandstanding and that he had every authority as commander in chief to do what he did. Anybody watching saw a little bit of the out-of-control fury Leon Cohan and I had been blasted with the year before.

Those working in my office may have been biased, but they thought I looked much better. But on Election Day, both the governor and I won by a landslide. Hundreds of thousands of voters split their tickets to vote Democratic for president and attorney general, and Republican for governor. What did that really mean?

Today, after many more years in politics, I'd have to conclude that politically, my very public spat with the governor probably helped both of us, to the extent it was a factor at all. People tend to love those whom they see as fighting for their own best interests. Romney was going after what he said were corrupt men in uniform, wasting public funds. On the other hand, there I was declaring that everyone has the right to a fair trial. My guess is that both of us would have won anyway, but the dispute helped raise our statewide visibility.

Legally, the record shows that I was right; it was wrong for the governor to discharge the officers without a hearing. Four days after the election, Romney reinstated the two top men, who were then suspended until formal charges could be drawn up. (The third had no legally defined position to which he had to be restored.) Eventually the case was solved by allowing them to retire honorably from the Michigan National Guard the next year. The little tempest was virtually completely forgotten within months.

But I clearly was going to have to keep working with Romney. To give him his due, his victory over my old friend Neil Staebler was one of the most impressive in state history. Think of it: Romney ran more than seven hundred thousand votes ahead of his party's hapless presidential candidate, Barry Goldwater.

I won easily, too, and for me, the best thing about that election was that it was the last time I would ever have to run for a two-year term; starting in 1966, state officers would serve for four years. This was also the last time we would be on the ballot in presidential election years. Unfortunately, while this never affected me, on balance that has tended to be a bad thing for Democrats seeking statewide office. As is well-known in political circles, Democrats have a harder time getting their voters to the polls in off-year elections.

With the election over, I decided, as Christmas approached, that it would be a good idea to call on Governor Romney and extend the olive branch. His secretary ushered me right in. "Governor, this is a visit of peace. Holiday time is a good opportunity to heal wounds and start afresh," I said. He started to warm up and reached for my hand. "Merry Christmas," he said. I told him I wished him and his family the same.

Then I added, "Governor, the people have elected you and me to our offices once again from our different parties—and mindful of our public disputes. I believe that means they want us to serve together, do the best we can and try to get along." Romney began to clearly and sincerely warm up. "I like your attitude, Frank. Let's try to start a new era of cooperation."

I had a sudden inspiration. Well, not that sudden; I had been thinking about ways to eliminate unnecessary friction. "Why don't we have Bob Danhof and my deputy, Leon Cohan, get together and work on defining the respective duties of our offices and identifying any potential areas of unnecessary conflict?" I suggested. By then Danhof, the man I had defeated in my first campaign for attorney general and a former U.S. district attorney for western Michigan, had become a top legal advisor to Romney.

We were never going to agree on everything, I told the governor, but why not avoid any potential unnecessary friction? By this time, the governor had to have realized that dismissing the National Guard officers without even a hearing was a legal, if not a political, blunder.

"That's a good idea," Romney told me.

And I have to admit he then offered a good idea: "Let's let them take their time, put it in writing, and then you and I can get together and agree to personally cooperate in all the areas covered."

That made sense to me. In the end, what started out as nothing more than a holiday greeting turned out to have lasting political significance—though one that took months to bear fruit.

Finally, after many meetings between our two deputies, they came up with a memorandum the press and political scientists later called the "Treaty of Lansing." The document was a masterpiece of brevity. It included a list of all the major duties of the Office of Governor, as well as a list of the statutory and common-law duties of the attorney general. Though the document was short, it covered all the conceivable areas of conflict and set out a framework to resolve them.

The treaty addressed the main cause of conflict between the governor and me this way: it recognized that the ultimate legal authority in the state of Michigan is the attorney general, the only one elected by a statewide vote of all the people. His or her decisions on state law can only be overruled by the state or federal supreme courts.

However, I did understand and appreciate the legal needs of the chief executive. As a result, we worked out a deal so that the governor could name an attorney to give him a confidential legal perspective on certain issues. Legally, however, this person would have to be part of my department, be sworn in by me, and be an assistant attorney general. That meant the attorney assigned to the governor could never publicly contradict me, thus eliminating any repeat of the problem that led to the explosion between George Romney and me in the first place.

When the final treaty was ready and I reviewed it, I was thrilled. I told Leon, "This is just what we need between our offices—short and sweet and to the point. I think if George approves this, we've set the stage for years of cooperation, not only between this governor and me but for future generations." Generations of attorneys general and governors to come, that is; I instituted the same arrangement with the next three governors I served, with equally good results for all concerned.

Romney's attitude was precisely the same as mine. When presented with his copy of the Treaty of Lansing, he told Danhof, "This is just what we needed. You and Leon did a fine job." With that, he signed the document.

What's more, from then on, for the nearly four years he remained governor before departing for a position in the Nixon cabinet, both Romney and I lived up to every position in the agreement. All avoidable differences were dealt with behind closed doors by both of us or by our agents.

The cynical might say that the treaty worked so well because by that time, it was pretty clear that both of us were politically secure in our jobs and shoo-ins for landslide victories when we next ran. That much was certainly true. But the provisions of the Treaty of Lansing remained long after Romney was gone and continued to operate, virtually unchanged, for the next thirty years I held office.

Incidentally, twenty-two of those post-Romney years saw me serving with two other Republican governors, one of whom—John Engler—was far more conservative than George Romney.

I believe the Treaty of Lansing was, and is, a model for bipartisan cooperation in a time of divided government. Half a century after we crafted it, I am still proud of it.

12

CONSUMER PROTECTION

Nobody becomes an expert at any job overnight.

When I was first appointed attorney general, I was young, but I was already an experienced trial lawyer. Fortunately I inherited a staff of devoted and dedicated lawyers, many of whom were true experts in one branch or another of law.

Handling the state's basic legal affairs was not that difficult, especially because back in the early 1960s, far fewer lawsuits were being filed against the state of Michigan than is common today. But I wasn't satisfied with merely maintaining the status quo. Right from the start, what made a powerful impact on me was the fact that people were being ripped off in an ever-increasing number of ways.

Earlier I mentioned some of the first scams we stumbled across: furnace companies that advertised free "inspections" then tried to sell consumers a new furnace whether they needed one or not and get-rich-quick property sales schemes to convince veterans and young couples to buy property they could build homes on that turned out to be miles from civilization or utilities.

Early on, Maxine Boord Virtue had convinced me to set up a small consumer protection division, but as time went on, several things became clear to me. One was that the need to fight to protect the consumer was a far more important task than almost anyone had imagined. Certainly most Michigan lawmakers didn't have a clue. When I first told the legislature that Michigan needed a consumer protection act, one Republican lawmaker called that communism! In fact, we had studies showing that it was far more likely for someone to be cheated or defrauded in a consumer transaction than to be the victim of a crime.

As it turned out, Michigan's landmark Consumer Protection Act wouldn't be signed into law until 1976. But long before that, I began urging my attorneys to do whatever they could to protect the public.

Getting fully up to speed took some time. When I became attorney general in January 1962, there were only about seventy-five staff lawyers—formally known as assistant attorneys general—to do all the legal work for the state's eight million people.

One thing I quickly discovered as attorney general was that I may have had priorities, but I couldn't really control my agenda. Not only did unexpected issues come up, anyone can sue the state at any time. We had to defend against thousands of such cases, the number of which has seemed to endlessly accelerate as our society becomes ever more lawsuit happy. In addition, perhaps half of all convicted felons appeal their sentences. When they do, that makes more work for the attorney general's office. Although the attorney general's office generally wins 95 percent of these cases, they still take a massive amount of staff time.

Back in those early days, there was another factor that cut into my ability to do as much as I would have liked, not only in consumer protection but other areas as well. I had to face three statewide elections in four years, 1962, 1964, and 1966, which meant just keeping my job took a great deal of time and energy. After that, however, things eased. The term was changed to four years by the new constitution, and by the 1970s my work on behalf of consumers had made me nearly a household name in Michigan. Though I always tried to run as if I needed every last vote, I never had another close election after the first one. In 1974, I won statewide by more than a million votes, a margin never equaled by any candidate for attorney general in this state.

Though much of everything was new to me, in the area of consumer protection especially, I was largely feeling my way in the beginning. I was taking on the establishment in ways they'd never been challenged before.

I initiated big cases with little or no precedent against consumer cheats, giant merchants, banks that were abusing interest laws, and utilities charging exorbitant rates. My office also went after big corporate polluters and enemies of the environment. We believed that they could and should be held accountable to the people, which was a novel concept at the time.

We did something else, too.

My office was among the first in the nation to start new and innovative cases in environmental law. There were few, if any, lawyers taking on such cases at that time, let alone state attorneys general. But we did. And before long, my office was winning millions in environmental cases. We also succeeded in getting court orders to force polluting firms to spend millions cleaning up their messes. No other state government was doing this on such a massive scale—though when we started winning awards and getting national recognition, others followed our lead. I began to be noticed and referred to as the top public attorney in the nation when it came to cases involving the environment, civil rights, and especially consumer protection.

Yes, we were winging it. More than once in those early days, my assistant prosecutors and I worked hard at looking brave and confident—though in truth, we were more than a little scared. However, as time went on and we became more experienced and started winning—and winning big—managing the office became easier and smoother with each passing year.

One of the things I learned after a few years on the job was what to expect—mostly—when it came to the legal challenges that constantly landed on my desk. Cases that looked impossibly complicated in my first year as attorney general seemed commonplace five years later.

Something else favorable happened, too. Over the next decade, which was generally a prosperous one for Michigan, I managed to get the legislature to let me nearly double the staff. Though I hired some seasoned lawyers with particular areas of expertise, mostly I had a different strategy: I decided to go after the best and brightest new law school graduates. I reasoned that what they lacked in experience we could teach them, and in any event their inexperience would be more than made up for with their energy and enthusiasm. Besides, I thought, new lawyers wouldn't have to unlearn some of the things they would have had drilled into them working for for-profit law firms, namely, to think of everything in terms of billable hours. We had the luxury of doing law in the public interest. Nobody was getting rich, but I was able to pay decent salaries.

I often visited law schools on recruiting trips, and when it comes to consumer protection, one of the best hires I ever made was a young man named Edwin Bladen, who was just graduating from Wayne State University after a stint in the army. Bladen became one of my assistant attorneys general in 1965, right out of law school, and was impressive from the start. He had a keen interest in consumer protection, and four years later, I named him to succeed Maxine as head of the consumer protection division.

Years later, long after he had gone on to serve as a federal administrative law judge, Bladen told my collaborator on this book, journalist Jack Lessenberry, that he was inspired to join and remain on my staff for years, mainly because "among state attorneys general across the nation, Kelley was a leader in establishing new frontiers for his attorneys to push the courts toward justice. He was at the forefront of the consumer movement," Bladen adding, emphasizing that it would be difficult to overestimate the impact of what we accomplished. "Before anyone ever heard of Ralph Nader, Frank J. Kelley established one of the nation's first consumer protection divisions and cracked down on charities that pocketed more money than they spent on good works and retailers whose price at the scanner didn't match the price on the shelf," he said.

Bladen probably gave me a little too much credit. But what he said is what we tried to do, right from the start. One of my first really major efforts took place even before Ed arrived on the staff.

When I took office, some of the biggest cons were home improvement scams in which crooks we called "tin men" or "storm and siding hustlers" set out to defraud the public. This was the fast-growing 1960s, when legions of young couples were making a little money, filling their ranch houses with babies, and constantly trying to improve their homes on a budget. They would be preyed upon by so-called salesmen who would pressure them into signing contracts for new garages, windows, roofs, and aluminum siding—relatively quick and easy construction jobs—telling them that if they signed contracts, they might well not have to pay because their home would likely be "used as a model." The contracts' fine print made it clear that this was nothing more than a cheap pyramid scheme, and the chance the young couple would end up not paying for their improvements was slim to none. These consumers could, in fact, get out of paying only by signing lots of other people up for the contractor to take advantage of.

But that wasn't the worst part. These unscrupulous salesmen would persuade the vulnerable homeowners to sign binding contracts—which the tin men would then sell to a bank. The bank then claimed they were innocent purchasers of these contracts ("holders in due course"), and that meant that the homeowner couldn't cancel the contract or challenge the terms. In fact, it inevitably turned out that what these contractors were charging unsuspecting consumers was considerably higher than a fair-market price—sometimes as much as 20 to 30 percent more than they should have paid! The original contractor then subcontracted the work and kept close to a third of the money as pure profit.

Homeowners, mostly working-class homeowners, were being taken for millions a year. I felt I had to do something. But my first efforts totally failed. For several years, I asked friendly legislators to introduce bills to write new laws to protect consumers. They did, but the bills went nowhere. The reactionary committee chairmen bottled up my efforts, claiming any law aimed at protecting consumers would be an intrusion on "commerce." You could just as well say that laws against drugs and prostitution also interfere with commerce, but I knew it would be pointless to try to make that argument to them.

Then I got an inspiration.

We had found that only a few banks were willing to buy the home improvement contracts from these scam artists and that the majority of banks had no interest in dealing with these scoundrels. So I invited the top executives of all the major Michigan banks to a meeting at my office in the capitol. They all showed up. When they arrived, I had Maxine Virtue explain how we'd been swamped with hundreds of complaints from citizens who were being duped every month by these "home improvement" rackets.

Then I took over and explained that they, too, had a lot at stake. I told them I felt their industry was being hurt by the fact that a few unscrupulous banks were in bed with these con artists. Somewhat to my surprise, the bankers listened attentively and did not argue. A few days later, they informed my office through their lobbyist that they would support a home improvement protection act that would protect both the public and the bankers' good names.

That's just what I had been hoping for.

We carefully drafted a bill that would prohibit certain scams and provide a cancellation period whereby consumers who discovered they'd been taken could cancel their contract without any obligation by merely sending a certified or registered letter. That bill, the Home Improvement Finance Act, was passed by the state legislature in 1965 and effectively stopped the home improvement racket cold (except for the occasional freelance crook who scams some elderly person into a phony roof repair).

I learned two valuable lessons from that experience: money talks, and powerful allies matter. Once the top bankers in the state gave their approval, the bill sailed through both houses without a hitch. There are, in fact, occasional cases where doing the right thing will benefit both the general public and a special interest group, in this case, the bankers.

Sadly, that doesn't happen often enough.

What I soon learned was that it if I wanted to get anything done, it was essential to look for such connections—and for powerful allies in the courts, legislature, Congress, and other elected bodies. Simply put, big industries have far more influence than the general public does. I realized that protecting consumers became far easier if I could show corporations that they would benefit, at least to some extent, as well.

Some of the other areas we targeted, Bladen remembered, were also ones where legitimate businesses had a vested interest in our locking up the bad guys—quick-buck pyramid schemes, for example, and unscrupulous automobile transmission shops.

I believe someone could write a doctoral dissertation on the history of consumer law by studying the major cases we litigated over the years. If I were to list and discuss all of them here, it would turn what is meant to be an autobiography into a consumer law textbook. But I do want to touch on some highlights of some of my most prominent and possibly most important cases: ones involving General Motors, auto repair scams, and tainted meat.

THE ROCKET ENGINES THAT WEREN'T

In 1977, Oldsmobile was riding high and selling well, primarily because of the company's then famous Rocket V-8 engines. There was only one problem: many of the cars not only weren't true Rocket V-8s, they didn't even have Oldsmobile engines! General Motors couldn't produce enough Olds engines to meet demand, so they decided to use Chevrolet engines instead—and conceal that from the public. They painted the Chevy engines the same color as Olds engines were supposed to be and pasted a decal on the air filter housing indicating that it was a Rocket V-8 Oldsmobile engine.

Trouble was, it wasn't, and the engines were substantially different enough that they used a different kind of oil filter. GM foolishly did not, however, change the specifications in the owner's manuals of the cars with the Chevy engines. That meant that if anyone with one of the bogus engines tried to change the oil, they would inevitably use the wrong filter. Result: A leaky mess all over the driveway.

We sued. General Motors reacted with their usual swagger—till they learned that I possessed the proverbial "smoking gun." It was an internal GM document from a meeting at which company executives discussed the need for the switch and covering it up, "so the consumer wouldn't know what they are getting." Once the company knew we had that document, GM had no choice but to reach a nationwide settlement, pronto. Consumers received a $400 cash payment and a supplemental, three-year, bumper-to-bumper no-cost warranty. That is the equivalent of more than $1,500 in 2014, an amount we agreed was sufficient to compensate owners for any additional costs incurred to repair or maintain their engines.

AUTO REPAIR SCAMS

We had barely begun our first consumer protection division when we were flooded with reports of auto repair scams, of shops ripping off people by charging them through the nose for expensive repairs that really weren't needed. So we decided to set up a single "sting" operation.

We took about a dozen different vehicles, a selection of those made by all the major manufacturers, and had a prominent, aboveboard testing laboratory rig them all with a simple defect: they wrecked one of the spark plug wires so that one of the plugs wouldn't fire. This meant one piston wouldn't work, and thus the car or truck would run very rough. Any competent, computer-trained mechanic would have been able to instantly recognize the problem and fix it by merely replacing the spark plug wires.

We had our inspectors take such vehicles to various suspect dealer service departments and repair shops, complaining that the cars in question were missing and acting funny. Sure enough, some of the shops wanted to charge our people through the nose for unneeded and terribly expensive repairs.

We soon managed to put together an extensive report that revealed substantial fraud in a number of dealer and brand-name auto repair facilities. When it was complete, we took it to the legislature. Not only did we tell them how bad things were, we went to the capitol with an Auto Repair Act, drafted by my consumer protection division. We called for all auto repair facilities and their mechanics to be licensed—and for them to be required to have met certain minimum educational and training standards.

The legislature quickly agreed and used the proposed bill we had drafted as a model. They ended up passing the Motor Vehicle and Service Act of 1974, which remains in effect today.

There seems to be no question that this has substantially eliminated fraud and sheer incompetence in car and truck repair. Our investigation—and the legislation that followed—has saved who knows how many people millions of dollars and thousands of hours of frustration.

THE "TAINTED MEAT" CASE (1966)

Few things are more important than knowing that the food we buy is safe. Like many Americans, I read about the horrible practices in Chicago slaughterhouses around the beginning of the twentieth century in Upton Sinclair's *The Jungle* when I was young.

I had naively thought that the progressives and muckrakers had long ago cleaned up the meat industry. Although Michigan had a law mandating that cattle that die on the range or in a barn can't be used for meat (because they might well have been sick), I soon learned that we weren't as far removed from the world of *The Jungle* as I had thought. My office started hearing rumors and then got an anonymous tip that there was a slaughterhouse in western Michigan, north of Holland, that was processing such carrion and then selling that meat to various local markets in the area. We decided that the best way to catch the crooked slaughterhouse was to run another sting operation, in which one poor cow would have to give up its life for the betterment of humankind.

Our plan was to buy a cow, kill it, leave the body in a field, and then call the facility in question to take it away. Although there were and are legitimate and legal ways to use a dead (fresh) cow found lying in a field (the bones can be used to make buttons and the fat to make soap), processing it for meat is illegal. However, we faced one formidable problem: how would we be able to prove that any particular meat that made it to the butcher's came from our cow?

Fortunately, we found an expert at Michigan State University who had the solution. He told us that a certain harmless florescent chemical substance could be injected into the cow's bloodstream and, after a brief time, the chemical would permeate all the animal's tissues. So we bought a cow from a rancher, injected it with the chemical, and then killed the beast. We then called the suspect facility, which also just happened to operate a dead animal removal service, and told them we had an animal lying dead in a field, perhaps struck by lightning. No problem, they told us; they'd come and take her away. After they picked up the dead cow, state police helicopters surreptitiously tracked them.

Sure enough, they went directly to the suspected illegal slaughterhouse. We waited a few moments before state troopers stormed into the facility, armed not just with guns but with a black light that would reveal any trace of the fluorescent substance.

They speedily began arresting anyone who had traces of the substance on their hands. They checked out the joint. There was a conveyor belt that went to a wall—and stopped. That seemed fishy, so they knocked down the wall and, in a scene straight out of Hollywood, discovered a sophisticated meat-packaging operation. They were told to go on grinding and packaging the meat. Then we checked each parcel with the black light. Everyone lit up like a Christmas tree. They had ground up our dead cow, all right. Next we told them to make their deliveries—which they did, accompanied by a state policeman in plainclothes. Every market buying meat from them had to be well aware they weren't dealing with a state-licensed butchering facility.

When the markets placed the meat in their display cases . . . bingo! The stunned owners and meat department managers were arrested on the spot. We then successfully petitioned Kent County Circuit Court for a one-man grand jury. Circuit judge Stuart Hoffius then issued indictments charging a number of the meat market operators with fraudulent sales. That certainly had a chilling effect on those who might be tempted to pull similar scams.

This case went to the heart of what consumer protection is all about. I like to think I set the right tone, but Bladen and my staff did a tremendous job on case after case, waging war on behalf of Michigan's consumers.

In this particular situation, nobody will ever know how many lives were saved or cases of food poisoning prevented by exposing the illegal use of animals lying dead in a field. And I suppose we should salute that poor cow we bought and had to kill. After all, sacrificing her life may have helped save human lives by making sure Michigan's meat supply would be clean.

We had many other cases, too, throughout my years in office. Whenever I thought I had seen it all, I learned that there is no end to the number of schemes people will come up with to try to cheat the public.

———

These cases—and others like them—soon established consumer protection as an important part of the attorney general's mission, in the view of my staff and the citizens. We were soon up to our eyeballs in more consumer protection cases than we could count.

Finally in 1976, after years of struggle, we managed to get the landmark Consumer Protection Act passed by the Michigan legislature and signed by Governor William Milliken, one of the most progressive and far-seeing Republicans I've ever known.

That was a good year, by the way, for the environment. That November, voters tired of roadside litter passed the state's "bottle bill," requiring a ten-cent deposit on virtually every canned and bottled beverage containers. Michigan now has the highest recycling rate for such containers in the entire nation.

The Consumer Protection Act defined fair business practices as well as "unfair, unconscionable and deceptive methods." It set standards for goods and services and advertising. Now, for the first time, we had a full arsenal of legal ammunition to go after the scam artists, especially those who prey on the elderly, the poorly educated, and the otherwise vulnerable.

Real estate scams, for instance. If you are young, you may not remember, but there were improper short sales and mortgage scams long before the Great

Recession in 2008–9. In the 1980s, in fact, my office put several fraudulent mort-gage companies out of business for ripping off borrowers.

In one landmark case, we sued Oakland County–based Diamond Mortgage Company for sticking buyers with a huge fee at closing and then increasing the amount of the loan to cover that fee—meaning they got their money right off the top. We took that case to the Michigan Supreme Court in December 1981. The high court considered the case for exactly a year—and then ruled that even though Diamond was a licensed and regulated business, they weren't exempt from the Consumer Protection Act.

The Michigan attorney general's office finally, on my watch, was acting as the attorney for all the people.

———

I am proud to say that one of the first journalists to really recognize what we did was none other than Michael Moore—long before he was the major docu-mentary filmmaker he is now. Today, Michael Moore is famous for films like *Fahrenheit 911*, *Bowling for Columbine*, and *Roger and Me*. But in 1985, when he was the founder of an alternative paper in Flint called the *Michigan Voice*, he put me on the cover to recognize our achievements in protecting the consumer and the environment.

"Frank J. Kelley has, as Michigan's Attorney General, been a leading advo-cate for consumers' and workers' rights," Moore wrote. He praised my "record as a consumer advocate and added, "He has been relentless in his opposition to . . . attempts by giant utilities to force rate payers to pick up the tab for failed projects. His record as a consumer advocate and environmentalist remains unmatched by any other attorney general in the nation," the future filmmaker added. How can you top that?

When I looked at his story again years later, it jogged my memory and reminded me of some other cases I had forgotten about. The one that really impressed Moore was an attempt by the former Consumers Power (now Con-sumers Energy) to build a nuclear plant in Midland. When they first proposed building the plant back in 1967, Consumers said it would cost $256 million. That was long before the Three Mile Island and Chernobyl disasters, and nuclear power was relatively uncontroversial. But the costs to the consumer weren't. I knew by then how the game worked with utilities. They almost invariably have cost overrun after cost overrun, with the idea of happily passing them on to the consumer.

By 1975, it was clear to me that the project was unnecessary and would cost way too much. But the utility wouldn't stop its efforts to build it. Finally, in

1980, we started what Hugh Anderson, the head of my Special Litigation Division, called an "all-out assault." We filed a three-way lawsuit against Consumers Power, Detroit Edison, and the Michigan Public Service Commission, which operated pretty much as a rubber stamp for any utility that wanted a rate hike. Eventually, Consumers gave up, and we dropped the lawsuit.

————

Now, I was never exactly naïve about human nature. I grew up on the mean streets of Detroit and among hard-drinking sailors when I was working on the car ferries.

I've had my money stolen, I've been in a few barroom brawls, and maybe I've even had one or two experiences in my youth I decided to leave out of this book. But even given all that, I still found myself stunned by the variety of ways in which human beings callously exploit each other.

And you probably won't be surprised to learn that that extends to health care as well. We've all become much more familiar with the issues surrounding health care in recent years, thanks to spiraling costs and the national debate over the Affordable Care Act.

But financial health care controversies started long before this, and my office became involved in one precedent-setting case in 1996. Michigan Affiliated Healthcare Systems had a hospital in Lansing that was having financial problems. At that time, all Michigan hospitals were nonprofit entities and thereby exempt from taxes. Suddenly we learned that an out-of-state, for-profit corporation, Columbia/HCA Healthcare Corp., was interested in buying half the Lansing hospital.

This would have been a sweetheart deal for Columbia—a form of "financial recycling." In other words, while the money Columbia would have spent in buying half the hospital would have been used for so-called charity care, all the services and supplies would have had to be purchased through Columbia.

We filed a lawsuit on the grounds that the sale was not in the public interest, since it would have resulted in the diversion of charitable assets for noncharitable purposes, which we felt violated Michigan's Non-Profit Corporation Act. The case went before Ingham County circuit judge James Giddings, who agreed with us fully and ruled in our favor. Columbia and the local hospital tried to find some way around this, but within a few months they abandoned their attempts.

The lawsuit got some national attention and led to my being interviewed by Mike Wallace, himself a former radio reporter in Detroit, in a *60 Minutes* segment, and I was invited to speak to groups around the country. This was a powerful reminder that properly representing the public interest is an immense force of good for society as a whole.

That's what I tried to do for thirty-seven years.

I was later asked why—if the Columbia deal was illegal—Vanguard Health Systems, a for-profit corporation, was allowed to buy the Detroit Medical Center (DMC) in 2010. The answer is simple: Vanguard did not partner with the DMC—it acquired it outright. Though I was no longer attorney general, the parties sought my opinion in the case. As I told counsel for the DMC, Judge Giddings ruled in 1996 that it would have been perfectly legal for a for-profit corporation to buy a nonprofit and change its status. But it had to be one or the other. Thus the purchase of the DMC was entirely lawful.

––––––

By the mid-1960s, I was forced to confront something more startling than abuses in the health care industry. I soon learned that the attorney general's office needed not only a consumer protection division but also an entire subdivision devoted to charity and charitable trust scams.

One of the most significant such scams involved the misappropriation of trust funds by the officers of a Detroit bank—the former Detroit Bank and Trust, which later was merged into what is now Comerica. They were administering an estate of several million dollars and were charged with building a home for elderly women. But instead of building the home, the bank's trust and corporate officers were supporting their elderly mothers with the income from the trust! When this was brought to my attention, we sued.

Eventually we won a complete victory. The courts found the bank officers guilty of conflicts of interest, misappropriation of trust property, and violation of their fiduciary duties. Every one of the officers who profited was assessed a surcharge equal to his mother's benefit. In addition, Detroit Bank and Trust was ordered to build the home, which still exists.

There were many other such cases. In the late 1960s, we investigated a charity called the Crippled Children's Fund of Michigan. What could be more heartwarming than trying to help disabled children? Except that's not where the money was going. One of the fund's employees, a young man who was himself physically challenged and had been hired to solicit funds from donors, tipped us off that something was wrong.

With his help, we were able to get his bosses to hire one of our investigators as another solicitor. Well, it didn't take him long to determine that the whole thing was the type of scam we used to see a lot of. They were operating what we called a telephone "boiler room," calling businesses, mostly in Macomb County. Whenever they could get someone to agree to give money, they promptly would send runners over to the business to pick up a check or, in some cases, to get the donation in cash. (This was before the days of widespread credit card use, let alone the Internet.)

None of the money went to disabled children. The operator kept what was left after paying the solicitors and the phone and utility bills. Within two weeks we had enough evidence to shut the fund down and bring charges. When he appealed, the high court affirmed his felony conviction.* We caught him quickly, but not before more than $15,000 given by warm-hearted but deceived small businessmen had disappeared into his pockets.

Cases like these caused us to successfully lean on the legislature to rewrite the charitable solicitation law to require solicitors to be licensed and to require fund-raisers and charities to be bonded.

That doesn't mean unscrupulous businesses aren't still out there. Nor does it mean that some of them still don't get away with their bad behavior, at least for a while. Defending the public against them also requires an attorney general fully committed to use the powers and resources of his or her office to make sure Michigan's consumers are fully protected. I'm sorry to say that some of those powers have been weakened by subsequent legislation and court decisions.

You may recall the case I mentioned earlier in which we were able to stop some lending abuses after the Michigan Supreme Court ruled in 1982 that just because a business is licensed and regulated doesn't mean it isn't required to live up to the rules set down by the Consumer Protection Act. Tragically, a very different Michigan Supreme Court issued a ruling in 1999, right after I finally left office, that the Consumer Protection Act did not apply to licensed and regulated businesses. This largely and effectively gutted what had been one of the best "people-protection" pieces of legislation in my lifetime.

Today we need a new consumer protection act with more teeth in it—and we need lawmakers and attorneys general who stand up for the people.

Fighting to see that the people are protected is a battle that future attorneys general are going to have to fight, again and again.

I would never claim that I came anywhere close to finishing the job. But I can say that we blazed a trail for consumer protection, and I left my successors a road map and at least some legal tools.

Now it is their turn to sharpen and improve them.

---

* *People v. Burnette*, 19 Mich App 336 (1969).

13

DEPARTURE: RUNNING FOR THE SENATE, 1971–72

One thing about a political career: no matter how important your position, no matter how good a job you are doing, there's one question everyone is always asking you.

So what are you going to run for next?

The president of the United States may be the only person who never gets asked that. Believe me, everyone else does—except maybe a few congressmen who are in their late eighties.

So what are you going to run for next?

Though I thoroughly enjoyed being Michigan's attorney general, there came a time when I listened to those whispers, too.

You have to understand one thing: when I was appointed attorney general on December 28, 1961, nobody had ever been our state's attorney general longer than five years. By 1967, I was the new longevity champ, and I couldn't very well compare notes with the man whose record I had just surpassed, Jacob Howard. That's because he had left office before the Civil War. Normally, the career path of attorneys general in our state had been for them to eventually join a large, prestigious law firm, especially if they were Republican, or wait for an appointment to a vacancy on the state supreme court, as my predecessor, Paul Adams, had done.

But in my case, things were complicated by a fluke. Exactly a year after John Swainson appointed me to the job, he left office, having been defeated for reelection by George Romney. No one knew that Michigan would not have another Democratic governor for twenty years. The Republicans who held that office in the meantime mostly got along fine with me. But they weren't about to do anything to help my career. When there were rare high court vacancies, they would appoint members of their own party.

Being governor never particularly appealed to me. I knew after a few years of being attorney general that the job isn't nearly as powerful as the public perceives it to be, and I feared I'd find it largely boring. Besides, incumbents George Romney and then Bill Milliken were popular politicians, and to take them on, I would have had to give up my job as attorney general and risk ending up an unemployed lawyer with a wife and three kids the day after the election.

But there was one logical race to make: U.S. senator. Republican Robert Griffin had been appointed by George Romney in 1966, after a Democratic senator, Pat McNamara, had died in office. Griffin then managed to win a full term that November, shocking many people by beating the father of the modern Democratic Party, G. Mennen "Soapy" Williams, for the full term.

Soapy Williams had won six straight two-year terms, starting in 1948. He had presidential ambitions in 1960, but after a nasty battle with the state legislature led to national stories about "Michigan on the rocks," any chance of his winning the nomination was effectively squelched. President Kennedy ended up making him assistant secretary of state for Africa, a job he did remarkably well, coining the phrase "Africa for the Africans." But when he came back to run for the Senate, he had been out of Michigan for more than five years.

He also had been ill and looked tired. Worse, 1966 was a big GOP year, and Soapy lost. He later became ambassador to the Philippines before ending his career as Chief Justice of the Michigan Supreme Court, resigning just before his death in 1988.

Griffin was going to have to run for reelection in 1972. Democrats badly wanted to take back that Senate seat. Within a year after Soapy Williams's defeat, they began talking about running me.

Leon Cohan, my very able deputy, and some of my closest friends began planning possible scenarios. One positive was that I wouldn't have to give up my job as attorney general to take him on; my term had two more years to run.

Finally, I felt I had to take the plunge—and I didn't believe in doing things halfway. Over a two-year period, we assembled one of the most brilliant campaign teams ever put together, which included future national stars like Jeff Greenfield, a former speechwriter for Bobby Kennedy, David Garth, and pollster Pat Caddell. We also had a vast corps of young volunteers, the star of whom was, in 1970, a twenty-eight-year-old assistant attorney general named Jim Blanchard. Little did I know that he would be Michigan's next Democratic governor ... a dozen years later.

Most felt I was a better speaker than my opponent. We executed a brilliant primary strategy designed to keep other Democrats out of the race and avoid splitting the party.

Everything we could control went as well as humanly possible. Unfortunately campaigns are often about things you can't control. Two such things blew up in that year's campaign, hitting the race with the force of a tornado. One was white suburban voters' fear of cross-district school busing. The other was the weakest Democratic political ticket in my entire lifetime. When it was over, you might say our operation was perfect. Unfortunately the "patient"—my candidacy—didn't make it.

But I am getting way ahead of the story.

―――――

Even as I was coasting to victory by a whopping 750,000 votes for a fourth term as attorney general in 1970, I was lining up support for a Senate run two years later. Much of labor backed me early, including Bill Marshall, successor to Gus Scholle as head of the AFL-CIO, and Leonard Woodcock, who succeeded Walter Reuther as head of the UAW. I'm sure Reuther would have been an ally, too, had he not been killed in a tragic plane crash up north near Pellston that May. It also didn't hurt that my beloved little brother Jimmy Kelley was in the building trades and a proud member of Local 58.

I even had good relations with the Teamsters, though they were outcasts of a sort then, with their longtime leader, Jimmy Hoffa, in federal prison. (Interestingly, the Kennedys had never asked me to become involved in any of their efforts to get Hoffa. My guess is that they may have thought taking on Hoffa would have given me political difficulties, since it was my home state and Michigan Democrats depended heavily on the union vote.)

I never met James Riddle Hoffa, though I did serve him with a summons once when I was working for the sheriff's office; he came to the door in a bathrobe and called me "kid." However, I got to know his son, current Teamsters president Jim Hoffa, whom I met as he was graduating from college; he was the roommate of another young man who worked for me. The younger Hoffa impressed me as a fine and decent young man, and I'm happy that he has become a successful and apparently completely honest head of the Teamsters on his own.

But back to my Senate campaign. Throughout 1971, I quietly locked up support from county chairpersons and party activists. My supporters in the Jewish community, including Philip Warren, Stuart Hertzberg, and Avern Cohn, began raising funds for my campaign. Other would-be candidates may have tested the waters but quickly withdrew once they found we had gotten there ahead of them and they were literally being left out in the cold.

But there was still one potential primary opponent we had to take seriously, a man I'd known since he was a teenager. That was the Honorable Jerome P. Cavanagh, by then the former mayor of Detroit, with whom I had been friends since Soapy Williams's famous first campaign. Jerry had once been a darling of the national news media after he won an upset victory in 1961 at the age of thirty-three and was elected mayor of Detroit.

The nation had a young Irish president; Detroit had an even younger Irish mayor, and many saw great things ahead for him, especially Cavanagh himself. But his reputation had been heavily damaged since he had been elected. He had let his ego get the better of him, a dangerous mistake for any young politician, and had run against Soapy Williams for the Democratic U.S. Senate nomination in 1966. That was a bad mistake. Williams beat him soundly, but there was a perception that Soapy had been weakened by the primary battle, and some blamed Cavanagh for Soapy's eventual loss in the general election. Far worse had happened to the peppy young mayor since.

The horrendous Detroit riot of July 1967 took everyone in Michigan by surprise and badly damaged Cavanagh's reputation. Despite the fact that America had been wracked by urban riots, nobody saw this one coming, least of all Cavanagh, who'd won an upset victory six years before, mainly thanks to the votes of black Detroiters.

To this day, I am somewhat baffled by the reasons behind that riot, but what nobody can deny is that it hurt Cavanagh's reputation. While cities from Newark to Los Angeles had major riots in the 1960s, Detroit's was the worst in terms of lives lost—forty-three—and property damage, which was initially exaggerated but in today's dollars was in the hundreds of millions.

The destruction and death were probably made worse because of politics. George Romney, Michigan's Republican governor, was hoping to run for president the following year and expected to run against Lyndon Johnson, the man in the White House. Although it soon became apparent that the U.S. Army would be needed to stop the violence, LBJ didn't want to do Romney any favors, and Romney at first didn't want to look weak by admitting that the state couldn't maintain law and order. Once the troops arrived the riot was quickly quelled. But the delay had made the final toll much worse.

Cavanagh had looked helpless and weak. What's worse, he went through a nasty divorce while he was mayor, with the sordid and embarrassing details splashed across the newspapers.

When his term expired in 1969, he didn't even try to run for reelection. But he still had a name and powerful ambitions, and the last thing I needed was a contested primary. That's why my supporters and I worked so hard to try to line up support.

Remarkably, it all paid off in the end.

Everything came down to a secret meeting of party and union heavyweights in Detroit's old Sheraton-Cadillac Hotel early in 1972. Cavanagh spoke eloquently for ten minutes. I did my best to follow. Then, after a moment of silence, Leonard Woodcock, the head of the UAW, said in his calm, softly strong voice, "Speaking for the union, we don't want a strong and able candidate so weakened in the primary that we lose the general election." He added that such a primary six years earlier had, in his opinion, cost Soapy victory in 1966. Then he looked at the former mayor. "You are free to run, Jerry, but I'm telling you now that we're going to support Frank Kelley from this meeting on and do everything we can to elect him." Cavanagh looked stunned.

Bill Marshall from the state AFL-CIO spoke next. "I agree with Leonard, and I am going to personally campaign and raise money for Frank." James McNeely, then Democratic state chair, finally spoke. "The party would be better served if we rallied around one particular candidate in this particular race because Griffin will be tough." Speaking carefully, he added that the party would officially be neutral if there was a contested primary. "But I believe the majority of our people are already committed to Frank," he said. The meeting then adjourned.

Soon afterward, Cavanagh announced he would not be a candidate for the U.S. Senate. Two years later, he ran for the Democratic nomination for governor but was beaten solidly by Sandy Levin. That was his last attempt at elected office.

Jerry and I were rivals then. But I want to say that we were never enemies. We had been friends since our college days—and Jerry remains my friend of fond memory. Tragically, not only did his political career end early, his very life was far too short. In 1979, five years after his last defeat, this young man who had shown so much promise died of a massive heart attack; he was barely fifty-one years old. Like many other politicians who made a splash when they were young, going back to Michigan's first governor, Stevens T. Mason, he proved a shooting star.

Nobody knew that then, however, and with an uncontested primary ahead, I had a lot of time to prepare. The early signs were promising. Though Griffin was in the Senate, I was at least as well-known. One early Democratic Party poll had me more than ten points ahead. Later on I learned that GOP polls showed much the same thing. Organized labor really wanted to defeat Griffin, who, when he was in the House in 1959, became the co-sponsor of the Landrum-Griffin Act, which was billed as an anticorruption act but which gave the government stronger powers to meddle in union affairs. For their part, union leaders saw the bill as a means to tie them up in red tape, thanks to a seemingly endless series of reports it required them to file with the federal government. They saw it as a way to help slow their organizing efforts, while increasing the chances of falling into some technical violation.

I took stock of my chances. Griffin and I were both about the same age—he was forty-eight; I was a year younger. Griffin held a higher office, but I had been elected statewide four times at that point to his one election. And he had managed to win at least partly on the coattails of Romney, who won in 1966 with a whopping 61 percent of the vote against Zolton Ferency.

But Democratic turnout would be much higher in 1972, which was a presidential election year. Michigan was trending increasingly Democratic. Four years before, Hubert Humphrey lost the presidential election to Richard Nixon—but won Michigan solidly. I had reason to think I had a very good chance.

I knew I would be heavily outspent. But I calculated that if I could raise a million dollars, I could win. Nowadays, the cost of taking on an incumbent senator might be thirty times as much. A million wasn't easy for a Democrat, but I felt I could do it.

Much later I learned that Republicans saw the same polls and reached the same conclusions. They knew how popular I was, and they knew they had to find some issue to do me in—not just something where voters might disagree with some position I took but something to scare people. They had to come up with an issue that would divide the traditional Democratic coalition and turn enough voters against me.

A few years earlier or later, they wouldn't have had a chance. But the early 1970s were an odd and divisive period in U.S. history, with the Vietnam War still on and the nation struggling with the aftermath of the civil rights movement. And those who wanted to beat me found their issue, all right: cross-district busing.

That was a long time ago, and if you weren't around then, it may be difficult to understand how intense the passions were that this aroused. So let me give you some background.

In 1954 the U.S. Supreme Court had issued its famous ruling in *Brown v. Board of Education* that legally mandated, or de jure, school segregation was unconstitutional. That was generally applauded in northern states like Michigan, which saw it as applying mainly to the South. But Michigan's public schools were, in many places, almost as segregated as those in the South because blacks were largely confined by custom to some very restricted ghettos, even within the city of Detroit.

In in the 1950s and 1960s, Detroit's black population rapidly increased, and black families were younger and larger than white families. By 1963, more than half the students in Detroit's public schools were black. By the time I was getting ready to run for the U.S. Senate, two-thirds of the students in Detroit public schools were black. White flight had sharply accelerated after the devastating civil disturbances of July 1967.

Even within Detroit, housing patterns meant that most schools were either nearly all black or all white. Suddenly some activists and NAACP officials started charging that this de facto segregation was just as damaging as the de jure segregation of the old South.

Michigan passed a law in 1969—Public Act 48—that would have broken up the Detroit school systems into eight smaller districts. This had broad support because it would preserve some white districts. It was supported by an odd coalition of whites who wanted majority white schools and some black power advocates—including the bill's main sponsor, a state senator named Coleman A. Young.

But the NAACP took a dim view of this bill, in part because it worked to maintain segregation. They filed suit against the state in U.S. District Court in August 1970, claiming Public Act 48 was unconstitutional primarily because it perpetuated segregation.

Remember: Michigan's attorney general, by law, is the top lawyer for the state. I had to defend the state and its chief officers whenever they were sued, regardless of my personal feelings. As legal scholar Jennifer Huff wrote many years later, "on one side stood the NAACP representing African-American Detroit parents and students. On the other side stood Governor William Milliken, Attorney General Frank Kelley, the State Board of Education, Superintendent of Public Instruction John W. Porter, and (Detroit Schools) Superintendent Norman Drachler."*

The case would come to be known as *Milliken v. Bradley*, since the governor was the top state official and Ronald Bradley was first on a list of Detroit students who were technically the plaintiffs. The case eventually went all the way to the U.S. Supreme Court and had a major impact in terms of how school desegregation remedies could be used in the United States.

But long before that, it would have a major impact on me. However, that wouldn't be clear for some time.

---

* Jennifer A. Huff, "The Only Feasible Desegregation Plan: *Milliken v. Bradley* and Judge Roth's Order for Cross-District Busing," *The Court Legacy* 15, no. 2 (May 2008).

But back to the early days of my Senate campaign. Both political parties took early secret polls in 1971 matching me up against Bob Griffin. Our polls indicated that I had a substantial lead of more than ten points—a lot for any incumbent to overcome, especially when facing a challenger as well-known as I was.

Later, I was to learn that GOP polls showed the same thing. Oddly enough, neither side wanted the results of these polls known. Republicans didn't want to know that it looked like their man was going down in flames. But I was even less eager for people to know I was so far ahead. I knew the race would tighten up; they almost always do. And as I said, I knew we needed to raise a lot of money, which is always harder for Democrats. If my supporters thought I was a sure thing, they might be less likely to give—and things looked like they were going my way.

Meanwhile, the *Milliken v. Bradley* case at first looked like it was going nowhere. U.S. district judge Stephen J. Roth, who had served briefly as Michigan's attorney general more than a decade before me, ruled that there was no evidence of either deliberate de facto or de jure segregation in Detroit's public schools.

But civil rights lawyers came up with another idea—what they called a "metropolitan solution." What everyone would soon call it, however, was "cross-district busing." What it meant was that students from Detroit would be bused to schools in mostly white areas, and many white students would be bused to Detroit. Even the idea of this provoked anger, horror, and ferocious hostility on the part of white parents throughout the community.

What I could instantly see was how unpopular this idea was. I also knew, however, that if the courts were to order such a thing, I would legally have to defend and enforce that ruling.

Which, politically, would be the kiss of death.

Sure enough, on September 27, 1971, Judge Roth ruled that segregation did exist and that government had combined with private institutions to "establish and to maintain the pattern of residential segregation throughout the Detroit metropolitan area." He ordered the Detroit School Board and the state of Michigan to develop a metropolitan-wide cross-district busing solution that would include Wayne, Oakland, and Macomb counties.

That would have been a massive undertaking requiring vast logistical planning, even if it had been widely accepted. But, of course, it wasn't. In Pontiac, members of the Ku Klux Klan fire-bombed school buses. Militant mothers chained themselves to buses. Parents yanked kids out of public schools.

Things were heating up, fast. And this wasn't going to be good for my campaign. Years later, two highly placed Republican sources, men now dead, told me the full story of how the White House did me in. Back then, the *Detroit News* had the largest circulation in the state, and Martin Hayden, its vice president and editor, was an influential and openly partisan Republican. During a telephone conversation in late 1970 or early 1971, Hayden told President Richard Nixon that Griffin was in trouble. "Don't worry," Nixon said. "I have the issue that will defeat Kelley and the Democrats." That issue was cross-district busing. It was said that Nixon suggested to the editor that he have a reporter ask James McNeely, the Democratic state chair, what he would do if the courts ordered cross-district busing.

The reporter did—and it is not surprising that McNeely tried to duck the question. But eventually he reluctantly said Democrats wouldn't oppose such a remedy if ordered. This led to screaming, scurrilous headlines that suggested the Democratic Party was in favor of cross-district busing. The irony of it is that I was, remember, the chief attorney defending the state against charges of discrimination. My assistants and I were in Judge Roth's courtroom arguing that there was no illegal discrimination in Detroit schools and that cross-district busing was an extreme remedy and a practically impossible solution. But that didn't come across in the media.

Senator Griffin spent more than twice the amount I did on TV ads—some $1.8 million against my $800,000. Many of his commercials showed yellow school buses picking up white children and busing them away down a sinister, foggy road.

Within days, my lead in the polls evaporated, and we were running even. I knew I had to broaden the scope of the campaign. I knew, too, that I needed to establish some knowledge of foreign policy. So Leon Cohan and I went on a world fact-finding tour in the fall of 1971. Though the trip was entirely political, it was one of the most memorable experiences of my life.

That was the height of the Cold War, remember, and we began by visiting West Germany and then crossed through the Berlin Wall to travel through East Germany, Poland, and finally to Moscow. Later, we went to Israel, Lebanon, and Cyprus before meeting up with my wife and daughter in Rome. We had no trouble gaining an audience with top political leaders; all their intelligence indicated I would soon be a U.S. senator, and from an influential state to boot.

When I returned, I threw myself into the campaign. But I am going to admit something I perhaps shouldn't: from time to time throughout my career, I have been torn with self-doubt, even a touch of self-loathing. Was I really good enough? Good enough to be attorney general? Good enough to be a senator? Was this really something I wanted to do?

But then I shook it off. Nobody could say I didn't work hard in that campaign. We had an amazing galaxy of past, present, and future stars. I mentioned my main speechwriter, Jeff Greenfield, who had written speeches for Bobby Kennedy, and David Garth, the wizard of political advertising. Our pollster, Pat Caddell, had just graduated from Harvard and later went on to fame as Jimmy Carter's pollster—and one of the first to make effective use of election night exit polls. Teddy Kennedy, the last prince of America's reigning political family, came in to campaign for me, which meant a lot.

All that didn't mean, however, that I didn't have lots of Michigan help. We had strong labor support. Mildred "Millie" Jeffrey, at that time the highest-ranking woman in the UAW union, helped with social and women's issues. African Americans turned out in droves, incensed at the Republicans' efforts to play racial politics. My own family threw themselves into the campaign. Sister Patricia ran the campaign headquarters and saw to it that every volunteer kept busy. My youngest brother, Dick, put his PR skills to work; brother Jim worked on his union colleagues. To this day, I believe it was a beautifully staffed and well-run campaign.

But though the operation was perfect, in the end, it couldn't save the patient. As if cross-district busing wasn't a big enough burden, I also had to run on a ticket headed by presidential candidate George McGovern, who would suffer the worst national loss in modern times.

Still, we were optimistic. We gave it our all. Until the final days, I was neck and neck with Griffin. This was before the era of televised debates; had we had them, the story might have ended differently.

The one debate we had was before the Economic Club of Detroit, a largely pro-business audience that mainly favored my opponent. I had spent hours practicing with Jeff Greenfield; I was raring to go. I came out swinging, telling the audience why Griffin didn't deserve to be elected, attacking his positions on the issues. When it was over, I sensed I had won some new respect. The Detroit TV stations all said things like "observers seemed to think Frank Kelley won the debate or "Kelley appeared to have made the most points." But it wasn't televised.

During those last hectic days, we managed to find the budget to rent an executive jet for a week, which meant, of course, that I got to work three times as hard in what were then all eighteen-hour-days.

I was kept so busy I couldn't even think. But I didn't want the campaign to end. Pat Caddell was telling me I was still at least a couple points down because of busing.

But my crowds were hugely enthusiastic. Trouble was, I was gaining votes retail, while Bob Griffin was going after them wholesale with his negative ads suggesting I wanted to bus little white kids to some scary, menacing ghetto.

His team flooded the airwaves with these ads in the final days of the campaign. Overall, his heavy outspending on television made the difference.

On Election Day, my wife and I voted and then flew to Detroit to wait out the returns in the city's old Sheraton-Cadillac Hotel.

There's a fascinating ritual to election nights in America, at least for major races. The candidate's family and closest advisors huddle with him or her in a private bedroom suite. Immediately next door are the closest advisors, paid and unpaid, along with top fund-raisers, contributors, spouses, and friends.

Below is a ballroom, where a band is playing and the candidate's regular supporters gather, awaiting the returns, celebrating, waiting for the candidate to come down and claim victory, though they know this also could be where he or she may have to concede defeat.

Mysteriously, in all cases, if the returns show the candidate is winning, the crowd continues to grow in both size and elation as the hours pass. But if the news turns bad, the ballroom crowd can just as mysteriously all but evaporate inside of an hour.

Early on election night, the news looked good. Normally Republican Alpena came in strong for me. By 9:30, I was ahead. That was an era when local television stations had full-time Lansing bureaus. Tom Greene, dean of the broadcast reporters, was saying that I might be a winner. Cheers erupted from the ballroom.

But it wasn't to be. Returns kept flooding in, and around 10:00 p.m. I got a call from my top analyst, thirty-year-old Jim Blanchard. I could hear the news in his voice before he gave it to me straight: "Frank, it's not good. You are trailing in too many places outstate where you shouldn't be. The suburbs are weak because of busing." He paused, and I heard the catch in his voice. "My numbers indicate we can't make it."

Intellectually I was prepared, thanks to the briefings I had gotten from Pat Caddell. Emotionally, it hurt.

I ended up consoling Blanchard. "It was your duty to tell me the truth, good or bad. I know you don't want to be the bearer of bad news." For some reason, I added, "Keep everything to yourself."

The truth didn't take long to be apparent on the huge election tally boards. My early lead disappeared. I fell behind by an ever-growing margin. Long before midnight, the ballroom was empty.

With tears in their eyes, my closest aides told me how sorry they were. Shortly before 1:00 a.m. I called Senator Griffin. "I believe it's time to congratulate you on your victory and to wish you well. It was a hard campaign, and I'm sure you're glad to have it over as well." His voice was gentle. "Thanks for this call, Frank, you are most gracious. I'm glad it's over, too. Thanks for the call, and good luck."

That was, I have learned, about par for concession statements. In most cases, they are painfully short in order to minimize the pain for the loser, especially if the election was, as mine was, in doubt.

That was the only election I ever lost. The final tally was 1,781,065 votes for Griffin and 1,577,178 for me. I had received far more votes in Michigan than did my party's presidential nominee, George McGovern, but it wasn't enough.

Losing was terribly hard, more so than I expected. I'm sad to say it also produced self-doubt and a personal crisis that affected my marriage and eventually led to the end of it. The details are not important, except that I accept all the blame for allowing stress and politics to infect my personal life.

Jo and I separated soon after the election, and various attempts at reconciliation failed. Eventually we divorced, and in 1980 I married Nancy, who was a civil servant and a librarian for the state of Michigan. Ironically, she had worked in the attorney general's office, though I didn't know her at all till we met socially.

We fell in love, and Nancy has taken wonderful care of me ever since. And I'm happy to say that my lovely first wife, Josephine, and I have again become close friends. She lives in Florida with our two daughters, Karen and Jane, and we get together every winter.

That my marriage failed is my life's biggest regret.

But apart from that, I have become convinced that losing that Senate race may just have been the best thing that ever happened to me.

No, I am not rationalizing my defeat.

Years later I was in Washington visiting an old friend of mine, Bill Saxbe, who was also a former attorney general (from Ohio) and who had been elected to the U.S. Senate in 1968. Though he was a Republican, I considered him a kindred spirit, an action-motivated guy who had been the prosecutor in the famous Sam Sheppard trial.

Saxbe told me that being a senator was boring. Nothing much happens, he said, except for endless committee meetings. Especially when you are new, you have little power and, most of the time, little to do. He realized he didn't have the slightest interest in running again and gratefully accepted an offer to become attorney general in the last months of the Nixon administration. Adlai Stevenson III, a Democrat from Illinois, told me he, too, found the Senate a bore.

Eventually I realized how important the job I had was and how much power I had as attorney general to do good for Michigan's people and consumers. Plenty of my friends thought I got a bad break. Without any doubt, I could have raised the money and support needed to run again.

But gradually I realized I didn't need to.

There's one thing you learn in politics that the textbooks never tell you: truth is nearly always stranger than fiction.

Less than two years after my defeat, I stood before the U.S. Supreme Court, arguing a historic case called *Milliken v. Bradley*. Though I had been defeated in the Senate race because I was smeared as being in favor of cross-district school busing, here I was arguing that such busing was not only a bad idea but unconstitutional.

Five months later, the high court sided with me. In a 5–4 decision, the justices said that Judge Roth's desegregation order was "wholly impermissible" and not justified by the landmark school desegregation decision, *Brown v. Board of Education*.

That was effectively the end of cross-district busing.

Six years after my defeat, it was Bob Griffin's turn to make the call I had made to him on the worst night of my political life. The next time he ran, he was beaten by Carl Levin, whose first job out of law school had been working in my office. The night Griffin's Senate career ended, the same voters were reelecting me attorney general by nearly a million votes! That night I got more votes than anyone on either ticket. I wonder if some of the voters were trying to tell me they were sorry.

I'll never know.

But what I do know is that exactly ten years after young Jim Blanchard called me to give me the bad news, it was my turn to go to him on election night. But this time, the story was very different. That night, I was able to congratulate him on being the first Democrat elected governor of Michigan in twenty years.

For the first time since my friend John Swainson left office, I would have a chance to work with a governor who was not only of my own party but a good friend—and one to whom I'd given his start.

Yogi Berra's famous saying is truer about politics than baseball: it really ain't over till it's over.

14

MY FIRST TWO GOVERNORS:
SWAINSON AND ROMNEY

During my nearly four decades as Michigan's attorney general, it was my pleasure (and occasional pain) to serve with five governors through what were tumultuous times in our state's history.

They were a very different lot. Two were Democrats; three were Republicans. They included brawlers and gentlemen; a war hero, one who tried to become president, and one who was an authentically tragic figure. Some were liberals; one, a hard-right conservative.

One—George Romney—was nearly old enough to have been my father. The last one, John Engler, was barely a teenager that day John Swainson changed my life by appointing me attorney general.

But I made it my business to know and get along with them all. That's in part due to something the first Frank Kelley told me, over and over. "Frank," Dad would say, "any fool can make enemies. It takes a smart man to make and keep friends."

True to that motto, I found ways to get along well with every one of them— though, as noted earlier, Romney and I had a little difficulty at first until we each agreed on what was our turf.

Here's a dirty little secret about politics and government that you won't learn in political science textbooks: governors are important figures, no doubt about it. But the fact is that much of the time they don't have all that much to do. Yes, they sign bills, push their programs, make deals, and try hard to talk new businesses into coming to Michigan, and try even harder—usually without much success—to talk established businesses out of closing plants or leaving the state. But there is a lot of down time, during which they visit cherry festivals, cut ribbons, and make appointments to highly important bodies such as—I kid you not—the state asparagus board.

Nobody, however, would deny that governors are often key figures in the history of a state, if only because they can and do tend leave their imprint on an era, just as presidents do. Nationally, we talk about the "Kennedy years" or the "Obama years." Those who know Michigan history instantly recognize the difference between the "Milliken era" and the "Engler era."

So here are my impressions—and memories—of the two men who governed Michigan during the years when I was its chief lawyer, John Swainson and George Romney.

By the way, if you ever meet one of a state's other current or former top elected officials, such as secretary of state or attorney general, don't ask them "which governor they served under." That's because I never served under a single one. I served with them. Michigan's secretary of state and attorney general are not like cabinet officers in Washington, who are appointed. We are nominated and elected separately and independently.

———

There are men and women today who have tragically lost one or both legs as children and remember being visited in the hospital by a man who was Michigan's governor. John Swainson would talk to them, listen to and encourage them, and sometimes even do a little dance in their room. Then he would pull up his pant legs and show them that he didn't have any legs at all.

Nobody will ever know how many children he inspired. As far as I know, he never turned down a request for a hospital visit.

Swainson, who was seven months younger than I was, had both his legs blown off by a land mine in France in November 1944. Three men with him were literally blown completely to bits. In addition, his ribs and jaw were broken and he was covered with lacerations. Nevertheless, through iron determination he not only survived but got himself through Olivet College and law school at the University of North Carolina before returning to Michigan to take the bar exam. We got to know each other a bit and had a beer together the day we were both admitted to the bar.

That day, Swainson told me he was interested in public service—and said he was thinking of joining the Young Republicans. Naturally, as a staunch Democrat, I was horrified.

As my good friend Larry Glazer relates in his excellent biography of Swainson, *Wounded Warrior,** I immediately came up with seventeen reasons why he shouldn't become a Republican!

Whether my arguments were the deciding factor I'll never know, but he became a Democrat. He was only twenty-nine when he captured a state senate seat. (Ironically, I had been approached first about running for the same seat, but I had made up my mind to move to Alpena.) Four years later, Swainson was elected lieutenant governor. This was back when state officers served only two-year terms.

In 1960, when G. Mennen "Soapy" Williams finally retired, Secretary of State James Hare was the man everybody expected to succeed him. But Swainson was a young man in a hurry. He outworked and outhustled Hare, won over key labor leaders, and won the primary going away. That November, he won a squeaker over two-time GOP candidate Paul Bagwell. He was barely thirty-five years old.

Everything seemed to be going his way. With his good looks, war record, and stunning electoral successes, a huge future, maybe even on the national stage, seemed all but certain.

But that's not what happened. Swainson was a good, honest, hardworking governor, but he followed Soapy Williams, a man seen by many as a superstar. What's worse, the legislature, as I noted earlier, was apportioned basically by geography. There was no rule dictating that all districts had to have the same population, and that meant Republicans had huge majorities in the state senate. They did not want to do the new governor any good, no matter how reasonable he might be.

The GOP, which by then had been shut out of the governorship for fourteen years, was anxious to take the statehouse back. And they figured they finally had the candidate to do it in George Romney, who had the square jaw and white hair of a matinee idol. Romney had gotten a lot of favorable national publicity while he was head of the American Motors Corporation (AMC), which years later merged with and was absorbed by Chrysler.

AMC pioneered America's first true compact car, the Rambler, and Romney served as the head pitchman, cleverly grabbing headlines by calling his car an alternative to the "gas-guzzling dinosaurs" made by the Big Three. Then in 1959, he led the successful drive for a new state constitutional convention.

---

* Lawrence M. Glazer, *Wounded Warrior: The Rise and Fall of Michigan Governor John Swainson* (East Lansing: Michigan State University Press, 2010), 24.

The newspapers loved Romney. Nearly all the owners and publishers were Republicans, and they were angry and frustrated that Democrats had held the governor's office for so long.

Nevertheless, Swainson did manage to accomplish some things. Some slight tax reforms were agreed upon, though not enough to take care of the needs of a rich and growing state. The legislature expanded the state's network of community colleges, something that would eventually become crucially important. They also agreed on a process of court reform.

Two years were not, however, enough for Swainson to make much of a mark. The wonder is not that George Romney beat him in 1962 but that Swainson kept it so close. In the end, he lost by a very small margin, 51 to 48 percent.

My heart broke a little as he conceded defeat. He was my friend and the man who had appointed me attorney general. But he was still young, and I felt he had a great future ahead of him—and for a while, that was exactly how things looked.

Within three years, he had been elected to a Wayne County Circuit judgeship. Five years later, in 1970, he was elected to the Michigan Supreme Court by a landslide, even running far ahead of Soapy Williams, who was also elected that day. When he became a Supreme Court justice he was barely forty-five. He might have gone on to be elected to the U.S. Senate when Phil Hart retired a few years later or to another nationally prominent post.

But fate had a few cruel tricks to play. Acting on a tip that a Supreme Court justice had taken a bribe to influence a decision, an ambitious prosecutor called for a grand jury investigation. Eventually Swainson was charged with accepting a bribe. He was acquitted but was convicted of three counts of perjury, in large part because of his own fumbling testimony.

I was convinced at the time that he was innocent and an honest man, a conclusion that was also reached by Glazer, himself a former judge, after he made an exhaustive study of the trial for his book, which I highly recommend for anyone interested in the tragic life of this man who gave and suffered so much.

Swainson did, however, have one weakness: he would meet with, socialize with, or talk to anyone who wanted to see him. That included some unsavory characters, and his having associated with them seems to have made a bad impression on the jury. His conviction destroyed his life.

His sentence was only a couple of months in a halfway house, but that was the least of his worries. He had to resign from the court and lost his law license. He became a serious drinker and twice had to face drunk driving charges before at last getting into a treatment program and getting his life turned around.

Slowly things picked up for him. Eventually, his law license was restored. He found work as a mediator, in cases where the parties wanted to settle out of court.

But I could tell he was still terribly sad and needed a lift. One day in 1977, I had an idea: I decided I would personally visit Henry Ford II, the grandson of the founder of the Ford Motor Company and its current chairman. I wanted to see if somehow, perhaps through the Ford Foundation, he could do something to make better use of Swainson's talents.

I called Ford's office, spoke to his secretary, who happened to be male, and told him that the matter I wanted to see Ford about had nothing to do with him or his business; I simply wanted a few moments of his time. Ford, it turned out, was out of the country.

Before long I received a follow-up call inviting me to meet with Mr. Ford. His office was located at the top floor of the chief administration building of the Ford Motor Company in Dearborn, known informally as the Glass House.

I wasn't surprised to find that it was a striking and beautifully appointed modern office. There was an apartment with a bedroom off to the side, which allowed Mr. Ford to stay overnight if needed. After we greeted one another, I sat down, and we enjoyed a few moments of small talk. I told him that one of my uncles had once been a high official at Ford but that he had been fired because they wanted to make room for the infamous Harry Bennett, who was an enemy of young Henry II when he took over the company.

Ford was very interested in that story, and it immediately eased things between us. We hit it off quite well.

He was a fascinating man. He had been released from the U.S. Navy early, near the end of World War II, to save the company from total ruin by his senile grandfather, the founder, who was under the influence of Bennett, who was regarded as little more than a thug. Hank the Deuce, as he was nicknamed, did that and rebuilt Ford into a worthy competitor of General Motors.

Eventually I broached the subject about which I had come to see him. Without mentioning any names, I told him about a good friend who'd been through all kinds of tragedy in his life, and I recounted the story of John Swainson's life. I'm sure that as I got well into the story, he knew whom I was talking about.

When I finally got to the end, I told Ford about how Swainson had lost the governorship and made a comeback that took him all the way to Michigan's highest court only to be put upon by a federal task force and have his life go down in flames . . . again.

I told Ford that the governor was pretty disheartened and depressed and that I was very worried about him. "I felt you might be able to identify with the situation and help," I said. I shall never forget his reply: "You know, when John Swainson was governor I didn't particularly like his politics. He seemed too pro-union. I'm not against unions, but he seemed not to understand the problems of management. However, when I see you come here today for your friend, Governor Swainson, and see that you are doing this strictly for him and to help him, I cannot respond in anything but a human way. I must do something in response as a human being. Would you please leave it to me? I want no publicity as to anything that might happen, but you can be sure that I will do something for Governor Swainson within a reasonable time."

That was that. We spent some time chatting about the automobile business, and then—I'll never forget this—he insisted on taking the elevator and walking with me all the way to the entrance.

I felt somehow that he had enjoyed putting aside the pressures of business for a few minutes and just talking about something he could easily improve: the situation of one poor human being. Ford himself had a hard time with media scrutiny of his private life and two divorces, something he eventually countered with the brilliant slogan "Never complain; never explain."

In less than a month, John Swainson was contacted by one of the Ford trusts, which offered him a position as a consultant on a project involving narcotic addiction, especially in children. Swainson was overjoyed—and not just because of the salary, which was a then-princely $40,000 a year. He had been managing to make ends meet financially between his mediation work and his military pension as a wounded veteran. But being retained by Ford made him feel like he had been accepted back into the world of public service.

That contract lasted for five years. It ended just as my good friend and protégé James J. "Jim" Blanchard was settling in as the state's first Democratic governor since Swainson.

Soon afterward, I asked the new governor to put Swainson on the Michigan Historical Commission, an unpaid but intellectually stimulating post. I knew that John would welcome the opportunity to work with those who would be writing the state's history.

I didn't have to ask, but I knew he was worried about his own legacy; he once told a reporter that he feared he would go down in history with an asterisk that said "convicted and died." But that didn't happen. Gradually his reputation improved. Sympathetic stories about him began to appear. He won respect for his work on the historical commission. He founded and became president of the Retired Judges Association. He successfully rebuilt his life.

When John Engler became governor in 1991, I asked him, as a courtesy to a fellow governor, to keep Swainson on the Michigan Historical Commission, and to his credit he did.

Swainson, tragically, did not have a long life. He was stricken with congestive heart failure in 1992 and had a stroke the following year. The years and the stress and the war wounds must have prematurely aged him. He was sitting at his kitchen table one beautiful morning in May 1994, when a massive heart attack hit him.

He was gone before the ambulance arrived. When I spoke at his funeral I said, "It was never to be easy for John Swainson." It never was, but he always rose to the occasion. Swainson was a good and decent man who, on the battlefield and in the courtroom, survived and overcame things that would have broken most people. He gave me my start.

He deserved better. He deserves to be remembered.

———

If you've read this far, you already know that I tangled with Romney early on in his administration when it was clear that he didn't understand that I was an elected official and had my own sphere of responsibility. And I wasn't at all that happy that Romney had beaten my good friend and mentor.

But my philosophy of how to make government work was shaped by my experience as a young country lawyer in Alpena—that, and my dad's wise barroom counsel. I learned that in order to understand and work with people, you can't remain partisan after the election is over—especially when you are governing for the good of the millions of people in the very diverse state of Michigan.

You have to make up your mind to work with people from different parties and very different philosophies. When you fail to do that, you get the kind of paralysis we've seen in Congress during President Obama's administration.

That wasn't my way. I firmly believed that when the people chose Romney as their governor and me as their attorney general, they wanted us to work together for the best interests of the whole state.

That is how I have always tried to operate, and it's a good thing, too: after that first election, the voters eight times chose me and a governor from the other party! Only twice did I have the good fortune to get elected along with a fellow Democrat.

So my mind was made up from the start that I would do my level best to get along with Romney and his Republican appointees. And, except for the dramatic clashes I described earlier, we did get along for the most part, especially on routine matters, and especially after we worked out the "Treaty of Lansing" described earlier.

Eventually I came up with a system where the governor would have on his staff an assistant attorney general who worked for him but who was technically on my payroll and part of my operation. That was constitutionally and practically sound arrangement, and I made similar arrangements throughout the tenures of all five governors. I felt it was good policy to try to prevent other departments from setting up their own legal staffs.

Our job was, in one way or another, to represent them all.

But even when things were working smoothly, I have to say that of all the governors I worked with, George Wilcken Romney was the most difficult for me to understand, or read emotionally. Part of that, I believe, was that he was completely a product of his Mormon religion—far more so than most people knew. He was actually born in Mexico, where his grandfather had gone to escape a new federal law outlawing the practice of polygamy. George's parents fled Pancho Villa and the Mexican Revolution, returned to America in 1912 when he was five, and knocked around the mountain west before ending up back in Utah.

My impression is that George Romney was shaped by the experience of growing up in the proud, defiantly different Mormon culture. He had an uncanny gift for sales promotion and self-promotion—not necessarily in that order.

Romney's ambition was far too great to be contained by Salt Lake City. He was still in his early twenties when he arrived in Washington to work, first as a congressional staffer then as a lobbyist for Alcoa, the aluminum manufacturer. He moved on to Detroit in 1939, where he was soon head of the Automobile Manufacturers Association; he spent World War II as the automakers' chief lobbyist. After the war, he jumped to what soon became American Motors Corporation, where in 1954 he became chairman and president, thanks to the sudden unexpected death that October of his mentor, George W. Mason.

There, Romney launched a famous gamble that paid off, big time. He denounced Ford, Chrysler, and General Motors as producers of huge, fuel-wasting vehicles and proclaimed that AMC would only sell compact cars. For a few years, things were touch and go.

Then his signature vehicle, the Rambler, took off. Suddenly AMC was making money hand over fist, the Rambler was the third most popular car in the nation, and Romney, who often appeared in and even wrote the Rambler ads himself, became both a millionaire and a folk hero. You have to say this for him: he had ambition, brains, and drive. He rose to the leadership of a car manufacturer without having a college degree. Americans have always loved self-made industrial leaders, and soon George Romney was on the cover of *Time* magazine.

Most men, at some point in their lives, are troubled by self-doubt. I don't think Romney ever was, certainly not when I knew him. He had a handsome face, movie-star chin, and shock of hair, and I have to say, he was hardworking and extremely confident.

He rigorously followed the Mormon practice of not smoking, swearing, or drinking alcohol or even coffee. He was totally devoted to his wife, Lenore, and gave vast sums to the Mormon Church.

But he was clearly devoted to himself as well, and anyone could smell that he wanted a political career. In 1959 he launched Citizens for Michigan, which was billed as a nonpartisan group formed to study the state's problems and produce new solutions.

He came to Alpena that year to speak about Citizens for Michigan, and I sat in the audience as just one more small-town lawyer. I listened closely, and it was clear to me that they only solution he had was to call a convention and write a new state constitution. Anyone with an ounce of political sophistication could see that Citizens for Michigan was designed to launch Romney into statewide politics as a crusading "reformer."

If that sounds a bit cynical, it's because I was, even then. But I have to admit George played the role superbly well. Campaigning in shirtsleeves, grinning at plain folks, and brandishing petitions, he managed to get a call for a constitutional convention on the November 1960 ballot—and got people to approve one. Then he ran for election as a delegate, naturally, a move that did accomplish one thing: it forced Romney to declare that he was a member of the Republican Party, which surprised no one.

Thanks in part to a lot of editorial support from the newspapers, his new constitution, as I noted earlier, narrowly passed in April 1963, a few months after he had taken over as governor.

Though we got off to a somewhat rocky start, I gradually developed respect for him. For one thing, despite claims to the contrary by his son Mitt, the 2012 presidential nominee, George Romney wouldn't have been welcome in today's GOP.

Michigan had no income tax when Romney came to power, in part because of entrenched opposition from legislative Republicans. But Romney was not an antitax zealot. He believed that a government, like a business, cannot run if it is undercapitalized. He worked hard on his fellow Republicans in the legislature, and in 1967, after being reelected to a third term by a landslide, he finally won passage of a corporate and individual income tax. That was hard, but not as hard as it would be today.

Michigan was a booming state in the mid-1960s. The automotive industry and the national economy were roaring. Taxes were not seen as evil, even among some Republicans. To be sure, those in the legislature did, it was true, fear the wrath of the farmers and the business sectors if they raised taxes. But there was no Tea Party and few fanatics who thought all taxes were bad. True, the income tax we got—originally a mere 2.6 percent—was not as fair as it should have been. Michigan's constitution outlawed any graduated income tax and still does. However, I have to salute Governor Romney for hanging in there and getting a necessary, if unpopular, measure passed. If George Romney was convinced of the righteousness of his cause, he would go through a brick wall fighting for it. By the time he got the income tax passed, I had developed a good deal of respect for Romney. This was in large part because he was sincerely and strongly progressive on civil rights.

When Barry Goldwater, his party's 1964 presidential nominee, refused to support the historic Civil Rights Act, Romney refused to support him. That may have helped him win reelection that year, but I don't think that's why he did it. Even during World War II, he had successfully fought the Federal Housing Administration to come up with better housing for black workers near the Willow Run plant. What made this more remarkable was that he took these stands even though his church at the time did not believe blacks were equal to whites and would not allow them to be members of the lay clergy.

But while our relationship became much stronger as time went by, the last two years of Romney's governorship were not especially happy ones for him. In the wee hours of Sunday, July 23, 1967, only a few days after he signed the income tax bills, a police raid on an after-hours drinking joint in Detroit's inner city mushroomed into what then became the biggest urban riot in American history.

This was happening just as polls showed that Romney was the leading candidate for the GOP presidential nomination the following year—and the Harris polls showed him beating President Lyndon Johnson,

Naturally, LBJ didn't want to do Romney any favors.

When the riot worsened, Romney and Detroit mayor Jerry Cavanagh wanted Washington to send troops. As a fellow Democrat, I called U.S. attorney general Ramsey Clark. He was sympathetic but told us he could only do that if Romney formally declared the city was in a state of civil insurrection. The governor didn't want to do that because that could have given insurance companies the loophole they needed to avoid paying for property damage. As they dithered, the riot got worse.

Early on, the police told the mayor the riot was out of control. Cavanagh, who was only thirty-nine years old, remained calm, cool, and collected. Though he and I were to have our differences, he was then the picture of courageous leadership throughout what he must have known was the worst crisis any mayor could face, one that, as he may have suspected even then, would forever damage his career.

Once he was told the police had lost control, he asked the governor to declare a state of emergency so that the Michigan National Guard could be called up to quell the riot. I immediately prepared a state of emergency edict. The governor signed it, and—under heavy police escort—took off for Detroit. I heard they were setting up a command post at Detroit's forbidding and spooky old police headquarters at 1300 Beaubien.

I was beginning to realize that I needed to see for myself what was going on. But before I could move, word came that both the governor and mayor wanted me in Detroit—right away. So Leon Cohan and I boarded a heavily loaded helicopter at state police headquarters in East Lansing. It was us, the pilot, and two state troopers armed with automatic weapons.

We didn't arrive in the city till after dark. We could see the fires burning in the riot area as we approached. Today many people talk about the riot as though it engulfed and destroyed the entire city of Detroit. In fact, nearly all of the rioting took place over two square miles, which amounted to a little more than 1 percent of the city's total area.

That, however, was more than bad enough. Even with the copter's blades whirring far above the scene, we could hear the crack of gunfire from the streets below.

Eventually we landed at Detroit City Airport, a relatively small facility on the city's east side. Two armed police troopers put us in an unmarked police car and told us to sit on the floor.

We soon learned that we were in far greater danger than we had initially thought—and it wasn't primarily the rioters' fault. We were shocked to hear one of the troopers who flew with us say that our helicopter was carrying several hundred rounds of live ammunition from the local armory. What's more, gunfire from the riot just missed our chopper as it began to descend for a landing. Now, I don't hold many grudges. But I have to say that I have never forgiven whoever was in command of the state police for sending his state's attorney general and his deputy into a riot zone in a helicopter that was a flying bomb. Had one bullet hit that ammo, had something sent one spark into that helicopter, you wouldn't be reading this story.

But though we survived, it was clear to me from the start that there would be no winners, politically or otherwise.

Soon after we landed, we saw another large helicopter arrive carrying cameras, photographers, and news crews from New York. "Before this is over, we're going to look like South Africa out of control," I succinctly told Leon, who was worried about the media. We were both right. Detroit's national image began to change that day, and not for the better, a slide that continued for decades, right up to the day that the city declared bankruptcy in July 2013.

Eventually I got to police headquarters and managed to commandeer a small room, where Leon and I set up shop, assisted by a couple of assistant attorneys general from our Detroit office. We did whatever was needed. I was involved in all the conferences that took place between Washington and Detroit.

President Lyndon Johnson and his special envoy, Cyrus Vance, spoke constantly to Governor Romney and Mayor Cavanagh.

I was there to offer whatever advice and legal counsel were needed. But I deliberately did not seek the spotlight, for a good reason. As I told Leon at the time, "There's no glory for those charged with putting down a riot." None, no matter what.

You don't have to be a political genius to see why. Television was bringing images of looters and rioters smashing store windows, stealing color televisions and furniture, and setting fires into people's homes. The viewing audience was not only disgusted and turned off by the violence, they were bound to be turned off by anybody connected with it—including the good people who were trying to stop it.

Finally, after a day and a half, LBJ ordered thousands of paratroopers from the U.S. Army's 82nd Airborne Division into Detroit. What was especially devastating is that he went on national television to announce his decision, referring several times to what he said was Governor Romney's inability to control the riot.

That certainly hurt Romney's campaign, though Lyndon Johnson didn't look very good either. But it was Romney himself who would fatally wound his brief presidential campaign. On August 31, 1967, barely a month after the riot ended, the governor went on Lou Gordon's popular local TV talk show. The war in Vietnam came up. Romney, who had previously been a supporter of the war, had visited South Vietnam in November 1965, soon after the United States began massive troop deployments. "When I came back from Vietnam, I'd just had the greatest brainwashing that anyone can get," he said. He then announced that he no longer believed U.S. participation in the war was a good idea. The problem wasn't so much his turning against what by then was a terribly divisive war but using the term "brainwashing."

Nobody likes the idea of being in the hands of a president who could be "brainwashed," especially in a nuclear age. Images came to mind of the zombie-like assassin from the movie *The Manchurian Candidate*. Political cartoonists had a field day. U.S. senator Eugene McCarthy, himself a Democratic antiwar candidate, uttered the most devastating comment: "I would have thought a light rinse would have done it."

Romney trudged gallantly on, campaigning through the snows of New Hampshire, but two weeks before the voting it was clear even to him that he didn't have a chance. He dropped out rather than face humiliating defeat. Richard Nixon won the primary, the nomination, and the election that November and then offered Romney the cabinet post of secretary of Housing and Urban Development (HUD).

Romney resigned as governor and took it. He served four years in Nixon's cabinet. Most accounts say he did a decent job as secretary, but HUD was never important to the Nixon crew, and he was never part of the "in crowd," which, given the people around Nixon, was a good thing.

The worst mistake he made during those years had nothing to do with Washington, ironically; it was his pushing his wife, Lenore, to run for the U.S. Senate against the popular incumbent, Phil Hart. Lenore Romney won the GOP nomination in 1970—barely—on the strength of her last name. But she lost by more than two to one, the worst defeat any Republican has ever suffered in a Senate race.

After Nixon's first term, Romney resigned, just in time to avoid the devastation of Watergate. He went home to Bloomfield Hills and lived an active life volunteering for various causes, taking care of his family, and advising his son Mitt on his budding political career.

Death took him while he was exercising on his treadmill one morning in July 1995, when he was eighty-eight years old. Nobody ever says this, but the best parts of George Romney's legacy were the state income tax and an enormous and utterly necessary expansion of state government.

Theodore White, the esteemed journalist and author of the *Making of the President* series, called Romney "an honest and decent man simply not cut out to be President of the United States." Add brash, headstrong, temperamental, and stubborn, and—at least based on my experience—that about sums him up.

But he was a man of integrity, and the voters knew it. And here in Michigan, he never lost an election. That's not a bad epitaph.

15

THE TUMULTUOUS 1970s:
THE MILLIKEN YEARS

When George Romney resigned to serve in Nixon's cabinet, it was the first time since World War II that a Michigan governor had failed to complete his term. The new governor would be Bill Milliken, who, thanks to Michigan's new constitution, was the first lieutenant governor in the state ever to be elected on a ticket with the governor. Before that, they had been elected separately. Had it not been for this, Romney might well have been succeeded by a Democrat. In fact, during his first two-year term, the lieutenant governor was a Democrat—the irrepressible T. John Lesinski, who, in an odd way, may have owed his success in part to me.

Back when we were both a couple of young law students, T. John was thinking about a run for the legislature. Except he was going to do so using his full first name, which was Thaddeus. "That won't work," I told him. "If you want to be a priest, you can be Thaddeus. If you want to get elected to anything, you'd better run as T. John." He took my advice and got elected in 1950 to the first of five terms in the state legislature.

He was elected lieutenant governor in 1960 and then, to George Romney's discomfort, managed to narrowly win reelection the day Romney beat Swainson. T. John used to have fun doing small things to needle Romney, who had little sense of humor. When the governor was out of state, for example, he would use his limousine and leave his cheap, smelly cigars in the ashtray. Other times, he would issue proclamations as the acting governor of Michigan. He knew those two years were his last as lieutenant governor; in 1964, he got himself elected to the Michigan Court of Appeals and served with distinction for a dozen years.

Bill Milliken then succeeded him. Milliken, who served four years as number two, was always incredibly boyish in appearance. His first experience in politics came after he was elected to the state senate in 1960. Though he was then almost forty, state capitol security stopped him more than once to say, "I'm sorry, Sonny. You can't use that elevator; it is only for senators." Rather than being offended, he thought that was funny. Bill Milliken was a throwback to a political type seldom seen in politics today, what I would call the "patrician aristocrat." This is someone born into wealth and privilege who, nevertheless, seeks political office usually, at least in part, because of a drive and a desire to serve his or her fellow citizens. The Rockefellers, for example, fall into this category, as do the Kennedys. However, throughout my long career, I met only two people from Michigan who were clearly aristocrats in politics.

One was the legendary G. Mennen "Soapy" Williams, who left the governor's chair about a year before I became attorney general but whom I came to know through various campaigns, and especially in working with him when he served on Michigan's Supreme Court. Though he was born into wealth and privilege, he became a New Deal–style Democrat committed to serving his fellow man.

But I worked much more closely with the other great patrician aristocrat of my career: William Grawn Milliken, the longest-serving governor in Michigan's history and one of the very best. Milliken came from a well-off merchant family in Traverse City; his grandfather founded what for many years was the largest department store in northern Michigan, J. W. Milliken, Inc. Both his father and grandfather had served in the state senate before him, and all were progressive, liberal Republicans. All three men had graduated from Yale. I have a hunch that in today's world all the Millikens would have been Democrats. But in the Traverse City of their era, Democrats were nearly as scarce as Dodo birds.

Bill Milliken was much tougher than he looked. He served with distinction in World War II as a waist gunner on a B-24 bomber. He survived crash landings, being wounded in the stomach by a shell fragment, and being shot at by Germans during fifty tough missions in Europe. Following the war, he expanded the family department store business, opening Milliken's first-ever satellite stores and vastly increasing the company's profits.

But politics was in his blood, and it was his turn to win his father's and grandfather's old senate seat in November 1960. My first real encounter with Milliken set the tone for our long—and pleasant—working relationship.

The Michigan Press Association had their annual meeting in Traverse City in the spring of 1962, just months after I had been appointed attorney general and only about a year after Milliken first was elected to the state senate. Civil rights struggles were much in the news then, and the press thought it might be interesting to have the young Democratic attorney general debate the new local Republican state senator on "civil rights problems in Michigan" at their annual dinner.

Well, if they expected fireworks, they were likely disappointed. What they heard wasn't really a debate but two men who were strongly pro–civil rights explaining their views.

We were both young—I was thirty-seven; he was just forty but looked much younger, as he did throughout his life. The only real difference between us was in the way we approached the problem.

What I remember, however, was that both Bill and Helen Milliken seemed to instinctively sense that I was the stranger there, and they both went out of their way to make me feel welcome. I liked them both immediately, and that feeling only deepened throughout the years. Perhaps because he came from a political family whose department store business depended on good relations with everybody, Bill Milliken understood the way in which people with differing views and background ought to treat each other.

His ability to get along with people was almost uncanny. He was a patrician aristocrat from a district that, he used to say, didn't have a single black voter in it when he was first elected. I was a hardscrabble, big-city kid who put himself through the University of Detroit while Milliken was going to Yale. Nevertheless, we got along, then and, essentially, always. That shouldn't surprise anyone who knows that, much later, Milliken developed both a close friendship and a political partnership with Detroit's first black mayor, Coleman Young, a man whose higher education was the streets.

But for me, having Milliken in the governor's seat was like a breath of fresh air. As I've said, my relationship with Romney was sometimes rocky. Milliken seemed to know instinctively that we had different responsibilities and represented different constituencies. He left me the space and turf I needed to carry out my legal agenda. In return, I never interfered in the slightest with his political agenda, which, if truth be told, was mainly an enlightened one.

Most of the time, our staffs worked together on complex problems. On those rare occasions in which we disagreed, we sat down together and quietly worked out honorable compromises. The Milliken years were, in fact, the closest thing to an "era of good feeling" Michigan politics has ever had, at least in my lifetime.

The voters seemed to appreciate his style, too. Less than two years after he stepped into George Romney's shoes, Milliken won an extremely close election against Sander Levin, then a rising young leader in the state senate. That 1970 election is notable because it was one of the nation's first punch-card voting disasters.

Detroit had gone to a system of punch-card voting that year, which was billed as the latest, most modern, fastest and best way of recording votes. On election night the punch cards were fed into a computer—which promptly got stuck and wouldn't spit them out.

It was three days before we knew for sure that Bill Milliken had eked out a narrow, 44,409-vote victory over Levin, in what was otherwise a solidly Democratic year. (Thirty years later, the nation would get a much more painful lesson in the hazards of punch-card voting with Florida's disputed votes in the 2000 presidential election.)

Four years later, in a 1974 rematch, Milliken defeated Levin again, this time by almost three times the margin of victory in the first election, something that was especially remarkable that year. Three months before, Richard Nixon had become the first and only president ever to resign. Soon afterward, Gerald Ford ignited another huge controversy by pardoning Nixon. That November was, as a result, one of the worst years for Republicans in history. But somehow partisan attacks barely touched Bill Milliken, perhaps because his administrations were virtually scandal-free.

As time went on, in fact, he seemed to the majority of voters to be an almost bipartisan or nonpartisan figure. What many people today most remember about his time as governor was the famous "odd couple" relationship and friendship Milliken forged with Detroit mayor Coleman Young.

On one level, it is hard to imagine a more unlikely pair: Milliken, the Yale-educated patrician from an upper-class family, who grew up in a city where there were essentially no African Americans, and Coleman Young, the street-tough, profane black politician who had been close to the far left in the 1940s and 1950s and whose favorite word was one best left abbreviated as MF—a word he wasn't shy about using every chance he got.

The two men forged a remarkable partnership, one in which Milliken did everything he could to help Detroit, from ordering state police to help patrol Detroit freeways to getting the legislature to help fund institutions like the Detroit Zoo and Detroit Institute of Arts. This was extremely unpopular with the right wing of his party but also led to Milliken's being the only GOP candidate for governor in modern times to carry Wayne County.

My respect for his decency and dignity steadily increased throughout the fourteen years he held the governorship and I was attorney general. We both served in our offices longer than anyone in Michigan history, and unless the term limits that were later enacted are ever repealed, those records are bound to stand forever.

However, although working with Milliken was pleasant, you may be surprised to know that as attorney general I didn't see him—or any of the later governors I worked with—all that often. Though I was technically every governor's lawyer for official matters as well as the state's top attorney, often I would meet personally and privately with each of them no more than once a month. That is, unless there was a crisis, and then we might be together for days, as I was with Romney during the Detroit riots.

The reason we did not have to spend more time together was because of a system I invented that evolved out of my earlier difficulties with Romney. In my first meeting with each new governor, I would tell him, "You can count on confidentiality from me on any matter before us. In time you'll find that you'll eventually have leaks from your own departments, but never will it happen from my office." That's a promise, I am proud to say, my staff and I always kept. Regardless of their politics, I regarded my relationship with any of my governors as a matter of attorney-client privilege. Over thirty-seven years, we never had a single violation of that trust.

The way I made things work was simple. I assigned to each governor an assistant attorney general who was technically on my payroll but who essentially reported to the executive. That helped eliminate confusion and streamline everything. At least once a week, my deputy, Leon Cohan, or later, Stanley Steinborn, would meet with the governor's representative to discuss any legal issues. They were also in frequent phone contact, and I would occasionally take part in those calls when they felt they needed me.

Milliken, I have to say, was easy to work with. Even in the midst of crisis, he remained calm, deliberative, and a good listener. I really got to know his style during the worst crisis his administration ever faced, the PBB poisoned cattle feed mess.

Ironically, though Milliken is remembered today as the most environment-friendly governor in Michigan's history, this was one of the state's biggest environmental disasters. Sometime in the spring of 1973, the Michigan Chemical Company in St. Louis accidentally shipped a fire retardant to Farm Bureau Services, which supplies thousands of farmers with cattle feed. The stuff contained a chemical called PBB (polybrominated biphenyl), which was highly poisonous. Thanks to mistakes made at the Missouri plant, the PBB had been labeled as cattle feed, and Farm Bureau Services sold it to farmers. Within months, farmers were reporting that something was terribly wrong with their livestock. It took a year to trace what the poison was.

Governor Milliken and I knew fairly early on what was happening, thanks to secret briefings we were given by the Michigan Agriculture Department. But neither the department's notoriously obstructionist director, B. Dale Ball, nor the governor himself moved fast enough to get out in front of the issue.

Years later, the governor, to his credit, admitted as much. "I wish I had more effectively carried the story to the public as an educational issue. I didn't adequately explain what happened," he told his biographer, Dave Dempsey. "No one deliberately set out to put the poison in cattle feed. People always (falsely) assumed it was due to some fault or failing of government . . . it got out of hand."* Out of hand it soon was, with angry farmers going to the press, and lurid images of dying cattle all over TV news broadcasts.

There was also a growing panic over the perceived public health threat, especially after tests showed that 95 percent of Michigan residents had residues of PBB in their bodies. I knew that a public relations disaster was building, but thanks to the principle of attorney-client privilege, I couldn't say very much in public. Early on, the governor and the agriculture department resisted calls to destroy severely infected cattle herds because that would mean destroying farm families' livelihoods. Gradually, however, it became apparent there really was no choice but to do just that. Before the crisis was over, according to a tally in the *Detroit Free Press*, the state would slaughter more than 23,000 head of cattle, thousands of sheep, pigs, and other animals, and 1.5 million chickens.

The big question, however, was what to do with all the dead cows. I sat in on one meeting with the governor and his Department of Agriculture officials, where their suggestions grew stranger and stranger, not to mention out of touch with all political reality. They were talking about either shipping the cows to Ohio, where they had found a landfill that would accept their bodies, and killing and burying them there or killing them first and then taking their corpses there. I couldn't believe what I was hearing.

Finally I asked if the room could be cleared so that I could speak privately with Bill Milliken for a few moments. When we were alone I said, "Look, Governor, shipping those cows out of state is absolutely the most ridiculous thing I have ever heard. I can tell you right now that the governor of Ohio, the senators from Ohio, and every politician in that state will be standing at the state line posing as heroes, saying, 'Thou shalt not bring those diseased cows into the sovereign state of Ohio.'" That would further mean, I argued, that we would be

---

* Dave Dempsey, *William G. Milliken: Michigan's Passionate Moderate* (Ann Arbor: University of Michigan Press, 2006).

portrayed on the national evening news as shady characters trying to send diseased cattle across state lines.

I didn't have to mention how that might affect his chances in the next election. Governor Milliken listened carefully. I knew he needed to hear an alternative. You don't have to have an MBA to know that it doesn't do any good to criticize an approach unless you have an alternative solution. Fortunately, I'd done my homework. "Governor," I said, "the experts tell us that PBB does not pass in the ground and won't get into the groundwater, that it's inert and whatever the disease is, it's not going to be passed through the ground. But in order to assuage the public and assure them, we can dig and put in a clay-lined pit on our own [state] property, in a rural or wooded area in the northern part of the state. We can get rid of the cows right there, bury them in the pit, bind them down with lots of earth, and the problem will be over. We're going to be ridiculed and criticized no matter what. Why not minimize the criticism and do what's scientifically sound and, from a public relations and political standpoint, allows us to maintain integrity?"

The governor seemed to think that made sense and said, "I'll think it over." Well, it wasn't more than a day or so later that I got word that Milliken had decided that was exactly right. As expected, when we announced our decision, there were noisy local protests.

We ended up burying the cattle in two landfills—one in Kalkaska and the other in Mio, in Oscoda County. The pits were excavated and dug, and the infected cattle were taken there, destroyed, and buried.

What impressed me most about Milliken's handling of the disaster is not that he took my advice but that he remained cool throughout the crisis. Neither then nor at any other time in his fourteen years in office did I ever see him have a temper tantrum of the sort Romney displayed. More important, Milliken wasn't interested in finger-pointing or trying to blame anyone else.[‡] On the contrary, he showed great courage. Angry Mio residents burned both of us in effigy near the burial site.

To his credit, the governor went there and spoke to an angry crowd, with his effigy swinging behind him, attempting, his biographer said, "to discuss and reason with them." Later he would quip, "But I was in good company. Frank Kelley was also being hung in effigy." That, indeed, I was.

[‡] Incidentally, I still feel bound by the rules of attorney-client privilege when it comes to all confidential discussions I had with any living governors. In this case, I asked for and received Governor Milliken's permission to discuss what went on behind the scenes during the PBB crisis.

The governor's unwillingness to point fingers didn't mean he wasn't politically astute. He went to Rick Halbert, a member of the family who first reported the PBB contamination, added him to his staff as an agricultural advisor, and stepped up efforts to have mechanisms in place to be ready to deal with other toxic hazards.

Gradually the PBB crisis was diffused. It occurred too late to affect the 1974 elections, but there were efforts made to use it against the governor in 1978. But by that time, most people in Michigan realized we had taken a sensible, balanced, and fair approach.

The crisis did cost the governor some votes in the affected rural counties. But he swept to victory by a landslide, and I won by an even larger margin, even carrying—to my astonishment—the counties where the dead cattle had been buried and my effigy had been hung.

Today, nearly half a century later, we still don't know what the human cost of the PBB contamination will be. Some studies have shown that women with the highest levels of PBB have a somewhat increased risk of developing breast cancer. But fortunately the massive birth defects and other consequences that some predicted have not come to pass, and there is general agreement that the crisis made Michigan much more ready to face and hopefully prevent future environmental disasters.

Bill Milliken and I continued to serve together for nearly a decade after that. He was by far the most bipartisan of any governor I served with. That doesn't mean we always agreed on issues—we didn't. That doesn't mean he wasn't a partisan Republican when he needed to be. I experienced that myself once.

Possibly my only real disappointment with the governor was when I asked him to appoint my old law partner from Alpena, John Mack, who was then a district judge, to a vacancy on the circuit court. Despite my plea, Milliken named a Republican instead. I was sorry but not angry; I realized the pressure on him from his own party to name one of their own had to be tremendous. Later he in fact apologized to me in a letter for not appointing my friend. Any other governor from the opposing party would likely have just ignored my request.

On the other hand, he once took the unusual step of naming me to head a state trade mission to Taiwan. Later he went out of his way to personally help save my reputation.

Investigative reporting became a big national fad in the years after Watergate. For a while, it seemed that every newspaper and broadcast outlet had to have its own investigative team. Some of these teams were on the level and did the public a service by exposing corruption. That was more than fine in my book. In cases that were clearly legitimate, we were happy to have the Michigan attorney general's office work with journalists to help them gather evidence and uncover corruption. This led to a number of important exposés.

We shared the credit for the good of the public. But there was one particular scurrilous radio reporter who got it into his head that I, Frank J. Kelley, was corrupt. He, I was told, had someone write a letter to the state highway department claiming I was up to no good and asking for an investigation. He then called the department to verify that the letter had been received. They confirmed that.

He then began broadcasting that he had learned from sources that the Michigan Highway Department was about to conduct an investigation into allegedly corrupt activities by Michigan attorney general Frank Kelley. I called the reporter himself, and then the station manager, and asked if they had any evidence of this. They did not, as I very well knew. I politely asked them to stop this sheer demagoguery. They refused, saying, "We know a letter went to the highway department on this matter."

The fact is, as anyone in state government can tell you, we are constantly deluged with letters alleging everything and anything, 99 percent of which have no validity whatsoever. We received letters saying that the governor was a Russian spy, while others claimed that space aliens control our every move. Nevertheless, the station kept it up, broadcasting this about me every weekend, when news was slow. Thousands of people were hearing this trash.

Finally, feeling desperate, I turned to Bill Milliken, explained the situation, and asked if he would call the station's owners and inform them that I was not being investigated by the highway department or any other state agency. "I think it is terrible that you are being subjected to that, Frank," he said. "Of course I will." He did exactly that, telling them that if anybody would know if I was being investigated it was the governor and that there was nothing whatsoever to this. Governor Milliken then virtually ordered them to stop, and this time they did. I'll never forget that.

Nobody ever has served the state as governor longer than William G. Milliken, and now that governors have term limits, no one ever will. I found him a fascinating man who, I believe, was in politics in part because of something instilled in him by his father and grandfather. Bill Milliken more than lived up to his family's expectations. He might easily have gone to the U.S. Senate or a cabinet post, but he had no desire whatsoever to do that. Toward the end of his final term, I noticed that he tended to leave for Traverse City earlier and stay away from Lansing longer whenever he could.

I wasn't surprised at all when, in late 1981, he announced he would not be a candidate for a fourth term. He retired gracefully and with dignity, and with a few rare exceptions, he stayed out of politics. Occasionally he would respond to press queries or issue an endorsement of some candidate he admired, but that was about it.

From time to time, we would talk and he would tell me, "Frank, remember that there is life after politics." He would add that he and his amazing wife, Helen, one of the major forces for feminism in her time, were enjoying themselves, and I believe they were.

I eventually realized that Milliken and I were different in one important respect. I am and always have been a people person. But Bill is, I believe, fundamentally a loner. After politics, he served on a number of boards, in Washington and elsewhere. He once told me that he loved leaving his home in Traverse City and driving long distances by himself across the country to corporate meetings. He said that those hours alone in his car were some of his happiest and most contented.

Michigan became a better place because of the career of William G. Milliken, and the standards of decency and civility he set are sadly missed today. After a long battle with cancer, Helen Milliken, to whom he had been married since he came back from World War II, died in November 2012.

One night more than a year later, the governor called me and said that I had been one of the five to ten most important people in his life. I was deeply moved.

Someday after I am gone, I only hope that someone writes that my performance and integrity deserve to be ranked with his.

16

MY PROTÉGÉ
BECOMES GOVERNOR:
THE BLANCHARD YEARS

One of the most satisfying things about my long career as attorney general was the opportunity I had to hire a lot of brilliant young lawyers who went on to have famous careers. They've included a U.S. senator, a governor, three congressmen, and many state senators, representatives, judges, and distinguished Michigan attorneys.

So many of my protégés have done so well, in fact, that I have probably gotten more credit than I deserve, as some sort of great "godfather" of Michigan politics.

Now, nobody ever said Frank J. Kelley didn't have an ego—just ask either of my wives or any of my three kids.

But the truth is that virtually all the young lawyers I hired who went on to greater things would have had fine and distinguished public careers even if they never knew me because they were all deeply motivated and talented to begin with.

Now I have to say that one of them, now-retired Ingham County Circuit judge Lawrence Glazer, would take exception to that. I initially hired him right out of law school in September 1968 to write my speeches. He was excellent but soon wanted to be transferred to legal work. He had a distinguished career on the bench and became a fine writer, as his biography of John Swainson shows. After reading an early version of this chapter, he wrote a note to the editor: "FJK is too modest here. He was a great role model, and a great mentor as well, for all of us who were interested in a public career."

Well, who am I to argue with a judge?

I suppose I helped some of my assistants with a bit of advice here and there or simply by trying to set a good example. I do know that I tried to be a good professional role model for them. I consciously tried always to act in the public interest and keep my doubts and insecurities to myself. It took me years to realize that every decent politician should always question him- or herself. History shows, after all, that nothing is scarier than people with power who believe they are always right.

What I tried to do is always be a man my father would have been proud of. And that meant, among other things, trying to give a hand up to the next generation. Those included a young Harvard Law school graduate I hired very early on, granting his request to work mostly out of our Detroit office. We soon made him head of our civil rights division, and he worked exceptionally hard.

Then one day in 1969 he asked for a meeting and told me he wanted to resign to run for Detroit City Council. He explained that he thought he could make more of a difference that way. Naturally I hated to lose him—but I frankly agreed. I always knew he was going places. His father was a lawyer; his uncle was a federal judge. His older brother, now a congressman, was gearing up for the first of two narrowly unsuccessful runs for governor.

Not surprisingly, my former assistant was soon Detroit City Council president. Nine years after he left my staff, he ran against the man who defeated me for the U.S. Senate—and beat him.

By now you may have guessed his name: Senator Carl Levin, who went on to become the powerful chair of the Armed Services Committee and serve Michigan well for a record thirty-six years.

Other distinguished Kelley alums on my staff early in their careers are too numerous to list here, but they include congressmen Bob Carr and Dennis Hertel, both young men with great ability.

But the man whose career was most linked with mine, both in legend and fact, also served in Congress—but is best remembered as the first Democratic chief executive of Michigan in two decades: Governor James J. Blanchard. I don't know whether he realizes it or not, but I considered Jim a special protégé—but not for reasons some think.

There is a now well-known—and totally silly—story about my relationship with Blanchard. The details vary, but according to the usual version of this legend, I originally hired him to carry my briefcase and be my driver. Eventually he got interested in politics. Next thing anyone knew he was in Congress, where he took charge of the 1979–80 "bailout" that saved the Chrysler Corporation (not for the last time) and then magically emerged as governor. Naturally all this was because of the contacts he had made driving around Frank J. Kelley, political master of the universe.

Flattering as that might be, there is very little truth in it. I did indeed hire Jim soon after he graduated from the University of Minnesota law school, but not as an assistant or a driver. Nor was this his first job; he had worked briefly for Secretary of State James Hare. Blanchard's original "godfather," in fact, was none other than my then-assistant Larry Glazer, who had known him since both men were teenagers and recommended him to me.

What is true is that when I hired him, Jim Blanchard, who was then twenty-seven, had the face of a teenager. But he was clearly smart, knowledgeable, enthusiastic, and mad about politics and government. Soon I found myself calling him into the office to handle special political or legal assignments for me. We talked politics a lot because I sensed this was his true passion. Also, I liked him. He was good company, and I began to sometimes take him with me to political appearances after hours.

After five years, he left my staff to run for Congress against U.S. representative Robert Huber, an extreme right-wing Republican. Huber was far too conservative for his district but had beaten my good friend State Senator Daniel Cooper in the same election that saw my candidacy for the U.S. Senate destroyed by the busing issue.

The landslide suffered by that year's Democratic presidential nominee, George McGovern, didn't do our party any favors.

But what a difference twenty-four months can make. Two years later, Nixon had just resigned, the GOP was tarred with the Watergate scandal, and Blanchard, then just thirty-two, narrowly won a crowded primary and went on to crush Huber by a landslide.

Flash-forward to seven years later. Jim was then in his fourth term and had won a lot of praise for helping save Chrysler.

That's when I went to Washington for a long lunch with my former assistant attorney general. We went, not to the House dining room, but to a restaurant where we could have some privacy. We talked politics for a while, but I was there with one of my trusted assistants—another young lawyer named Kelly Keenan—and an agenda. I wanted Jim Blanchard to consider giving up his seat in Congress to run for governor of Michigan.

Blanchard, I could see, was not only intrigued by the idea; it was obvious to me that he had already been thinking about it.

Know how I knew? As we talked, he unwrapped and lit up a cigar. For years he had been a fairly heavy cigarette smoker, and for years I had been trying to get him to quit for health reasons. Besides all the well-known risks of smoking, it was bad for the kind of stamina you'd need for a statewide campaign. I had told him that if he moved to cigars, it would then be easier to quit altogether.

Naturally I was pleased. If you think I was reacting somewhat like a father, you are right. Which goes to the heart of the relationship between the two of us. Blanchard's father left the family when he was nine years old. Walked out and was barely in the boy's life after that. But you would never have known that from the way he acted. He never showed a trace of self-pity. Instead, from the time he was a youngster, Blanchard, with the strong support of his mother, Rosalie, determined he was going to be a success—and he was.

But I knew how important my father was to me, as anyone who has read this far knows. My dad was a big part of my life till the day he unexpectedly died when I was already a lawyer, husband, and father. I've continued to miss him ever since.

I reasoned that it must have been damaging to Blanchard's psychology to have a father who just suddenly abandoned him when he was a nine-year-old boy.

My guess is that he saw me as something of a father substitute, professionally at least. Actually, I both consciously and—I am sure—unconsciously encouraged all my young lawyers to think of me as something like a father figure. My philosophy was, whenever possible, to hire young bright people fresh out of law school.

This gave me an opportunity to exercise my impulses to teach. But the learning wasn't just one way; my lawyers often came armed with some of the freshest developments in the law. They were also eager, idealistic, energetic, and a bargain for the state of Michigan. By that I mean that I could hire them for far less than I would have had to pay a highly experienced lawyer. Nor would they have to unlearn all sorts of bad habits. That had certainly been the case with the young Blanchard. But I knew something else, too.

No matter how well I treated him or any other young man who worked for me who had been abandoned by his father, he would never completely trust me. The closer we became, the more their subconscious fears would be stirred that I, too, might abandon them. Which meant they had to psychologically protect themselves from that possibility. You may scoff at this as amateur pop psychology, but over my long life, I have made a study of this.

I've seen patterns, over and over again. Naturally everybody has something in life they must overcome, and it is certainly true that what doesn't destroy us makes us tougher. But in the case of essentially fatherless sons, what I have seen is that they are never really able to trust men old enough to be their fathers. As a result, they tend to surround themselves with people who are basically their age or younger. That can be a weakness.

We saw this with President Bill Clinton, another fatherless child, who staffed his first administration with people his age or, in many cases, considerably younger, with disastrous results.

Jim Blanchard made many of the same mistakes, with similar consequences that almost—but not quite—ruined his governorship before it began. But that was all in the future the day the three of us had lunch in Washington.

It was clear that the young congressman was tantalized by the possibility of running. He wanted to know what a successful race would cost. The good news, I told him, was that I had strong reason to believe Bill Milliken wasn't going to run again. Winning would cost far less if he didn't have to take on an incumbent. This was a year after Ronald Reagan had become president. The economy was poor nationally, and it was worse in Michigan, where the state budget was running a deficit. Republicans, who had controlled the governorship for twenty years, were deeply unpopular.

Every sign pointed to a Democratic year. But I told Blanchard that he could not afford to delay. "You've got to make up your mind and announce early, if you are inclined to do this," I told him. Because of his successful leadership of the Chrysler rescue, I added, "There's nobody back home who is thinking of running as a Democrat who is as well-known as you are now." I told him that if he announced early, he would be able to line up endorsements, perhaps scare off any major competitors, and get a leg up on fund-raising.

Blanchard nodded slowly and then played devil's advocate, mentioning all the potential drawbacks. He would have to move back to his native Pleasant Ridge and put his son Jay in Michigan schools. While he talked, I reflected on a memo he had written me back when he was on my staff, detailing how I could run a successful race for governor. That was the last thing I wanted to do at that point. But his analysis was excellent, and reading it, I had realized how much Jim Blanchard loved politics and that he was a brilliant student of both the theory and the practice of politics and government.

By the time we left that very long and pleasant luncheon, I was smiling inside. I had no doubt whatsoever that he would run. Indeed, before long, he called a press conference and declared his candidacy for governor. Thanks in part to solid UAW support, he romped to victory in the Democratic primary, beating the party's previous nominee, Bill Fitzgerald, by three to one. Zolton Ferency, who as we've seen once had held considerable power behind the scenes, lost five to one.

Blanchard then ran a solid campaign, helped by a serious split among the Republicans, many of whom were angry conservatives who had increasingly resented Bill Milliken's moderate approach. They decisively turned down Milliken's choice to succeed him, Lt. Gov. James Brickley, and nominated a flamboyant insurance executive, Richard Headlee, who had a penchant for putting his foot in his mouth—as when he publicly insulted Helen Milliken, the governor's proudly feminist wife. L. Brooks Patterson, who was then the flamboyant young Oakland County prosecutor, was a close third.

In that primary election, 70 percent of Michigan Republicans essentially turned their backs on the moderate Milliken era. Ronald Reagan was in the White House, and the GOP nationally and in Michigan was rapidly moving to the right, something that continues today.

The general election campaign was marked by smooth professionalism on the part of Blanchard and a series of embarrassing missteps by Headlee, a newcomer to politics.

On election night, my onetime eager new assistant attorney general won a relatively easy victory. I was ecstatic. For the first time in two decades, I would be working not only with a governor of my own party but with someone whose career I had helped swing into high gear.

But Governor Blanchard would have a rocky start. When he took over in January 1983, the state was still mired in the aftereffects of stagflation and recession. Unemployment was high, and to make things worse, the state budget deficit was far worse than anyone imagined: $1.7 billion.

Soon after taking office, Blanchard asked the legislature for a steep temporary income tax increase, from 4.6 percent to 6.35 percent. Democrats narrowly controlled both the state house and senate, and the bill squeaked through. This turned out to be excellent public policy—and terrible politics. Few remember now, but the temporary tax hike solved the deficit problem brilliantly.

Today, confronted with such a shortfall, the politicians running things would probably have severely cut education and child-care programs. That didn't happen under Blanchard. The deficit was solved, the economy came roaring back, and the tax rate was returned to its original rate months ahead of schedule.

But not before Republicans cleverly pounced on the issue to launch recall campaigns that ousted two Democratic state senators in swing districts. They screamed the now-familiar GOP argument that any tax increase was bad and that Blanchard was going to tax Michigan into economic ruin and the poorhouse.

Republicans had then only recently started to revive that theme—and the mantra that we are all paying too much in taxes proved to be political dynamite. What could be more popular than that?

To my dismay, the new governor and his team didn't seem to know how to fight back. Just as I feared, his inner circle included no veterans of the state government wars. What was clear to me was that the "kids" around the governor were smart but too naïve and inexperienced to know how to counter the Republicans.

Democrats—including the governor himself—didn't take the recall drives seriously until it was too late. Under Michigan's constitution, it is ridiculously easy to recall legislators. All one has to do is collect a few thousand signatures—one-quarter of the number of people in the district who voted for governor in the previous election—and then voters are simply asked whether they want to remove the lawmaker in question or not.

That's not how most states do it. When recalls are held in Wisconsin, say, the officeholder faces a new election against a rival candidate. This gives the person voters are trying to recall a better chance to survive. After all, some voters are bound to like the officeholder's opponent even less. But whenever people get the chance to toss a particular politician out, with no thought to the consequences, they are far more likely to say yes. It's human nature, after all, to say, "Throw the bums out!" And that's just what happened to two fine Democratic state senators. Phil Mastin and David Serotkin were removed and then, under the recall law, were ineligible to run for reelection. When special elections were held to fill their seats, demoralized Democrats lost both races.

That gave control of the state senate to the GOP. What nobody imagined then was that, thanks to lucky breaks and gerrymandering, they would keep control for more than thirty years.

The Republican triumph would soon thrust into prominence the man who orchestrated it—the new Senate majority leader, thirty-five-year-old John Engler, a farm boy who had been elected to the legislature while still a student at Michigan State University. Despite lacking personal charisma and, in the early years, many social graces, he had evolved into an amazingly skilled political operative who eventually became one of Michigan's most powerful governors.

I confess I can't say I suspected how high Engler would rise when he took over the state senate in the fall of 1983. But I did know Blanchard was headed for serious trouble. Other Democratic Party leaders knew it, too. Blanchard's poll numbers and approval ratings were in free fall. Many old-timers were far harsher about his staff than I was, though I knew they weren't getting the job done. After being out of power for twenty years, the last thing Democrats needed was another one-term, failed governor.

They asked the governor to talk to me, and one day in late August, I was summoned to his office. I knew, even before that meeting, that Jim Blanchard's main problem was not policy related, his lack of political savvy, or an inability to govern. He was failing at public relations. Those around him, the group of neophytes he had hired, simply did not know how to convey to the public the positive things the governor was doing for Michigan. They didn't know how to get along with the media or get their story out to them. Something drastic had to happen.

Why didn't a bright guy like Blanchard see this and fix it?

Simple. His problem was that being governor—especially a new governor in a time of financial crisis—was so overwhelming a challenge, personally as well as politically that he didn't have time to handle and manage his relationship with the media as well.

Blanchard needed two things: a skilled, seasoned PR expert and an equally competent and tough office manager/chief of staff.

Fortunately I had part of the answer for him. Stanley Steinborn, who became my deputy in 1973 after Leon Cohan left for the private sector after my Senate bid, had good people sense. He told me about a bright young professional named Rick Cole who was exactly what Blanchard needed. Then in his early thirties, Cole had already started his own political public relations firm and had served as executive secretary to the state senate majority leader. What's more, he had managed to earn both a master's and a doctoral degree in education from Michigan State and was currently working in marketing and public relations in the Department of Commerce. I knew enough to trust Steinborn's instincts.

I also suspected strongly, as I have said, that Jim Blanchard would be very reluctant to seek help from someone he saw as a father figure. Because he was in fact seeking my help, I knew he was desperate.

After a few minutes of small talk with the governor and one of his staffers, I politely asked if I could speak to him in private. When we were alone, I launched right in: "Jim, you know as much about practical politics as anyone. We both know you are in trouble, and some drastic moves have to be made to improve your public image and approval ratings." He nodded. "You and I know that perception is everything. These right-wing attacks are being exaggerated by the media, and that's bringing your popularity down," I said. Governor Blanchard listened carefully. "That's right," he finally said. "Do you have a solution?" Now it was my turn to pause a few seconds. "Governor, you've got to improve your PR operation immediately. You have to replace your press person and your chief of staff—now." I told him he had to trust my judgment and that he had to make those moves that morning—"and by nightfall hire a young fellow you might have heard of, Rick Cole."

Suddenly it was as if I was arguing in court. "Jim, I believe this fellow has the PR instincts to turn around your image, take you off the defensive, and get you moving up in the polls. Make him your chief of staff. Let him come with ideas, hire any assistants he needs."

Blanchard thought briefly. "Frank, I think you are right, but are you sure?" I told him I was putting all my best judgment and experience on the line over this. He finally said okay.

But then he said he worried about letting down the staff. "I'll need a couple of days," he said. That, I knew, was dangerous—I had to get him to take action that day. If he vacillated, there was a good chance he would not go through with it or do it halfway. I worried he might hire Cole but leave the old team in place, which would almost be worse than not doing anything at all.

I pulled out my biggest gun and cast civility to the winds. "Jim," I said, surprising myself a little, "if you don't do this today, don't ask me to help you down the road. I know I'm right on this one, and you've got to do it now. I'll have Rick Cole standing by." I stood up. "I'll leave you now, Governor, but I'm calling you every hour today until I hear you have taken these steps to save your political ass." Harsh, perhaps, but I needed to get his full attention. Then I added, "I love you like a son, and all I want for you is success. And I believe you know that." I could see he did. Finally, he said, "I'll do it your way, Frank, because I am convinced you are right on this one."

I felt a deep sense of relief. Within a day or two, Governor Blanchard brought in Rick Cole, as press secretary at first, though he soon had a major policy-shaping role. Later, in his second term, Cole would become the governor's chief of staff. Soon things began changing, in the papers and in the polls.

Turning perceptions around takes time. The improving economy helped accomplish this, and voters could see Blanchard was keeping his promise to again lower the tax rate. When reelection time dawned in 1986, many of the GOP heavy hitters who might have been tempted to take on a weakened governor three years earlier found other things to do.

In the end, he was left with only a handful of possible credible opponents. Brighton-area businessman Dick Chrysler was the front-runner until he was derailed by a last-minute scandal involving unemployment insurance claims. Eventually Wayne County Executive William Lucas emerged as the GOP nominee. Lucas, who also had been county sheriff, was an African American who switched parties to run against Blanchard. His supporters hoped he could win by adding historically Democratic black votes to the Republican base, but Lucas managed to lose Republicans while failing to win more than a fifth of the black vote.

In November, Blanchard won the greatest gubernatorial landslide in modern history, garnering almost 69 percent of the vote. Lucas was a weaker-than-normal candidate, but it was clear that Blanchard would have romped to victory against any Republican that year. Barely three years earlier he had looked like a one-term failure.

I've often paused to reflect that, ironically, Jim Blanchard's career may have been saved by the Michigan Constitution of 1963—the one that changed the terms of most statewide elected officials from two to four years. Had Blanchard had to face the voters in 1984, he might very well have lost. His reputation hadn't yet been fully restored, the tax increase was still in force, and that was the year Ronald Reagan, as part of his forty-nine-state landslide, swept the state by 722,000 votes.

On the other hand, had the four-year term kicked in a little earlier, my friend Governor John Swainson, who served only two years, might never have lost to George Romney. But we'll never know. What I do know is that James J. Blanchard was a good governor, without a doubt, and a person of integrity and intelligence. During his second term, he focused on economic development.

The *Almanac of American Politics 1990* correctly praised him for trying to revitalize and diversify the economy by concentrating "on using Michigan's existing manufacturing expertise to specialize in high-skill, capital-intensive, flexible manufacturing." He also won nationwide praise for establishing the Michigan Education Trust (MET), the nation's first statewide college tuition guarantee program, which has helped thousands of parents afford to send kids through school. "Blanchard is the commanding figure of Michigan politics," that same article concluded, predicting he could easily match or eclipse Bill Milliken in terms of both accomplishments and years served.

But it was not to be.

Tragically, Jim Blanchard got somewhat out of touch with the people toward the end of his second term. To many, he seemed somewhat pompous and removed from their everyday struggles. He seemed to take a third term for granted.

Other problems surfaced. Eight years previously, he had selected Martha Griffiths, a longtime congresswoman, as his running mate. That was a brilliant political move. But by 1990 she was seventy-eight and had visibly slowed down, and the governor—probably correctly—felt it was time for a change.

What few realize is that replacing her was the responsible—not the safe—thing to do. What if President Bill Clinton had appointed Blanchard secretary of transportation upon taking office? Would it be right to leave one of the nation's most important industrial states with an ailing, eighty-one-year-old chief executive? Unfortunately Martha didn't step aside gracefully, and the highly publicized spat hurt Blanchard—even though he eventually nominated a younger woman, Libby Maynard, for the second spot.

Before all that, however, Jim and his wife, Paula, went through a divorce. It wasn't that messy as political divorces go, but Paula wrote a book about the breakup of their marriage, *Till Politics Do Us Part*, in which she mentioned rumors that her husband had been having an affair during his governorship with his secretary, Janet Fox, whom he soon married after the divorce.

How much that hurt his reelection chances is hard to say—but it didn't help. Ironically, his opponent in that race had also been recently divorced—the same John Engler who had become Michigan Senate majority leader. Even more ironic is the fact that his ex-wife, Colleen Engler, who had been a state senator, also wrote a memoir but never found a publisher for it.

What may have been more damaging than the book, however, were quarrels between Blanchard and Detroit mayor Coleman Young, who felt he and his city had been slighted. You might say the mayor didn't exactly overexert himself to get out the vote in the 1990 election.

Still, I can't believe the mayor thought Blanchard would lose. Nobody did. The weekend before the election, one poll even had Blanchard ahead of Engler 54 percent to 40 percent.

But I had a bad feeling about this. I heard from a pollster I respected that the race was getting tighter and that the governor could conceivably lose by half a percentage point—which is almost exactly what happened.

Turnout was abysmal. On election night, I soon saw that while I was beating Cliff Taylor, a future chief justice of the Michigan Supreme Court, by almost two to one, Blanchard and Engler were neck and neck. The next morning, it was clear that Jim Blanchard had lost, by a razor-thin final margin of 17,595 votes, in an extremely low turnout. Understandably, he was crushed.

Later he told an interviewer, "The legislature was tired of me, the press was tired of me," and he said he hadn't been so sure himself he wanted a third term. Fortunately he eventually bounced back, finding a new life as a lawyer and lobbyist in Washington.

President Bill Clinton appointed him ambassador to Canada, an experience Blanchard wrote about in an excellent memoir, *Behind the Embassy Door:*

Canada, Clinton and Quebec (1998). To this day, many Canadians say he was the best ambassador the United States ever sent to Ottawa.

History should be kind to Jim Blanchard. He was a dedicated and honest governor who had the guts to raise taxes to pull the state out of a financial crisis and helped lead it back to prosperity.

Today, I don't think anyone would be able to pull that off.

But what I was thinking about right after his defeat was this: once again, I would have to work with a governor of the other party.

This time, however, it would be very different than before.

17

SERVING JOHN ENGLER—
AND TURNING A PAGE

Can a liberal get along with a conservative in government?

My experience with John Engler indicates the answer is yes.

Politically, we had next to nothing in common. Our entire backgrounds and outlook were different. I came from the brawling, big-city streets of Detroit. He came from a cattle farm in a place called Beal City, near Mount Pleasant, in the north-central part of the state.

Engler was young enough to be my son. I was born in 1924; he came along in 1948. Although we were both raised Roman Catholic, that was pretty much where the resemblance ended. Though he eventually earned a law degree, his entire adult life had been spent in the legislature. Matter of fact, he was elected to the state house while he was still an undergrad at Michigan State.

Being in the legislature was something that never appealed to me. When my father failed to be elected to the Michigan senate when I was a boy I concluded that it had to be a cesspool of corruption. My entire career had been spent in pursuit of justice for the consumer, the citizen, the little man.

On the other hand, Engler thought he could improve society with tax breaks for business and by keeping government small and taxes low. Philosophically, we were oceans apart.

Nevertheless, he was the governor and I the attorney general, and we had both been put in our jobs by a vote of the people of the state of Michigan. My philosophy, ever since the tumultuous Romney days, had been to extend an olive branch to any new governor.

I intended to do the same with John Engler, but he actually reached out to me first. Not long after he had been elected, I was contacted by Richard McLellan, an attorney who was the head of his transition team, and remained a close aide after the election. He told me that the governor was going to an MSU basketball game and suggested that I might want to stop by and have a beer with him. "You know, you and the governor ought to get along," McLellan told me. "You both hate gambling."

Well, he was absolutely right about that. Detroit is one of the most impoverished areas in the nation, and the city's three casinos suck millions of dollars a day out of the pockets of those who can least afford it. Detroit's casinos don't attract the high rollers and investment bankers who gamble. They go to Vegas or some exotic foreign oasis to lose their money. Detroit's casinos lure poor, desperate people who come to lose their rent and grocery money. If that isn't a moral crime and an outrage, I don't know what is. Unfortunately the casinos seem here to stay.

But back to my relationship with John Engler. When I did sit down with him that first time, I was pleasantly surprised to find that he respected my experience. After the usual small talk, I told him the story of my early stormy relationship with George Romney and how we had finally solved that by setting up a communication channel. The key was to have my most trusted person develop a relationship with his most trusted person, something that he, as other governors before him, had agreed made sense. In this case, his intermediary was Lucille Taylor, his chief counsel. My representative was Stanley Steinborn, who had succeeded Leon Cohan as my chief deputy. I assured Engler he would never be blindsided by me or my office. That doesn't mean I endorsed his legislative agenda. Far from it. He was an apologist for just about anything any major corporation wanted to do. He was a fervent believer in low to no taxes and minimal to no regulation of business.

But I knew I wasn't going to change him, nor was he going to change me, and as a Democrat I knew—and he knew—I would have to speak out occasionally against his policies. We worked that out, however. Every few months I would see the governor in his office, and we'd agree on just how much criticism he was going to have.

Don't get me wrong. I would have been very, very happy if Jim Blanchard had won a third term. However, my job was to do the state's business. I would never pull any punches on a legal ruling. Nor would I hesitate to file a lawsuit to stop some outrage if I thought it was merited, even if that meant a public feud with the governor, such as the ones I endured, early on, with Romney.

But it made sense to get along as much as possible. I told Engler the story of how I was selected by a bunch of Republicans to be the city attorney in Alpena. After that, I told him: "I want you to know that I certainly don't have any personal animus against you. We ought to find some things we can agree on."

Turns out that besides gambling, there was another big issue on which we found common ground: capital punishment. Virtually every study that has ever been done on this subject shows that capital punishment is no deterrent to crime. Nor does it save the citizens money, as is sometimes claimed. The appeals process in capital cases can take years and cost a state millions. Michigan has never executed anyone since it was admitted as a state in 1837. Though capital punishment was technically legal at first, nine years later, executions were formally outlawed. There have been none since, though the federal government, which is beyond our jurisdiction, did hang a murderer in Milan in 1938. Michigan is one of a few states with no tradition of capital punishment. Nevertheless, from time to time, some demagogue looking to stir up the public starts loudly calling for a constitutional amendment to allow executions.

John Engler knew how to get and use power better than any governor in my time, and there's no telling what might have happened if he had supported capital punishment. Fortunately, he opposed it both on moral grounds as a fairly devout Roman Catholic and for practical reasons; like me, he knew it didn't work.

I told him in one of our early meetings that if he ever got any grief over his stand on capital punishment, I'd be happy to do whatever I could to help back him up. I think he appreciated that. But he was also smart enough to know he couldn't defeat me—I wasn't going anywhere, and getting along would be to the considerable advantage of both of us. Nevertheless, I was happy to hear that when he held his first annual meeting with all his appointees at the end of 1991, he spent the first three minutes talking about what an excellent relationship he had with Frank Kelley.

Nevertheless, though we got along well enough, most of the policies of the Engler years were dismaying to me, to say the least. He was on a crusade to cut services to the poor as much as possible, and he largely succeeded. He privatized services, closed some of the state's mental hospitals, ended general assistance welfare, and ended most state aid to the arts. Granted, many of the programs that had been going on for decades needed reform. Nobody doubts that there were abuses. But much of what was done struck me as particularly mean-spirited; it seemed as though a meat ax was being used where a scalpel was what was called for. But unless the constitution was being violated, I could do nothing. Occasionally I managed to blunt some of Engler's efforts.

For example, in January 1997, I issued a formal opinion stating that a law passed by the legislature requiring voters to show ID was an unconstitutional interference with citizens' right to vote.

There was—and is—no doubt in my mind that requiring voters to show ID at the polls is a violation of the equal protection clause of the Michigan constitution. My opinion had the force of law for ten years until the Michigan Supreme Court overturned it in July 2007. Our highest court has, unfortunately, become very partisan over the years, and on a party-line vote, the justices held that the voter ID law that I had effectively squelched was perfectly legal. That was long after I had retired, but this attempt to weaken one of the most important rights any citizen has still angers me.

What was also discouraging was that the Engler years were also years of weakness for the Michigan Democratic Party. Republicans controlled both houses of the legislature most of that time. Democrats seemed almost punch-drunk in their efforts to oppose Engler and his polices. For a while, they told themselves his election had been a fluke. They tried to blame it on Blanchard. True enough, the governor had run a poor—you might even say lousy—reelection campaign. He never seemed to take Engler seriously as a challenger—but then again, almost nobody else did either. Less excusably, he had failed to mend fences with Detroit mayor Coleman Young, who had felt taken for granted. Blanchard needed Young to make sure Detroit voters showed up on Election Day. In the end, far too many of them did not.

There was, as I said earlier, the divorce issue, but also a perception that Blanchard had become arrogant and disconnected from the average voter. That may not have been true, but in politics, perception is reality. My fellow Democrats told themselves Engler was an accidental governor and that they'd retire him after one term.

At first there were some grounds for believing that might be so. There were no signs that John Engler had any great personal popularity. His victory had been so narrow that he didn't even get a majority of the vote. Turnout was also shockingly low, which was the only reason he managed to win at all. Consider this: when Engler won the first time, he got more than 110,000 fewer votes than Blanchard's first opponent, Dick Headlee, had gotten in losing eight years before!

Unfortunately Blanchard's vote had fallen by more than 300,000, indicating that few Michigan voters were in love with either of them. But a win is a win . . . and here's what Democrats overlooked: John Engler was a master of governmental process. He had grown up in the legislature. He knew every member, their strengths and their weaknesses. He knew how to make the machinery work and how to stop his foes from making it work for them.

That's how he managed to get so much controversial legislation through in his first term, even though Democrats held the House of Representatives. Democrats howled in protest, but they were mostly ineffectual. Four years later, there was a major battle for the Democratic nomination for governor.

Debbie Stabenow, then a state senator, was the early favorite, but she had been damaged by a bill she had introduced to abolish the state's system of education funding. Engler jumped at the chance to change the system. Probably to her shock, Republicans helped pass her bill and then went to work on revamping the way public education works.

They asked voters in March 1994 to shift the responsibility for most school funding to the state, which would pay for the schools largely through a sales tax increase. Homeowners, however, would get a break on their property taxes. That part was wildly popular.

Democrats and teachers favored a different scheme that would have funded the schools through the income tax, rather than a boost in the sales tax, which falls heaviest on the poor. But harried homeowners couldn't resist the thought of a property tax cut.

On the ballot, the governor's scheme was listed as Proposal A, a name that would go down in history after the people embraced it by a more than two-to-one margin. Many saw it as the solution that would save public education for years to come.

Those who understood public education, however, knew better. Prior to Proposal A, schools were funded mainly by millages leveled on property in local districts. Voters in affluent districts, like the Grosse Pointes or the Grand Rapids suburbs, were more easily able to vote more money for their schools. Voters in poor districts, especially in impoverished Upper Peninsula areas, weren't.

To be sure, there were working-class districts in which voters staunchly supported their schools, and richer ones where stingy residents turned down millages. But mainly the system in place resulted in public schools in rich neighborhoods that were better than those in poor areas. That had probably always been the case, but it became a statewide embarrassment when some districts— most notably Kalkaska in the northern Lower Peninsula—started running out of money and closing down long before the school year ended.

Proposal A was supposed to fix all that for good. However, what it really did was put all public schools pretty much at the mercy of the state, which had the power to set the per pupil "foundation grant" that would determine the majority of their funding. Worse, it severely limited the ability of school districts to raise more money through millages, even if the voters wanted to.

What this meant is that this was very good for the poorest districts, like Kalkaska—for a time. But the best-funded districts were doomed to a slow decline. And eventually it was bad for all the schools when recessions hit or when legislators who were hostile to public education gained power. They balanced budgets by cutting the per pupil "foundation" grant. And parents and school districts were powerless to do much about it. That wasn't clear to voters in 1994, however; they thought John Engler had done something great for their schools.

However, the teachers' unions weren't happy with Debbie Stabenow, and as a result, she lost that year's Democratic primary for governor to Howard Wolpe, a former congressman from Kalamazoo whose seat had been eliminated by redistricting. Theoretically he should have been a strong candidate. A native of Los Angeles, he had moved to Michigan to be a political science professor at Western Michigan University. He decided to get into politics himself and was elected to Congress from what had been a Republican district. People found him warm and engaging.

But once he won the primary, his campaign turned bizarre. The thing Wolpe cared most about was Africa, and he was stunned when, after he jumped into the governor's race, Donald Riegle, Michigan's Democratic U.S. senator, unexpectedly decided to retire. That was the job Wolpe really wanted, but he couldn't very well drop out of the governor's race and run for U.S. Senate. But his heart didn't seem to be in it. During the campaign, he was much more eager to talk about South Africa than school financing and potholes.

Not only that, but 1994 turned out to be the worst year for Democrats since the New Deal. Inspired by Newt Gingrich's "Contract with America," Republicans won both houses of Congress for the first time since Dwight D. Eisenhower was first elected.

Wolpe lost by a landslide, getting barely 38 percent of the vote. Even worse, longtime Michigan secretary of state Richard Austin lost, too, to Republican Candice Miller. Dick Austin was a good and decent man who almost became Detroit's first black mayor.

Many people have speculated as to how history might have been different if Austin hadn't lost the Detroit mayoral election to Roman Gribbs by a whisker in 1969. Some believe had Austin been the Motor City's first black mayor, his much less confrontational personality might have eased tensions. But we'll never know.

The next year, he was elected secretary of state. He was a good, honest, and solid public official but eventually began to show signs of age.

His defeat left only one lonely statewide Democratic official: me.

Despite the GOP trend, I had again won easily, beating a little-known lawyer by nearly half a million votes. That was personally gratifying, but I knew that my days were numbered, and not for the reasons you might think.

Two years earlier, Michigan voters passed some of the most severe term limits in the nation. This would eventually be disastrous for the state legislature in particular, eliminating any institutional memory and helping lead to both dysfunction and irresponsibility. Under the new law, politicians could serve no more than six years in the state house of representatives and eight in the senate. Then, no matter what happens, they can't run again—ever, no matter how long they live, no matter how much the voters might want them. After those few years, everyone is barred from service for life. Term limits are a bad idea to begin with. Democracy has built-in term limits: regularly scheduled elections.

Any of us—liberal, conservative, independent—can name officeholders we think shouldn't be there. But if the voters of, say, Cadillac want to keep electing Joe Blow to represent them in Lansing, why should we take away their right to do that? Term limits have another very harmful effect on any organization. They are an open invitation to pass the buck on hard decisions and sweep problems under the rug.

Some actions, or inactions, have long-term consequences. Let's say that as a legislator you have two choices: responsibility tells you that you should tackle a difficult and expensive problem now, but no matter how brilliant your solution is, it will cost money and make people mad. However, what if you can also put things off for a decade? The second choice may end up being much worse for the state in the long run. For your career, however, the results will be great. Ten years later, when things blow up, you will no longer be in office. The results are easy to see.

This is largely why, as I am writing this in 2014, Michigan's roads are among the nation's worst. For years, legislators refused to fund them adequately, because doing so would have meant raising taxes. As a result, the state's competitiveness was damaged, and in the end, the citizens will eventually have to pay even more to make up for years of neglect.

Higher education has become largely unaffordable for even middle-class kids, unless they are willing to graduate burdened with crippling debt. Revenue-sharing cuts have helped drive many cities, including Detroit, into state-controlled emergency management.

Term limits, however, didn't apply only to legislators: starting in 1994, the governor, attorney general, and secretary of state were officially limited to two four-year terms. That included me. The new law meant that once I began my tenth term in January 1995, I knew that I could serve, at most, only one more term.

Should I run that one final time? For most of the next few years I didn't think much about it. There was the people's business to do: consumers to protect, rights to defend. No matter how often and effectively you go after scam artists, new ones keep springing up. What's more, those final years saw what some are convinced will go down as my most meaningful and important case—what is known as the Tobacco Master Settlement Agreement.

Early on in my time as attorney general, I learned that class-action suits were often an extremely effective way to win victories for consumers. When I was president of the National Association of Attorneys General, I began to rally my colleagues to join me to take on causes that were clearly in everyone's interest.

Tobacco was the largest and greatest of these. As someone once said, it is the only legal product that, when used as directed, is almost sure to kill you. Every state in the union has been crippled by the financial repercussions of tobacco, from increased medical costs to lost productivity.

When we had clear scientific evidence that tobacco was a health care hazard, we sued the industry on the grounds that, as Mississippi attorney general Mike Moore put it, "you caused the health crisis, you pay for it." Nearly every state joined in.

We found defenders in Congress, and for a while it looked like there would be a legislative solution. That failed, however, and we attorneys general got back into the fray. Finally, we won.

Eventually, during my last year in office, we negotiated a stupendous Master Settlement Agreement with the nation's four major tobacco manufacturers. They agreed to pay an unheard-of $206 *billion*—not million, *billion*—over the following twenty-five years.

Michigan's share over that time would be $12 billion. Elmer White, the author of a definitive work on Michigan accident law, later wrote in the *Michigan Bar Journal* that "Frank Kelley was instrumental in organizing a national effort by the attorneys general of dozens of states to file a class action lawsuit against the tobacco companies. This is the largest lawsuit settlement in Michigan history, a stunning achievement."*

---

* Elmer E. White, "Michigan Lawyers in History—Frank J. Kelley: The Eternal General," http://www.michbar.org/journal/article.cfm?articleID=87&volumeID=8 (accessed October 18, 2010).

The settlement was not yet finished but was moving toward a final resolution in December 1997. Thirty-six years before that, half my lifetime ago, I had been stunned when Governor John Swainson invited me to his home, offered me a glass of champagne, and told me he intended to appoint me attorney general of Michigan.

Now he was gone, my kids were grown, and I needed to decide whether to run for office one more time. There was no doubt that if I wanted the job, I would have been renominated and reelected. But did that make sense? That December I realized the answer was, finally, no.

Over the years, I had completely made over the attorney general's office. I had personally hired all but a few of the hundreds of assistant attorneys general who were doing the state's business. We had established civil rights, consumer protection, and environmental divisions and had broken new ground in many areas. There were more women and minority lawyers than ever in the department's history. I had, long since, established the record for service by any state attorney general in the nation.

Although I would turn seventy-four on the very last day of my term, I didn't feel old. I have always exercised, kept trim and fit, and I barely drank any alcohol. But I didn't want to be seen as one more old politician, clinging to power to the very last minute, incapable of letting go. Washington is full of that kind of politician today, and they are pathetic. I was also still energetic enough that I wanted to try something new.

Frankly, I also wanted to make some honest money. I had spent my life in public service and had put my three kids through college, and I had virtually nothing set aside for the future. What I did have was knowledge that virtually no one else had about the state—about how government functions and about the personalities both onstage and behind the scenes. However, I didn't want to start a firm on my own or oversee one that was perceived as a partisan operation.

But I had an idea. I reached out to Dennis Cawthorne, a Harvard law school graduate and a former Republican floor leader in the Michigan House who was fifteen years my junior. I knew he was a man of integrity. What about opening a law firm with me? He would appeal to Republicans; I would bring in Democrats. He also knew about and loved financial matters and knew far better than I did how to run an office, set rates, and invest money. He was more introverted than I and was reserved and thoughtful, with an encyclopedic knowledge of Michigan and political history.

My sense was that we would be a great combination. He was at first stunned by the suggestion, then intrigued and excited.

There was no reason to hurry to announce my retirement. Oddly enough, in Michigan, candidates for attorney general and secretary of state are not chosen in statewide primary elections; they are picked by delegates to the Democratic and Republican state conventions, which are held in late summer. Plus, if I announced too far in advance that I was leaving, it might have lessened my ability to press some of our hard legal cases.

Finally, in May 1998, I announced that I would not seek another term. Some of my staff members had tears in their eyes. Others couldn't quite believe it. I had virtually no regrets. Long ago, I learned that you should always leave a party a few minutes before anyone wants you to go. Now was the time.

That fall, I threw myself into an effort to help a brilliant young woman named Jennifer Granholm win the office I had held since she was three years old—Michigan attorney general.

That wouldn't be easy.

Nationally, it was a far better year for Democrats than four years earlier had been—but not in Michigan. Our party's nominee for governor was a man who had never been in politics before: Geoffrey Fieger, best known as the flamboyant attorney for Dr. Jack Kevorkian. Fieger is a brilliant courtroom attorney. At that time he had won more multimillion dollar medical malpractice cases than I could count.

Over and over again he got juries to find his most famous client not guilty, even though he confessed to breaking the law. But Fieger had no idea whatsoever how politics work or elections are won.

When the votes were counted, he had lost by more votes than even the hapless Howard Wolpe had. The Democratic nominee for secretary of state had done even worse, even losing Wayne County.

But Jennifer Granholm had narrowly won.

"I owe it to you, Frank," she told me. In fact, she was a highly appealing and charismatic candidate. However, I do think that I may have had a little something to do with it.

As January dawned, I stood in the crisp air on the steps of the state capitol as my successor was sworn in. Four days later, Dennis Cawthorne and I announced we would be founding and leading a "new governmental affairs and regulatory law firm."

I left on a high note. Without any doubt, I felt I had left the office I inherited so long ago in better shape than I had found it.

Now it was time for a new adventure.

18

FAMOUS PEOPLE I'VE KNOWN, IN POLITICS AND OTHERWISE

On the morning of the Tet Offensive, when Viet Cong invaded the U.S. embassy compound in Saigon and all hell was breaking loose, I met with President Lyndon B. Johnson in the Oval Office.

How did that happen?

Well, to begin with, partly by chance, I was fortunate enough to spend a lot more time with national political figures than most state politicians, especially state attorneys general, ever could imagine. One reason for this was that Michigan had Republican governors for all but nine of my thirty-seven years on the job. That meant that the state's two highest-ranking Democratic officials were the attorney general and the secretary of state. Secretaries of state, however, are primarily concerned with local matters—driver's licenses and plates; voter registration. They mostly aren't concerned with national events.

On the other hand, attorneys general argue before the U.S. Supreme Court and frequently get involved in legal cases with national implications. After my first decade in office, I had more seniority than any other state attorney general in the nation. That gave me some national standing with my peers, something enhanced by the fact that Michigan was a big industrial state crucial to the outcome of presidential elections. When presidential candidates came courting, I was, de facto, usually the highest-ranking Michigan Democrat on the scene.

That's not how I happened to be in the Oval Office that bleak day in January 1968, however. The top three officers of the National Association of Attorneys General were in Washington for our annual conference and were scheduled to meet with the president. This was an annual meeting we had about law enforcement concerns. (Today, sadly, this no longer happens; instead the chief executive meets briefly with all the attorneys general, an event about as meaningful as a speech to a service club.)

That morning, however, when we heard what was going on, we quickly told the president's aides that we could postpone the meeting.

"Hell no," LBJ said. "Show them in." The president, a tall man with immense presence, stood up from his desk and came over to shake hands with me and my two colleagues, Bill Saxbe of Ohio and Arthur Sills of New Jersey, both now deceased, I'm sad to say. We sat down on two couches and he pulled up a straight-backed chair to face us.

What followed was an exciting meeting that lasted for three-quarters of an hour and was punctuated by phone calls from the secretary of state, from the Pentagon, and from Vietnam.

"You gentlemen represent the law throughout the United States," LBJ said. "As a nation we are trying to restore order in a beleaguered country halfway around the world. But of equal if not greater importance is the fact that in the face of a crime wave here at home, we must maintain law and order on every street and byway in our country."

That may sound like standard political rhetoric, and it was. He went on to say, essentially, that if we supported him on Vietnam, he would support funding for whatever local crime initiatives we backed.

Politics as usual, you might say. But my two fellow attorneys general and I were deeply impressed that on a day of crisis, he took the time to meet with us.

"He's impressive, and certainly in full charge," said Saxbe, the only one of us who was a Republican. Sadly and ironically, it wasn't true. Vietnam had overwhelmed his presidency, as that day showed.

I do want to note that while JFK was my all-time hero and the most charismatic man I have ever met, LBJ made a powerful impression and had an appeal of his own. He had a melodious Texas drawl that was quite charming—at least in small doses.

When he fixed you with his gaze, it was utterly riveting. He would look you in the eyes and make you feel as though he was hanging onto your every word. Whatever his faults, I am convinced that he was basically a decent man who wanted to leave a legacy of accomplishment. And he did.

President Johnson got more civil rights legislation passed than Kennedy ever could have. He did more for the poor than any president, with the exception of Franklin D. Roosevelt. But Vietnam destroyed him. Two months after our meeting, in that same room he announced to the nation that he wouldn't run for reelection. Five years later, he was dead.

He was followed in the White House by Richard Nixon. Since I was the state's top law enforcement officer, I was sometimes invited to the White House by Republican presidents—Nixon and Gerald Ford, Ronald Reagan and George Herbert Walker Bush.

However, you might say that my reception was never quite as warm as it was when Democrats were in power. I remember the first time I saw Nixon as president. He looked like some woeful stand-in, sent out to check the microphones till the real president arrived.

I did get to know the man who almost beat him the year of the Tet Offensive: Hubert Humphrey. The attorney general of his home state of Minnesota, Walter Mondale, introduced us. One of the later ironies of history is that Mondale would follow in Humphrey's footsteps, becoming first a senator and then vice president, and then losing a presidential election on his own. Mondale was an exceptionally decent as well as capable man whom I believe might have been a fine president if he hadn't been unlucky enough to run against Ronald Reagan in 1984.

In April 1977, soon after Mondale became vice president, I joined him in Marquette, up in the Upper Peninsula, and flew with him on Air Force One to the Jefferson-Jackson Day dinner in Detroit. Mondale, my former colleague, had the use of the presidential plane for this trip. He invited me to sit up front with him, where the president would normally ride, while we each puffed a cigar.

"Only in America, eh, Frank? A minister's son and a saloon keeper's son ending up here!" He grinned and turned to a lieutenant, who was serving as steward, and ordered us two cheeseburgers.

But back to 1968 and his Minnesota mentor. Humphrey was an able man, and I think somehow he would have found a way out of Vietnam far earlier than Nixon did. But that was not to be, and I was not at first a supporter of his that terrible spring. Robert F. Kennedy, my mentor as attorney general, announced he was a candidate for president that March.

Less than three weeks after Kennedy got into the race, Martin Luther King Jr. was assassinated. That was quite a blow. I can't pretend to have known King well, but I had met and talked with him at least a couple times. What I remember best is that he projected great dignity.

Two months later, as he won the California primary, Bobby Kennedy, too, was gunned down. It was all way too much.

If you aren't old enough to remember these events, you may not realize the devastating impact those three murders had on this nation: John F. Kennedy, Robert F. Kennedy, Martin Luther King Jr. Each of them tried to make this nation and world a better place. Each was murdered for it. When they were alive, millions and millions of people genuinely believed that democracy and our system of government worked, or could be made to work.

When they were killed, we lost our innocence and we lost our way politically—and in my opinion, we've never completely recovered. Suddenly it became difficult to get many young and idealistic Americans involved in politics, a problem that persists to this day. I certainly lost some of the hope and idealism I had always had, and I've never quite gotten them back.

That doesn't mean I've stopped believing completely. Edward M. "Teddy" Kennedy, may he rest in peace, put it in perspective when he spoke at the 1980 Democratic National Convention: "The work goes on, the cause endures, the hope still lives, and the dream shall never die."

We have to believe that. But it wasn't all that easy when we were left with the likes of Richard Nixon and Spiro T. Agnew.

Fortunately there were lighter moments, even in that dreadful year. One I'll never forget was when Ed Muskie, Humphrey's choice for vice president, was campaigning in Michigan that fall. He was a craggy-faced senator from Maine and a truly charming man. I met him at Detroit Metropolitan Airport in October to escort him to Cobo Hall. Suddenly, a crisis developed: Muskie suddenly looked very uncomfortable. He confided that he had forgotten to relieve himself on the plane, and he really had to urinate.

"I know the feeling," I said, thinking quickly. "Tell the Secret Service agent in charge that you have to stop at a Detroit fire station to congratulate a local heroic fireman. There's one just a mile from here." Squirming, Muskie did exactly that.

We stopped, he ducked into the restroom, and then he came out and talked for two minutes to the surprised and delighted firemen. Gratefully he turned to me and said, "You are a great practical politician, Frank." Humphrey and Muskie lost that election, though they did carry Michigan easily. Muskie went on to become one of the Senate's most distinguished members and finally secretary of state. To the end of his days, whenever we saw each other, he'd say, "There's Frank Kelley, the practical politician."

One thing I've never talked about is that for a few months in 1976, there seemed to be a chance that I might end up a different kind of attorney general—U.S. attorney general, that is, the chief law enforcement officer of the United States of America.

Here's what happened. There was huge interest that spring in the Democratic presidential nomination. We'd gone through Watergate, and Gerald Ford was widely seen as an accidental president whose popularity had been permanently damaged by his stunning pardon of Richard Nixon. That winter I heard from Jim Blanchard, who was then completing his first term in Congress.

Senator Henry Jackson of Washington was expected to be a major contender for the presidential nomination. He was my kind of Democrat. He stood for a strong foreign policy and had been one of the earliest and strongest supporters of civil rights legislation. His team was looking for a strong Democrat to head his campaign in the Midwest. Would I be interested? I thought it over for a few days. Meanwhile, Blanchard mentioned my name to the Jackson inner circle, and they were very interested. Within days, the senator himself called me.

What some may not remember now is that "Scoop" Jackson was one of the Senate's most respected figures. Strong and ethical, he sometimes won reelection with more than 80 percent of the vote.

I told him I was very interested and soon flew to Washington to meet with him. Everybody knows that every senator and congressman has an office in Washington, but what is not common knowledge is that the most powerful members have second offices and are much closer to the center of power.

Senator Jackson, the chair of what was then the powerful Interior Committee, had one of these, a few feet from the Senate chamber. He had then been in the Senate for nearly a quarter of a century, arriving about the time I began practicing law. Regardless, he treated me as an equal and a political ally of great value. I do remember one interesting thing about that meeting. He had sent out for a couple of steak sandwiches that we could eat while we talked. They arrived with a silver coffee service, and they were delicious. Then suddenly a bell rang. Jackson had to jump up and scurry to the floor for a vote. I was left to enjoy my lunch while his got cold. This was sometime in 1975, less than three years after I lost my election for the Senate to Bob Griffin.

While I ate, I reflected on how lucky I was. As attorney general, I wasn't tied to my desk. I could basically control my own schedule. Had I been elected to the Senate, my office wouldn't have been near the Capitol; it would have been blocks away. I would have spent years dropping lunches and running to vote on legislation that I would have very little power to shape until I accumulated seniority.

Believe me, this wasn't sour grapes. I suddenly realized that for me, losing had been a blessing. Eventually, Scoop Jackson came back. The more we talked, the more I respected and liked him. I was determined to do everything I could to help him. Early on, things appeared to be going great. He won the important New York and Massachusetts primaries; he had skipped the Iowa caucus and the primary in New Hampshire. They had been won by an obscure former governor of Georgia who wasn't taken very seriously then, a man named Jimmy Carter. Today it is clear that skipping those contests was a fatal mistake.

But that wasn't clear at all then. Nobody had heard of the Iowa caucuses before 1976. The previous two winners of the New Hampshire primary hadn't come close to winning nomination.

What was crucial was labor. The senator flew to Detroit, where he met with Doug Fraser, then the second-in-command of the UAW, and his top aide, Sam Fishman. Leonard Woodcock, head of the UAW, was supposed to be there, but he wasn't. Later, I learned that he had already secretly made up his mind to support Jimmy Carter.

The labor leaders made it clear that they'd have absolutely no problem with Scoop Jackson, who had as fine a record on their issues as anybody. They liked his tough foreign policy stance. But they told him they weren't going to endorse anyone that early. What worried them was something that also worried me. The senator was warm and compelling in person but came across as stiff and distant on television. If he had a weakness, it was that—and that he didn't realize how important that had become.

But he still seemed an extremely strong candidate. He told the labor leaders, "You know, gentlemen, if I am elected, I think Frank Kelley would make an excellent attorney general." They seemed to like that. Was he serious? You might think he was just trying to win over my crowd. But I learned that he repeated that to his assistants and others when I wasn't there. I know how politics works, and I certainly can't say that Jackson would have appointed me U.S. attorney general.

But I do think that, at the very least, I would have been an influential legal counsel and administration insider. Alas, it wasn't to be. Carter beat him badly in the Pennsylvania primary. Money dried up quickly, and by May Jackson's campaign was over.

I did support Carter that fall but was never especially impressed by him. Though he won, he lost Michigan in November, and before long, his presidency was in trouble.

Four years later, I supported Senator Ted Kennedy's challenge to President Carter for the Democratic nomination. How could I do anything else? I had been loyal to his brothers, and they made me feel as if I were part of something great.

When I had run for the U.S. Senate in 1972, Teddy Kennedy had voluntarily come to Michigan to campaign for me. "I'm so glad to be in Michigan to help my friend and the friend of my brothers, Frank Kelley, in his campaign for the Senate," he had told them. The crowds had roared with excitement and approval.

This was three years after the incident at Chappaquiddick, but it was clear that whatever the journalists wrote, millions still believed in the Kennedy magic and message of hope.

Scoff if you want to, but I will be convinced to my dying day that the youngest Kennedy brother was also a great man who was denied our nation's highest office because of one tragic mistake. Had Mary Jo Kopechne gotten out of that car, I believe that Edward Moore Kennedy would have been president and a damned good one for the people of this nation. But in national politics, people hold you to an impossible standard. They don't realize you are mortal and have a hard time excusing you when you make a transgression.

Long ago I learned that we all have feet of clay—most of all, perhaps, me. I let stress and defeat destroy my first marriage, as I have said. I long ago repaired relationships with my family.

Although I will always have regrets, campaigning for Kennedy in the 1980 primaries and caucuses is not one of them. I was proud to do so. But you can guess how popular that made me at the Carter White House. Kennedy did narrowly win the Michigan caucuses, but he lost the nomination. A few months later, Ronald Reagan beat the hapless Carter in a landslide.

Fast-forward eight years, to 1988.

Democrats had taken two terrific beatings at the hands of Ronald Reagan. Now we were going to face his vice president, George H. W. Bush. Jim Blanchard, who was then governor, and I were not convinced that another northern liberal could win. But we felt we knew a man who might be an extremely strong candidate. He was the successful governor of a southern state but not a Jimmy Carter. Gregarious and charismatic, he was a Rhodes Scholar and had a brilliant, attractive wife from Illinois, a Yale law school graduate who was as smart—or maybe smarter—than he.

I had known him longer than most politicians had because he had been elected attorney general of Arkansas when he was just thirty years old. I flew down to meet with him, which meant meeting with them. I compellingly—and I think eloquently—listed all the reasons he should make the race. They listened attentively.

Finally, Hillary Clinton spoke. "That may all be true, Frank. But we don't have the money." She was right. Nobody was going to put up millions that year for a little-known governor of Arkansas. Instead Democrats nominated Michael Dukakis, who lost forty of the fifty states.

Four years later, it was Clinton's time. He defeated President Bush and went on to be the first two-term Democratic president since Franklin D. Roosevelt. I was never a true Clinton insider and won't attempt to add to the many assessments of his administration here. But I do want to note that when he signed the Tobacco Master Settlement Agreement in the Rose Garden in 1998, my last year in office, he unexpectedly went out of his way to praise me: "Mr. Kelley, I know you are retiring this year as the senior attorney general of America. We served together back in the dark ages, and I can't imagine a more fitting capstone to your career than the fact that you've been part of this, and we thank you."

That absolutely delighted me.

Not all of the impressive people I met were political, of course, or even Americans. When I had decided to run for the U.S. Senate, Leon Cohan and I took a whirlwind foreign tour in 1971 designed to orient me more on foreign policy and world problems.

I'll never forget one evening that especially tested both my political acumen and my acting skills. We were in Israel, where I visited the Knesset and within an hour had a chance to chat with four of the most impressive people in Israel: Prime Minister Golda Meir; Abba Eban, then ambassador to the United States; Defense Minister Moshe Dayan; and General (later Prime Minister) Ariel Sharon.

Dayan made perhaps the biggest impression on me. He told me that the Israeli army wasn't big on saluting and spit-and-polish. The country was so small, in fact, it relied heavily on part-time volunteers. He told me about a man named Max who owned a tailor shop but trained as a tank commander three times a week. Whenever he saw Dayan, at army drills, for example, he didn't salute. He just said, "Hello, Moshe, how are you?" That would have been intolerable in any other army, but it didn't bother Dayan. "We show our discipline by unquestioned bravery and dedication in combat," Dayan said, adding, "I'm not interested in superficial posturing. It's thorough training that counts."

That evening made an enormous impression on me, even though I was suffering horribly from a painful stomach flu, or possibly food poisoning, and had to carry out strategic reconnaissance to make sure I was always within striking distance of a restroom. Had I been home, I can assure you I would not have left my bedroom that night, even if I was supposed to argue before the U.S. Supreme Court. But this was a one-in-a-million chance to meet some of the most impressive figures in Israel and, in fact, in the world.

I wouldn't have missed it for anything.

That's not to say I wasn't deeply impressed by many people I encountered during the other stops on our trip, which included visits to the Soviet Union, Eastern Europe, France, and what were then the two Germanies.

I'll never forget the beauty of Lebanon and the utter decency of its people in those days before that nation was ripped apart by its tragic civil war. My trip there had been arranged by my friend Mike Berry, a highly respected attorney of Lebanese descent who later won high praise for his running of Detroit Metropolitan Airport. He was so respected in Lebanon, the country his parents came from, that when I arrived in Beirut, the mayor greeted me on the tarmac, and when I disembarked a sixteen-piece band was playing and signs were waving saying "Welcome Frank Kelley."

But perhaps the most impressive person I met on that trip was the late Archbishop Makarios III, the leader of Cyprus. Makarios was at that time head of the Greek Orthodox Church on that embattled island but had been Cyprus's first president after it won independence from Great Britain in 1960.

Being the first head of a newly independent nation is never easy. But his job was far harder still. Cyprus had a large Turkish minority, and some of them were none too happy at having to be ruled by a Greek. He had survived one assassination attempt shortly before I met with him, and that wasn't the only one. Nevertheless, he was serene, warm, and well informed.

Though he received me in Cyprus's elegant presidential palace, he told me that every night he slept in a small bedroom in the simple parish church where he had been assigned as a lowly assistant priest, many years before.

"I try as a priest first not to succumb to materialism," he said. "I believe this lifestyle permits me to have a better perspective for exercising my temporal role in government and politics." He was, without any doubt, absolutely sincere—and down to earth at the same time. I told him I brought greetings from the Greek Cypriot community of Michigan. After remarking that there were few of these, he stunned me by saying, "As a matter of fact, there is one less since you arrested X," and named a notorious criminal who had been indicted for bribing police officers. However, before I could say anything, Makarios smiled widely. "Don't worry. I know the story. Mr. X had it coming."

Diplomatic incident avoided, I relaxed. We then discussed Greek immigration and migration around the world and how very successful so many of their descendants had been.

What was very clear to me was that this very impressive yet saintly man, with his gray-flecked black beard, black robes, and black crown, was capable of inspiring virtually everyone he met.

Unfortunately his life took a tragic turn a few years later. He was ousted from power by a Greek military coup in 1974, and in response, Turkey invaded and occupied the mostly Turkish northern half of Cyprus. Makarios fled to London for a few months but returned when worldwide rejection of the new government allowed him to regain power. The military plotters fled, but the Turkish army remained.

For the next two years Makarios tried unsuccessfully to persuade the occupiers to leave and to restore the integrity of Cyprus as one nation with one government. Then, perhaps because of the stress, he died in 1977 of a sudden massive heart attack.

His memory is revered still.

Leon Cohan traveled with me on that worldwide tour and had helped make many of the arrangements. The morning after our meeting with the archbishop, when we were dashing off to catch a place for the next country on the list, he said to me, "In our whole life, Frank, we meet only a few great humble human beings. Archbishop Makarios was one of them." I agreed and added, "Leon, I think we are going to meet most of our lifetime's allotment of truly great people on this trip."

For once, I was totally right.

19

LIFE AFTER POLITICS

When I rolled out of bed on Saturday morning, January 2, 1999, it was the first time since the early Kennedy administration that I was not an elected public official. No longer was I attorney general.

I wasn't Michigan's chief lawyer anymore. Hundreds of assistants weren't standing by to carry out my instructions.

Reporters weren't waiting for me to announce news. I no longer had a tax-payer-funded car and driver.

No legislators called to ask my advice on how to make bills they were about to introduce pass constitutional muster. And I was just fine with all of that.

I've always been a social animal. Long before I ever thought of entering politics—something I did by pure accident—I knew there was a secret to being popular at parties: you always leave a few minutes before anyone wants you to. You want your hosts and friends saying, "Don't you wish Frank had hung around just a little longer?" You don't want them saying, "My God, isn't that old fart ever going to retire? Doesn't he realize it's time for someone new?"

When I voluntarily chose not to run for reelection, I left a job I had always loved and could have had for four more years. But I had absolutely no regrets. I knew, too, that if I retired then I would be in a much better position to start a new venture than if I was four years older, couldn't run anymore, and was forced to find something new to do.

When I announced my decision to retire, I told a jammed press conference, "My late father told me that a good public man or woman leaves before they have to go." And I also quoted Harry Truman, who, when he voluntarily stepped down from the presidency, was asked how he felt about leaving the highest office in the land. "You must be mistaken," Truman said. "I'm going to be a citizen. That's the highest office in the land."

True enough. However, I was also a citizen who had to make a living. Within a few weeks, Dennis and I got our firm, Kelley Cawthorne, up and running. Originally it was called Kelley, Cawthorne and Ralls. William Ralls, a Harvard-trained lawyer, was briefly a partner, but it wasn't a good fit and we all amiably parted company.

Dennis knew every Republican in the state and many of them elsewhere in the country. I knew more than my share of Democrats. To my mild discomfort, we legally had to register as lobbyists. I wasn't about to do any lobbying as I understood that term, buttonholing lawmakers to ask them to vote a certain way on bills.

What I was willing and eager to do was get back to practicing law. It turned out my skills weren't all that rusty. Among the many interesting cases I handled was the sale of the Cincinnati Reds baseball team, a complicated transaction with many moving parts.

Part of my success in my new venture—as well as attorney general—was certainly due to my secretary, Pat Anderson, who worked with me throughout my entire career as attorney general. Then, an apparent glutton for punishment, she followed me to Kelley Cawthorne and stayed with me till I finally ended my time as not only a founding partner but a consultant after we sold the firm.

I could have spent this entire book saying good things about her, and it still wouldn't have been enough.

Dennis Cawthorne was no more eager to be a lobbyist than I was, but we soon realized we needed that service and began to hire some lobbyists. The firm grew. We started to win recognition as one of Lansing's top legal and legislative consulting services.

There is a common misconception, by the way, as to what firms like ours do. Kelley Cawthorne didn't take legislators to a bar, get them drunk, buy them steaks, and try to get them to cast votes they didn't believe in on behalf of fat cats who wanted to get richer. We were, in fact, more like a private think tank. We would, for a fee, take on a client and do what we could to try to get their message and point of view across. We didn't lie, we didn't pressure, and we didn't behave in the slightest like the politicians in the wildly successful Netflix political thriller *House of Cards*.

Frankly, we would have lost all our effectiveness and credibility if we had tried. What we had to sell were our names, our prestige, and our knowledge. Yes, on occasion I would ask an official if he'd be willing to meet with one of my clients, if I felt it justified.

But we never promised anything or pressured anyone.

That is why we turned out—to my mild surprise—to be amazingly successful. Soon I was earning far more than I ever had when I was being paid by the taxpayers—which was a good thing, seeing as how I had very little in the way of savings when I retired from my first career at age seventy-four. After all, it would never do to have a former attorney general of the state of Michigan holding a sign saying "Will trade legal opinions for food."

Dennis and I ran the firm for a decade and then sold it to some of our associates, but we remained on for a few years as consultants.

By the way, leaving office didn't mean I was completely finished with public service. As I indicated previously, I seldom saw eye-to-eye politically with John Engler, but we got along personally. When I was leaving office, he began asking people, "What can I do for Frank Kelley?" Well, he ended up giving me a beautiful silver tray, which I treasure. But he also did something else. He appointed me to the Mackinac Island State Park Commission. Now, if you know much about Michigan, chances are that you at least know about Mackinac Island. Anchored in Lake Huron, it is famous for its fudge, horse-drawn carriages (cars are banned on the island), and the Grand Hotel, which has the largest porch in the world. The island is one of the state's most popular vacation spots, and the Grand, run for years by the Musser family, is a popular venue for state and national conferences.

There's an interesting tidbit of history few know about the island: it was once a national park. Michigan donated it to the nation in 1875. Twenty years later, however, Washington gave it back. Seems they decided it was too small to be a national park. Instead it then became Michigan's first state park. Being rejected by Washington was somewhat embarrassing, however, and the governor at the time, a Republican named John Tyler Rich, needed to save face. So he appointed a blue-ribbon board of commissioners, most of whom were already big shots, to run it.

That commission continues to this day, and serving on it is seen as a mark of prestige. My partner Cawthorne was already on it by the time I joined the seven-member commission, and for years we took turns serving as chair. The position is unpaid but interesting, and we each get to get to spend a few weeks on the island, supervising.

Retirement from active service has not meant complete retirement from politics either. In 2002, four years after I stepped down, my successor, Jennifer Granholm, ran for governor. I campaigned hard for her, and she ended up prevailing, becoming Michigan's first female governor in a close election in which Democrats lost the other major statewide offices. "I owe so much to you, Frank," she said on election night, and her door was always open to me during her eight years in office. The only sad thing about that election was that she defeated my other great protégé, James Blanchard, in that year's Democratic primary. He, too, wanted my support, but I had already pledged it to Granholm, who would probably have won that year no matter what I had done. Fortunately, there was no bitterness.

Today Granholm lives in California, where she is a law professor and sought-after news analyst, and Blanchard is a highly successful attorney with DLA Piper, the Washington-based law firm, and has homes both there and in his beloved Michigan.

As I write this, another of my protégés, U.S. senator Carl Levin, is winding up his career as chair of the Senate Armed Services Committee. Like me, he could have easily stayed another term. But also like me, he has come to the conclusion that there is life after politics. I have assistants and former assistants scattered throughout government, private industry, and enjoying retirement. Often I hear from them. Sometimes they ask my advice. Sometimes we reminisce about the old days, old campaigns, old crooks we put in jail, and one or two who got away.

What is gratifying is that I haven't been completely forgotten. In fact I have been baffled by the number of honors that have come my way in recent years. To my great delight, in October 2013 the walkway between the capitol and the Hall of Justice where I worked was designated the Frank J. Kelley Memorial Walkway.

Ethics always have been important to me, and I am especially proud to note that scandal never touched me or my administration while I was attorney general.

Later, recognizing my reputation, Governor Granholm named me to the state government ethics committee for a number of years. Michigan State University established the Frank J. Kelley Institute of Ethics and the Legal Profession, as well as a Frank Kelley Endowed Chair in Ethics at their law school. (By the way, this is the school that was, till it moved to East Lansing in 1997, the Detroit College of Law.) Endowed chairs are usually named after multimillionaires who put up the money out of their own funds. But in my case, friends, corporations, unions, and law firms helped me pledge more than $700,000 to raise the money to support the chair.

That was a truly humbling experience.

My adopted city of Alpena has even gotten into the act, honoring me in the summer of 2013 with a ceremony and a beautiful plaque within the courthouse, commemorating me more than a half a century after I left town. Why? Judge Michael Mack, the son of my old law partner, told a reporter, "I think if one kid from Alpena saw that and . . . went out and tried to do something better, it will be worth every penny."

Usually a man doesn't get such honors until after he dies. And as I write this, on the cusp of my ninetieth birthday, I know that I am a very fortunate man. Best of all, since I stepped down as attorney general, I have had more time to spend with my wonderful family: Nancy, my wife; my son, Frank, who has spent most of his career in state government, with the Michigan Department of Transportation; my daughter Karen, one of Florida's top travel agents; and my youngest daughter, Jane, who is retired from Delta Airlines. Both my daughters and my first wife, Jo, now live in Naples, and Nancy and I spend winters there with them.

But we are dedicated Michigan residents and always intend to be. Sometimes I think of the men who had the biggest impact on my early life and career: John Swainson, who made it all possible by his surprise decision to appoint me attorney general so long ago; John and Robert Kennedy, who inspired me and got me excited about public service in a way it is now sadly hard for the young to imagine; and most of all, my father, Frank Edward Kelley.

They are all long gone now.

But I can remember, as if it were yesterday, JFK saying, "One person can make a difference, and everyone should try." That's what the Kennedys and my father believed. That's what I always believed. I hope they would all agree I made a difference.

I do know that I tried.

20

LESSONS FROM A LIFE
IN PUBLIC SERVICE

So why did I write this book?

Simply, to convey this message: a life of public service, a life lived in the service of your fellow man, is worth living.

You are not likely to get rich doing it. You are bound to suffer defeats, disappointments, and setbacks. The good guys don't always win. But sometimes, if you work hard and smart, they do.

Today we see so many problems and politics is sometimes so frustrating that it is good to remind myself—and anyone reading this book—that there have been huge victories for justice in my lifetime.

When I was born, a black kid couldn't even live in most parts of Detroit. The year I was born, the Ku Klux Klan held a major parade down Woodward Avenue. In some states, a black man would have been lynched for even whistling at a white woman.

If you've read this far, you will remember that when a young black man named Grady Little was knifed to death in October 1961, the Wayne County prosecutor didn't even want to bring charges. Despite my intervention, his killer ended up walking free—and I got a tongue-lashing from the judge for "interfering" in the case.

But I will celebrate my ninetieth birthday in a nation where a black man, a baby who was two months old when Little died, is president of the United

States of America. And as I write this, the odds seem good that our first African American president—Barack Obama—may be succeeded by our first-ever female president.

I'll bet you can even guess her name.

Whatever they tell you, this is a world where courageous and smart people can still make a difference.

Thanks to those who fought hard and who didn't take no for an answer, Americans have a lot of rights, freedoms, and protections they couldn't even imagine when I was a boy: Social Security. Medicare and Medicaid. Clean air and clean water. My own contribution was modest, but we did help clean up the meat supply here in Michigan and prevent the utility companies from gouging consumers for second-rate service.

We did send some of those who cheated and preyed upon the weak to prison and scared others into going straight or leaving the state. True, I never became a major force in national politics, though I have known most of the main players for more than half a century.

But I did win some major victories for the public in my great state of Michigan, a state that, in 2014, had more than twice the population all of America did in George Washington's day.

As attorney general, I established two of the first consumer protection and environmental protection divisions of any state in the nation. I am proud of that. But I did little on my own, except this: I recruited and trained the best public interest lawyers I could find.

Together we fought to limit nuclear power in Michigan and keep what we had safe. We won battles to ensure clean air and water, to limit highway billboards—what I liked to call "litter on a stick"—and to generally make life better for the common man.

Not too bad, I'd say, for a saloon keeper's son who grew up in Detroit. I like to think my father would be proud of me. What would I tell him if he could magically reappear?

I think I would probably say, as I did when they honored me in Lansing recently, "Well, Dad, I tried my best. I did have a great life with moments of joy and some disappointment, but I remain optimistic about the future for my fellow man."

Optimistic, yes. Starry-eyed, no.

The future is up to you who are reading these words, and all your neighbors and friends. If this thing called democracy is going to continue to work, we need a new generation of young people to get involved. We need inspired, dedicated, and committed young people who are in many cases tougher, smarter, better educated, and more driven than my generation. Today the challenges are even bigger.

For example, we have to prevent the power of corporations from strangling our democracy. This is a bigger threat, in my opinion, than it has ever been. By the way, I am fairly well-read in economics. Socialism is a wonderful ideal, but we animals known as Homo sapiens aren't sufficiently evolved enough to make it work. Again, my father put it beautifully. Today I can still hear him saying, "Frank, you can be as radical as you want. Just remember one thing: You can't beat money."

Capitalism will always win, in other words, unless and until human nature changes for the better. And if you want one entirely safe prediction, it is that none of us is going to live to see that.

So even if I am a socialist at heart, in the real world, I am in favor of private enterprise. I strongly believe in and support a free-market system driven by the profit motive.

The fact is that my retirement has been made comfortable by the fact that I started and ran a very successful business in my later years.

The capitalist system has created great plenty and great innovation in all types of products. Anyone who, as I did, toured the Soviet Union in the old days saw how that system utterly failed.

But that doesn't mean corporations and the profit motive don't need regulating. That's the government's duty and obligation.

Automobiles are good and necessary things, but nobody thinks it is an outrageous denial of our freedoms for government to say you can't run red lights or use your car to haul garbage and dump it in our national parks.

But we have politicians today who say that we don't have to fix the roads or worry about what happens to the poor, or the sick, or the elderly. We have a political movement that seems to believe that all taxes are outrageous. Well, I have news for them.

Taxes, as Oliver Wendell Holmes said, are the price we pay for a civilized society. Holmes, by the way, who lived from 1841 to 1935, was one of the most revered U.S. Supreme Court justices, a Civil War hero, and a deeply conservative Republican.

You get what you pay for.

I am a lawyer. But I've been fascinated by anthropology, as well as philosophy and sociology, and have read deeply in those subjects all my life. And here's what I can tell you: human beings are, by their very nature, herd animals. Mentally far superior to the rest, no doubt. Capable of rational thought and stunning intellectual achievement, certainly.

But we are still creatures of habit and instinct. For our own protection, we will stay with the herd even when our leaders take us down paths we suspect are wrong. That tendency has led to some of mankind's worst moments. Nazi Germany. Stalin's Russia. The Detroit riots. Religious cults like that of Jim Jones in Guyana and the Branch Davidians in Waco, Texas.

Religious leaders and great philosophers have recognized this for millennia. Christians, Muslims, Jews, and Buddhists all recognize that humans can be greedy and cheat each other, even in our own families.

Sometimes we are even capable of murder—something no other herd animal ever does. That's why we need restraints. Checks and balances, police and courts, lawyers and judges. That's why we need governments and social safety nets.

America's great gift to philosophy was the knowledge that we needed all these things and freedom, too. The story of our history is the story of our constant striving for balance.

And this is a battle in which there are bound to be no final victories—but one in which we must keep struggling against defeat.

Everybody remembers the famous line from John F. Kennedy's inaugural address: "Ask not what your country can do for you; ask what you can do for your country." That's the best-remembered thing that he said. But Kennedy said two other things in that amazing speech that sum up what my life has been about. He reminded us that "if a free society cannot help the many who are poor, it cannot save the few who are rich." Then, after summing up what he intended to do to make life better and more just, he said: "All this will not be finished in the first hundred days. Nor will it be finished in the first one thousand days, nor in the life of this administration, nor even perhaps in our lifetime on this planet. But let us begin."

———

My public service career began that year. Now, what I'd like to say to all those in generations after mine is: It's your turn. Your turn to begin and, this time, do it better.

You may not realize it, but old men have dreams, too, and here's mine: that some young person will read these words and think: Wow. This guy spent his life in public service. He didn't come from much money, but he got through law school, had a fascinating life, and met some of the world's greatest figures.

And he helped make people's lives better.

That's what *I* want to do.

That's why I wrote this book. Thank you for letting me tell my story. Now, whoever and wherever you are, go work on your own.

APPENDIX

ATTORNEY GENERAL FRANK KELLEY:
TEN SUCCESSFUL ELECTIONS

1962	Frank Kelley: 1,386,583	Robert Danhof: 1,268,462
1964	Frank Kelley: 1,800,056	Meyer Warshawsky: 1,231,028
1966	Frank Kelley: 1,232,149	Lawrence Lindemer: 1,091,892
1970	Frank Kelley: 1,644,338	William Farr: 893,438
1974	Frank Kelley: 1,739,466	Myron Wahls: 736,975
1978	Frank Kelley: 1,833,854	Mel Larsen: 962,588
1982	Frank Kelley: 1,707,064	L. Brooks Patterson: 1,238,755
1986	Frank Kelley: 1,585,999	Robert Cleland: 707,835
1990	Frank Kelley: 1,565,686	Clifford Taylor: 890,925
1994	Frank Kelley: 1,717,591	John Smietanka: 1,273,330
Total Kelley	16,212,786	61.2% (average)
Total GOP opponents	10,295,228	38.8% (average)

INDEX